CHAPTER 4

Edit Text

Do you want to edit the text in your document or check your document for spelling and grammar errors? This chapter teaches you how.

INSERT AND DELETE TEXT

You can easily add new text to your document and remove text you no longer need.

Word is an efficient editing tool. When you insert new text, the existing text moves to make room for the new text. When you remove text, the remaining text moves to fill the empty space.

INSERT TEXT

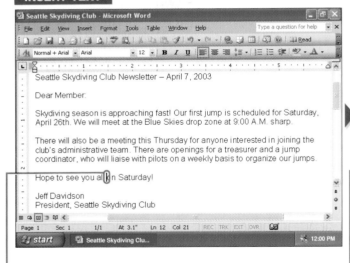

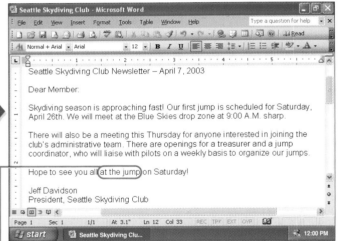

1 Click the location in your document where you want to insert new text.

■ The text you type will appear where the insertion point flashes on your screen.

Note: You can press the ←, →, ↓ or ↑ key to move the insertion point one character or line in any direction.

2 Type the text you want to insert.

■ To insert a blank space, press the **Spacebar**.

■ The words to the right of the new text move forward.

Why did red and green underlines appear under the text I inserted?

Word automatically checks your document for spelling and grammar errors as you type. Misspelled words display a red underline and grammar errors display a green underline. For information on checking spelling and grammar in your document, see page 62.

Why does the existing text in my document disappear when I insert new text?

You may have turned on the Overtype feature, which will replace existing text with the text you type. When the Overtype feature is on, the **OVR** status indicator at the bottom of your screen is **bold**. To turn the Overtype feature on or off, press the [Insert] key.

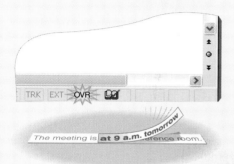

DELETE TEXT

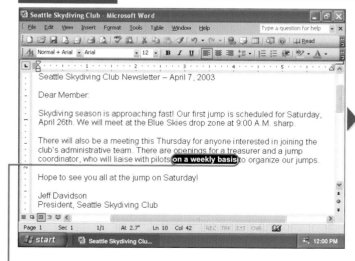

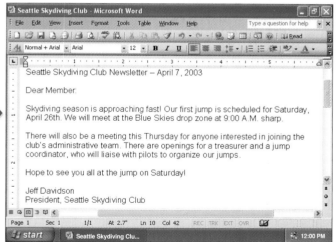

1 Select the text you want to delete. To select text, see page 8.

2 Press the [Delete] key to remove the text.

■ The text disappears. The remaining text in the line or paragraph moves to fill the empty space.

■ To delete a single character, click to the right of the character you want to delete and then press the [◄Backspace] key. Word deletes the character to the left of the flashing insertion point.

MOVE OR COPY TEXT

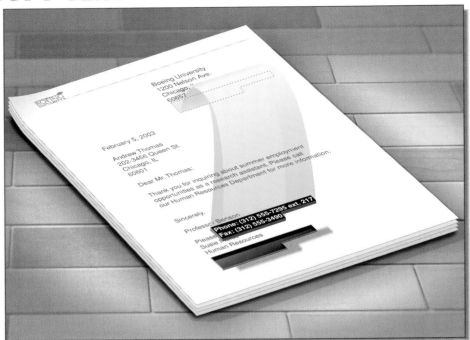

You can move or copy text to a new location in your document.

Moving text allows you to rearrange text in your document. When you move text, the text disappears from its original location.

Copying text allows you to repeat information in your document without having to retype the text. When you copy text, the text appears in both the original and new locations.

MOVE OR COPY TEXT

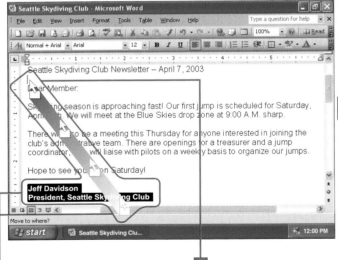

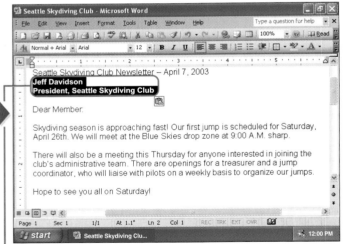

USING DRAG AND DROP

1 Select the text you want to move. To select text, see page 8.

2 Position the mouse over the selected text (I changes to ↔).

3 To move the text, drag the mouse ↔ to where you want to place the text.

Note: The text will appear where you position the dotted insertion point on your screen.

■ The text moves to the new location.

■ To copy text, perform steps **1** to **3**, except press and hold down the **Ctrl** key as you perform step **3**.

How can I use the Clipboard task pane to move or copy text?

The Clipboard task pane displays up to the last 24 items you have selected to move or copy. To place an item that appears on the Clipboard task pane in your document, click the location in your document where you want the item to appear and then click the item in the task pane. For information about task panes, see page 14.

Why does the Paste Options button (📋) appear when I move or copy text?

The Paste Options button (📋) allows you to change the format of text you moved or copied. For example, you can choose to keep the original formatting of the text or change the formatting of the text to match the text in the new location. Click the Paste Options button to display a list of options and then select the option you want to use. The Paste Options button is available only until you perform another task.

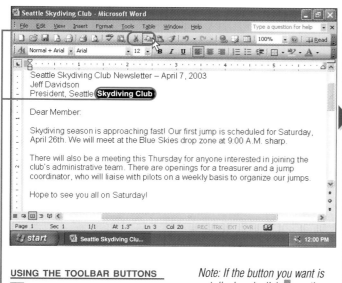

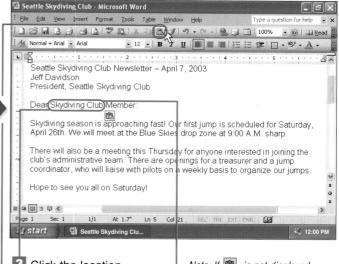

USING THE TOOLBAR BUTTONS

1 Select the text you want to move or copy. To select text, see page 8.

2 Click one of the following buttons.

✂ Move text

📋 Copy text

Note: If the button you want is not displayed, click ▸ on the Standard toolbar to display the button.

■ The Clipboard task pane may appear. To use the Clipboard task pane, see the top of this page.

3 Click the location where you want to place the text.

4 Click 📋 to place the text in the new location.

Note: If 📋 is not displayed, click ▸ on the Standard toolbar to display the button.

■ The text appears in the new location.

53

UNDO CHANGES

Word remembers the last changes you made to your document. If you regret these changes, you can cancel them by using the Undo feature.

The Undo feature can cancel your last editing and formatting changes. For example, you can cancel editing changes such as deleting a paragraph and cancel formatting changes such as underlining a word.

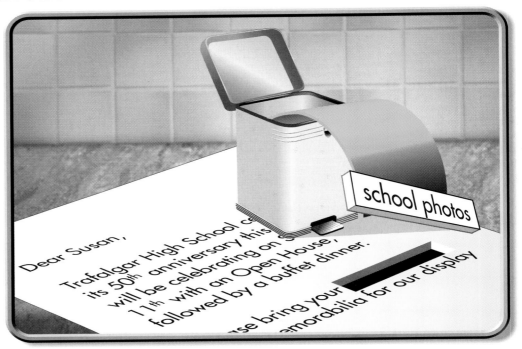

UNDO CHANGES

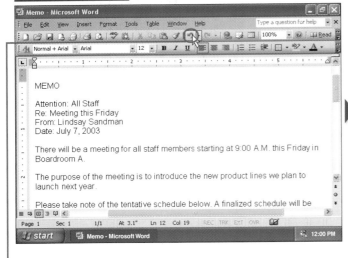

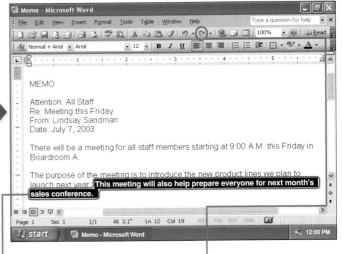

■1 Click 🔄 to undo the last change you made to your document.

Note: If 🔄 is not displayed, click ⁚ on the Standard toolbar to display the button.

■ Word cancels the last change you made to your document.

■ You can repeat step 1 to cancel previous changes you made.

■ To reverse the results of using the Undo feature, click 🔁.

Note: If 🔁 is not displayed, click ⁚ on the Standard toolbar to display the button.

INSERT THE DATE AND TIME

You can insert the current date and time into your document. Word can automatically update the date and time each time you open or print the document.

Word uses your computer's built-in clock to determine the current date and time.

INSERT THE DATE AND TIME

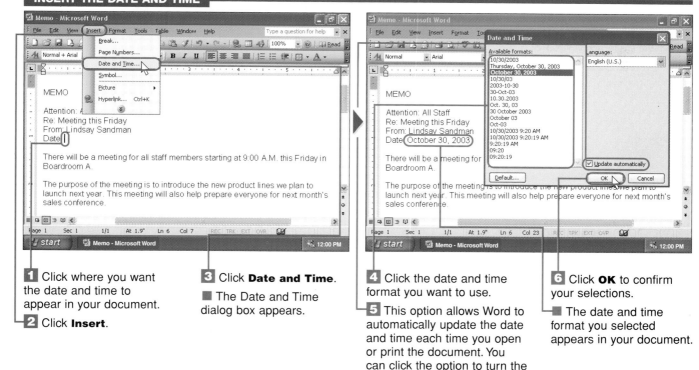

1 Click where you want the date and time to appear in your document.

2 Click **Insert**.

3 Click **Date and Time**.

■ The Date and Time dialog box appears.

4 Click the date and time format you want to use.

5 This option allows Word to automatically update the date and time each time you open or print the document. You can click the option to turn the option on(☑) or off(☐).

6 Click **OK** to confirm your selections.

■ The date and time format you selected appears in your document.

COUNT WORDS IN A DOCUMENT

You can have Word count the number of words in your document. Counting words is useful if you have a document that must contain a specific number of words, such as a magazine submission.

Dear Susan:

Trafalgar High School celebrates its 50th anniversary this year. We will be celebrating on September 22nd with an Open House, followed by a buffet dinner.

Please bring your school photos and memorabilia for our display table.

Word Count

When counting the number of words in your document, Word also counts the number of pages, characters, paragraphs and lines in your document.

COUNT WORDS IN A DOCUMENT

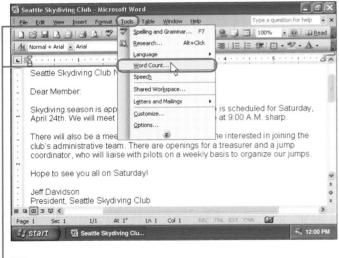

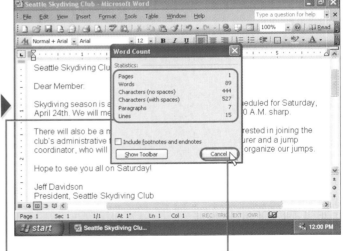

1 Click **Tools**.

2 Click **Word Count**.

■ The Word Count dialog box appears.

■ This area displays the total number of pages, words, characters, paragraphs and lines in your document.

3 When you finish reviewing the information, click **Cancel** or **Close** to close the Word Count dialog box.

How can I count the number of words in only part of my document?

To count the number of words in only part of your document, select the text before performing the steps on page 56. To select text, see page 8.

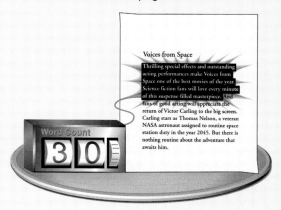

Is there another way to display the Word Count toolbar?

Yes. While reviewing the information in the Word Count dialog box, you can click the **Show Toolbar** button to display the Word Count toolbar.

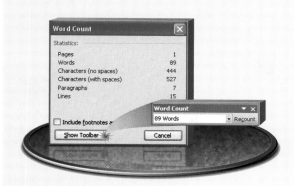

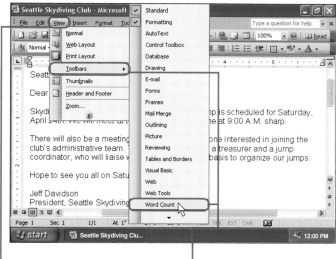

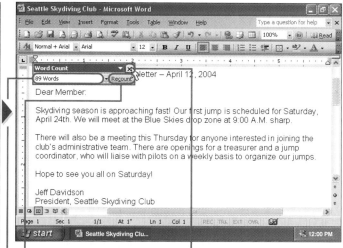

USING THE WORD COUNT TOOLBAR

The Word Count toolbar allows you to quickly recount the number of words in your document as you edit the document.

1 Click **View**.

2 Click **Toolbars**.

3 Click **Word Count**.

■ The Word Count toolbar appears.

4 Click **Recount**.

■ This area displays the total number of words in your document.

■ To display the number of characters, lines, pages or paragraphs, you can click this area to select the type of information you want to display.

5 To update the word count as you edit your document, repeat step **4**.

6 When you finish using the Word Count toolbar, click ✕ to hide the toolbar.

FIND TEXT

You can use the Find feature to quickly locate every occurrence of a word or phrase in your document.

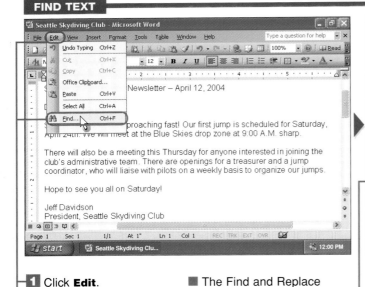

1 Click **Edit**.

2 Click **Find**.

■ The Find and Replace dialog box appears.

3 Type the text you want to find.

4 Click **Find Next** to start the search.

*Note: A dialog box appears if Word cannot find the text you specified. Click **OK** to close the dialog box and then skip to step 8.*

58

Can I search for part of a word?

When you search for text in your document, Word will find the text even when the text is part of a larger word. For example, if you search for **place**, Word will also find **place**s, **place**ment and common**place**.

Can I search only a specific section of my document?

Yes. To search only a specific section of your document, select the text you want to search before starting the search. To select text, see page 8.

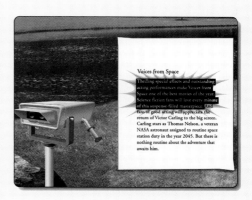

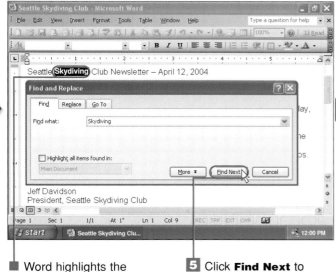

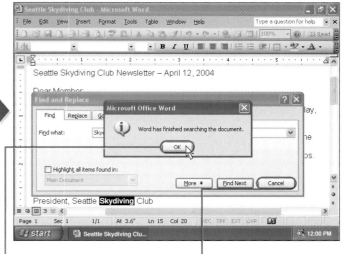

■ Word highlights the first matching word it finds.

5 Click **Find Next** to find the next matching word.

Note: To end the search at any time, click ***Cancel***.

6 Repeat step 5 until a dialog box appears, telling you the search is complete.

7 Click **OK** to close the dialog box.

8 Click **Cancel** to close the Find and Replace dialog box.

REPLACE TEXT

You can find and replace
every occurrence of a
word or phrase in your
document. This is useful
if you have frequently
misspelled a name.

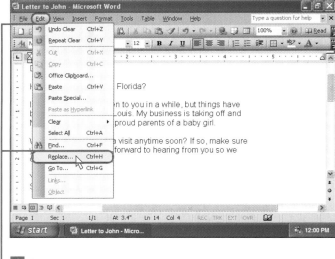

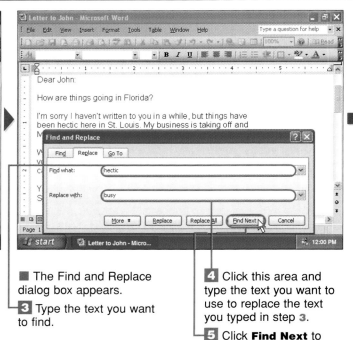

1 Click **Edit**.

2 Click **Replace**.

*Note: If Replace does not
appear on the menu, position
the mouse Ⓚ over the bottom
of the menu to display the
menu option.*

■ The Find and Replace
dialog box appears.

3 Type the text you want
to find.

4 Click this area and
type the text you want to
use to replace the text
you typed in step **3**.

5 Click **Find Next** to
start the search.

How can the Find and Replace feature help me quickly enter text?

When you need to type a long word or phrase, such as University of Massachusetts, many times in a document, you can use the Replace feature to simplify the task. You can type a short form of the word or phrase, such as UM, throughout your document and then have Word replace the short form with the full word or phrase.

How can I quickly display the Find and Replace dialog box?

You can press and hold down the **Ctrl** key as you press the **H** key to quickly display the Find and Replace dialog box.

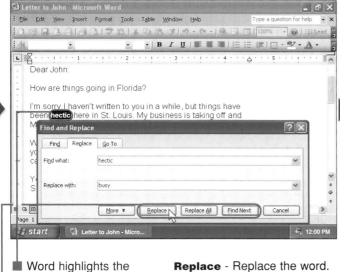

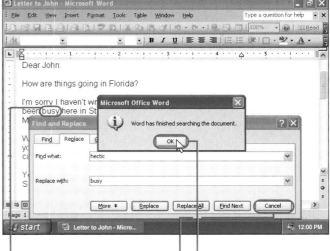

■ Word highlights the first matching word it finds.

6 Click one of the following options.

Replace - Replace the word.

Replace All - Replace the word and all other matching words in the document.

Find Next - Ignore the word.

Note: To cancel the search at any time, press the **Esc** *key.*

■ In this example, Word replaces the word and searches for the next matching word.

7 Replace or ignore matching words until a dialog box appears, telling you the search is complete.

8 Click **OK** to close the dialog box.

9 Click **Close** or **Cancel** to close the Find and Replace dialog box.

CHECK SPELLING AND GRAMMAR

You can find and correct all the spelling and grammar errors in your document.

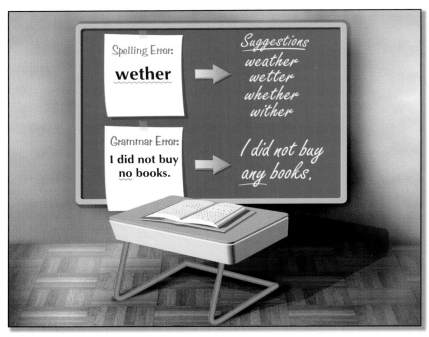

Word compares every word in your document to words in its dictionary. If a word does not exist in the dictionary, the word is considered misspelled.

Word will not find a correctly spelled word used in the wrong context, such as "My niece is **sit** years old." You should carefully review your document to find this type of error.

CHECK SPELLING AND GRAMMAR

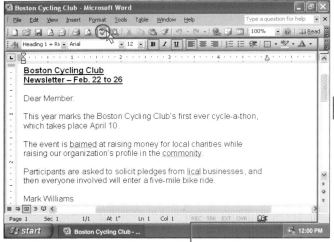

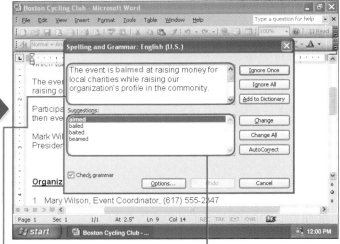

■ Word automatically underlines misspelled words in red and grammar errors in green. The underlines will not appear when you print your document.

1 Click 🔤 to start checking your document for spelling and grammar errors.

Note: If 🔤 is not displayed, click ⁙ on the Standard toolbar to display the button.

■ The Spelling and Grammar dialog box appears if Word finds an error in your document.

■ This area displays the first misspelled word or grammar error.

■ This area displays suggestions for correcting the error.

Why did Word underline a correctly spelled word?

The underlined word does not exist in Word's dictionary. You can add the word to the dictionary so Word will recognize the word during future spell checks.

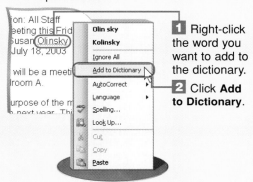

1 Right-click the word you want to add to the dictionary.

2 Click **Add to Dictionary**.

How can I quickly correct a single misspelled word or grammar error in my document?

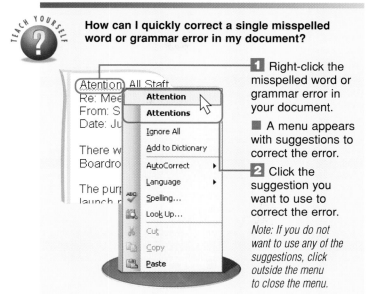

1 Right-click the misspelled word or grammar error in your document.

■ A menu appears with suggestions to correct the error.

2 Click the suggestion you want to use to correct the error.

Note: If you do not want to use any of the suggestions, click outside the menu to close the menu.

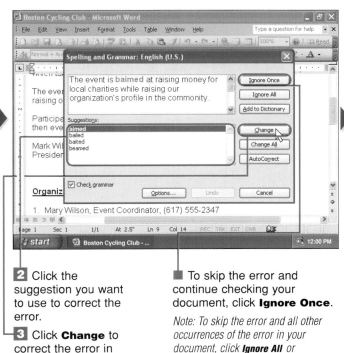

2 Click the suggestion you want to use to correct the error.

3 Click **Change** to correct the error in your document.

■ To skip the error and continue checking your document, click **Ignore Once**.

*Note: To skip the error and all other occurrences of the error in your document, click **Ignore All** or **Ignore Rule**. The name of the button depends on the type of error.*

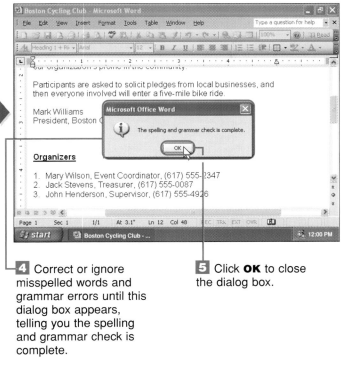

4 Correct or ignore misspelled words and grammar errors until this dialog box appears, telling you the spelling and grammar check is complete.

5 Click **OK** to close the dialog box.

TURN OFF SPELLING AND GRAMMAR CHECK

You can turn off Word's automatic spelling and grammar check features. This is useful if you are distracted by the red and green underlines Word uses to indicate errors in your documents.

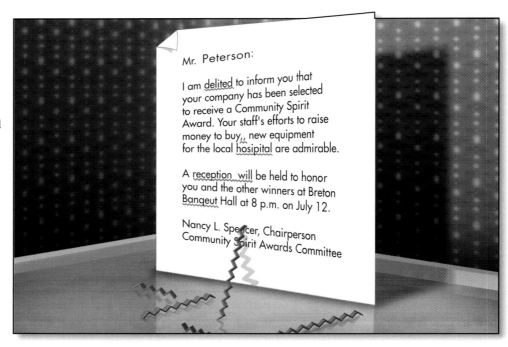

Mr. Peterson:

I am delited to inform you that your company has been selected to receive a Community Spirit Award. Your staff's efforts to raise money to buy,, new equipment for the local hosipital are admirable.

A reception will be held to honor you and the other winners at Breton Banqeut Hall at 8 p.m. on July 12.

Nancy L. Spencer, Chairperson Community Spirit Awards Committee

TURN OFF SPELLING AND GRAMMAR CHECK

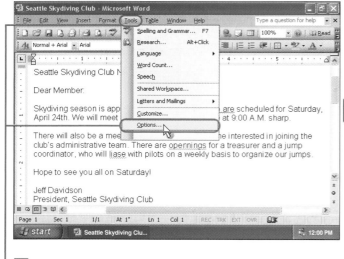

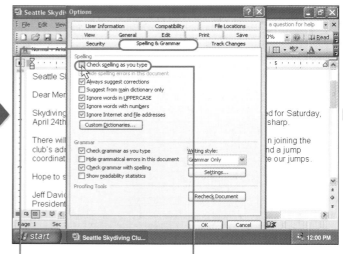

1 Click **Tools**.

2 Click **Options**.

■ The Options dialog box appears.

3 Click the **Spelling & Grammar** tab.

4 Click this option to turn off the automatic spelling check feature for all your documents (☑ changes to ☐).

How can I find errors in my documents after I turn off the automatic spelling and grammar check features?

You can check for spelling and grammar errors in your documents at any time. For more information, see page 62.

Can I hide the red and green underlines for only the current document?

You can hide the red and green underlines for the current document without turning off the automatic spelling and grammar check features for all your documents. Perform steps **1** to **6** below, selecting **Hide spelling errors in this document** in step **4** (☐ changes to ☑) and **Hide grammatical errors in this document** in step **5** (☐ changes to ☑).

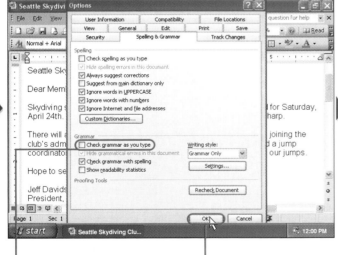

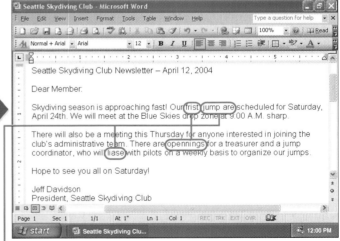

5 Click this option to turn off the automatic grammar check feature for all your documents (☑ changes to ☐).

6 Click **OK** to confirm your changes.

■ The spelling and grammar errors in your document are no longer underlined.

TURN ON SPELLING AND GRAMMAR CHECK

■ To turn on the automatic spelling and grammar check features, repeat steps **1** to **6** (☐ changes to ☑ in steps **4** and **5**).

USING THE THESAURUS

You can use the thesaurus on Word's Research task pane to replace a word in your document with a more suitable word.

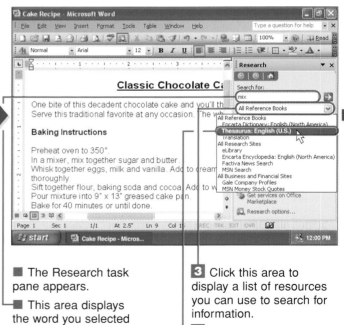

The thesaurus can replace a word in your document with a word that shares the same meaning, called a synonym.

Using the thesaurus included with Word is faster and more convenient than searching through a printed thesaurus.

USING THE THESAURUS

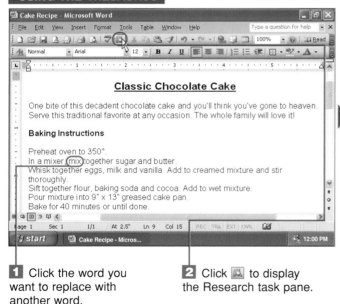

1 Click the word you want to replace with another word.

2 Click ◩ to display the Research task pane.

■ The Research task pane appears.

■ This area displays the word you selected in step **1**.

3 Click this area to display a list of resources you can use to search for information.

4 Click **Thesaurus**.

What if the Research task pane does not display a word I want to use?

You can look up synonyms for the words displayed in the Research task pane to find a more suitable word. Click a word in the task pane to display synonyms for the word.

*Note: If you click a **bold** word in the task pane, you will hide or display the list of synonyms for the bold word.*

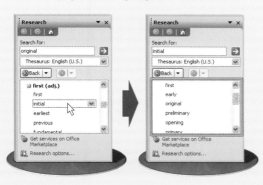

How can I quickly replace a word in my document with a synonym?

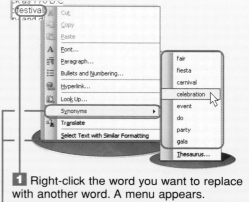

1 Right-click the word you want to replace with another word. A menu appears.

2 Click **Synonyms** to view a list of words with similar meanings.

3 Click the word you want to replace the word in your document.

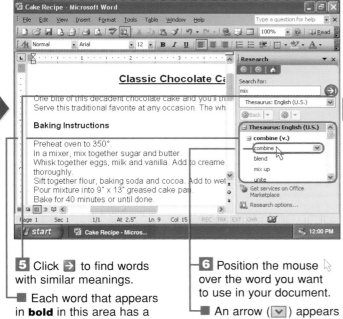

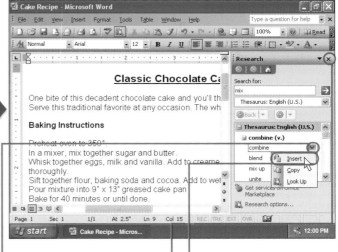

5 Click ➔ to find words with similar meanings.

■ Each word that appears in **bold** in this area has a similar meaning to the word in your document. Each word below a bold word offers a synonym for the bold word.

6 Position the mouse over the word you want to use in your document.

■ An arrow (▼) appears beside the word.

7 Click the arrow (▼) beside the word you want to use.

8 Click **Insert** to replace the word in your document with the new word.

9 To hide the Research task pane, click ✕ .

USING AUTOCORRECT

Word automatically corrects hundreds of typing and spelling errors as you type. You can create an AutoCorrect entry to add your own word or phrase to the list of errors that Word corrects.

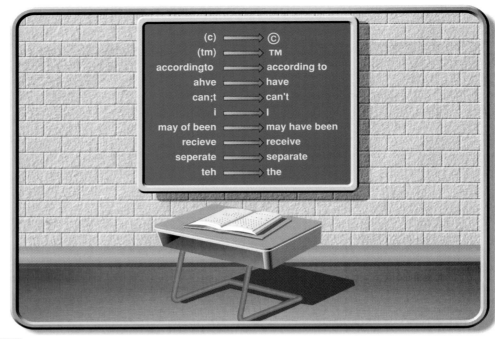

USING AUTOCORRECT

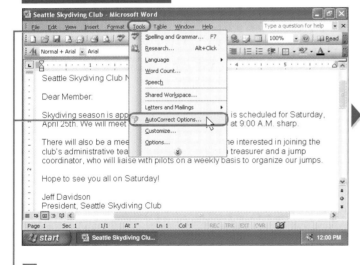

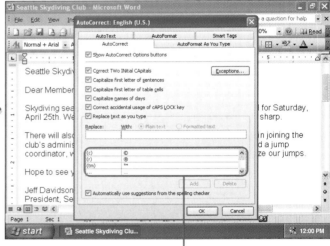

1 Click **Tools**.

2 Click **AutoCorrect Options**.

Note: If AutoCorrect Options does not appear on the menu, position the mouse ⬚ over the bottom of the menu to display the menu option.

■ The AutoCorrect dialog box appears.

■ This area displays the list of AutoCorrect entries included with Word.

What other types of errors does Word automatically correct?

When you type two consecutive uppercase letters, Word automatically converts the second letter to lowercase. When you type a lowercase letter for the first letter of a sentence or the name of a day, Word automatically converts the letter to uppercase.

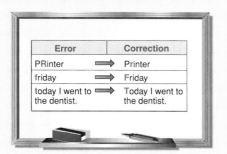

Error		Correction
PRinter	⟹	Printer
friday	⟹	Friday
today I went to the dentist.	⟹	Today I went to the dentist.

How can I reverse a change that Word has automatically made?

The Home Development Association (**HAD**) will be offering a ho... ying

↺ Change back to "HDA"

Stop Automatically Correcting "hda"

Control AutoCorrect Options...

■ A blue rectangle (▬) appears below text that has been automatically corrected.

1 If you do not want to accept the correction, position the mouse I over the blue rectangle to display the AutoCorrect Options button (🗲).

2 Click the AutoCorrect Options button to display a list of options for the correction.

3 Click the option you want to use.

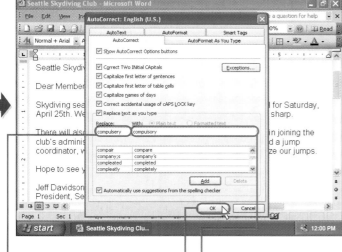

3 To add a new entry to the list, type the text you want Word to replace automatically. The text should not contain spaces and should not be a real word.

4 Click this area and type the text you want Word to automatically insert into your documents.

5 Click **OK** to confirm your change.

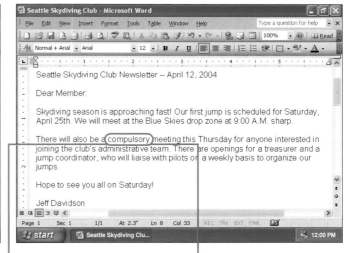

INSERT AN AUTOCORRECT ENTRY

■ After you create an AutoCorrect entry, Word will automatically insert the entry each time you type the corresponding text.

1 Click the location where you want the AutoCorrect entry to appear.

2 Type the text Word will automatically replace and then press the **Spacebar**.

■ Word automatically replaces the text with the AutoCorrect entry.

USING AUTOTEXT

You can use the AutoText feature to store text you frequently use, such as a mailing address, legal disclaimer or closing remark. You can then insert the text into your documents.

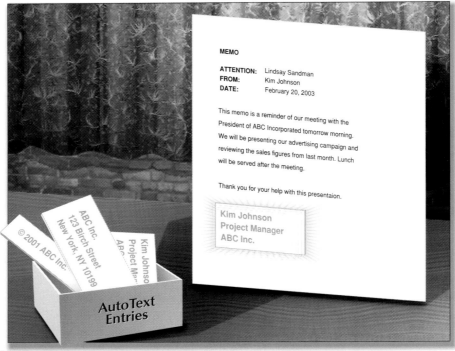

Using the AutoText feature saves you from having to type the same information over and over.

USING AUTOTEXT

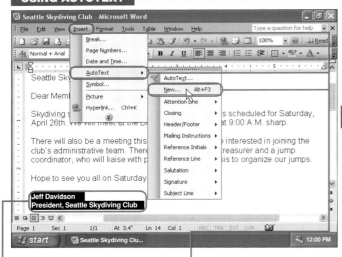

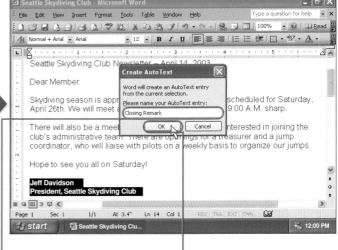

CREATE AN AUTOTEXT ENTRY

1 Type the text you want to store as an AutoText entry.

2 Select the text. To select text, see page 8.

3 Click **Insert**.

4 Click **AutoText**.

Note: If AutoText does not appear on the menu, position the mouse ⌖ over the bottom of the menu to display the menu option.

5 Click **New**.

■ The Create AutoText dialog box appears.

6 This area displays a name for the AutoText entry. To use a different name, type the name.

Note: The name of an AutoText entry should be at least four characters long.

7 Click **OK** to create the AutoText entry.

Does Word come with any AutoText entries?

Word comes with several AutoText entries that can help you quickly create a letter.

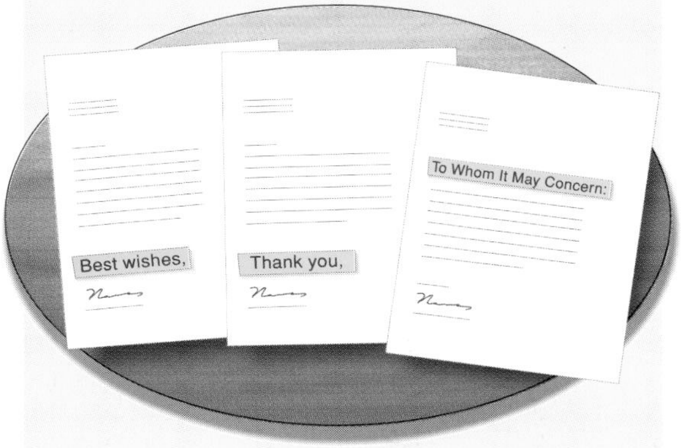

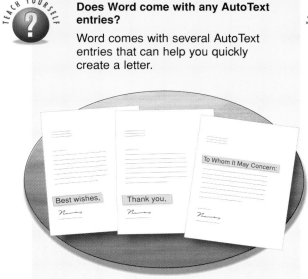

How can I quickly insert an AutoText entry into my document?

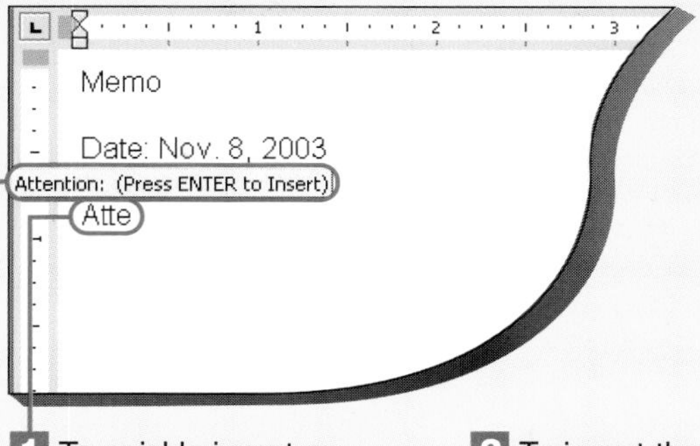

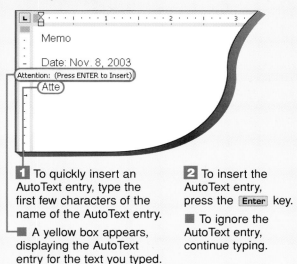

1 To quickly insert an AutoText entry, type the first few characters of the name of the AutoText entry.

■ A yellow box appears, displaying the AutoText entry for the text you typed.

2 To insert the AutoText entry, press the Enter key.

■ To ignore the AutoText entry, continue typing.

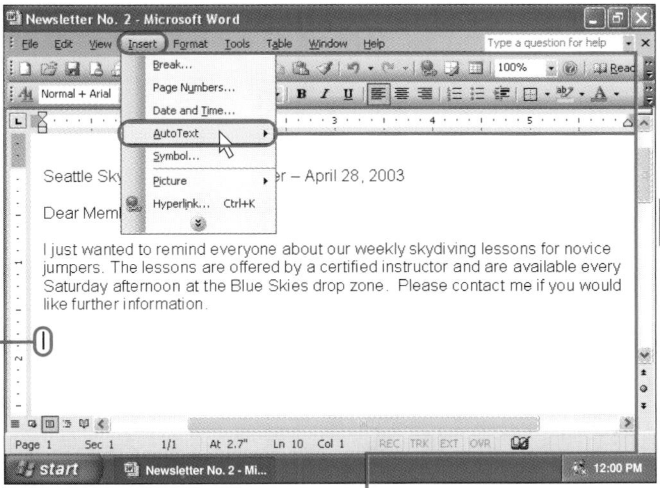

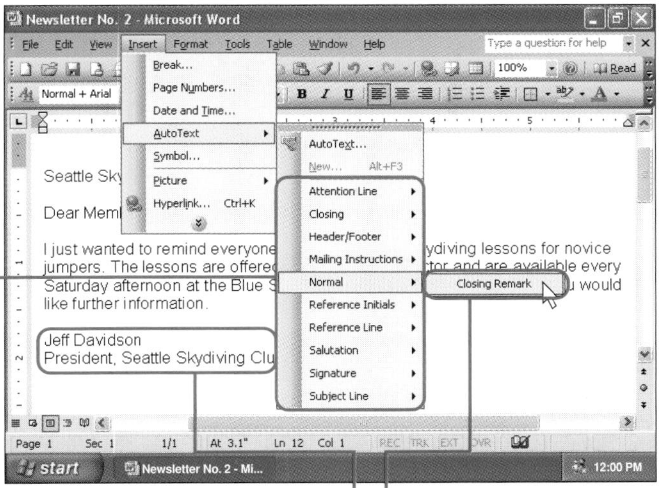

INSERT AN AUTOTEXT ENTRY

1 Click where you want the AutoText entry to appear in your document.

2 Click **Insert**.

3 Click **AutoText**.

Note: If AutoText does not appear on the menu, position the mouse over the bottom of the menu to display the menu option.

4 Click the category that stores the AutoText entry you want to use.

Note: The Normal category stores most AutoText entries you have created.

5 Click the AutoText entry you want to use.

■ The text appears in your document.

USING THE RESEARCH TASK PANE

You can use the Research task pane to gather reference material without ever having to leave your Word document. For example, you can look up a word in a dictionary or search through an encyclopedia on the Web.

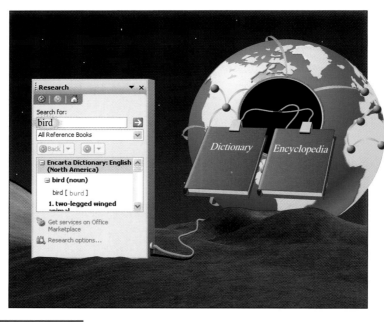

To use some of the resources offered in the Research task pane, your computer must be connected to the Internet.

Links to Web sites in the Research task pane that are preceded by a money icon (💷) require you to register and pay before you can view the information.

USING THE RESEARCH TASK PANE

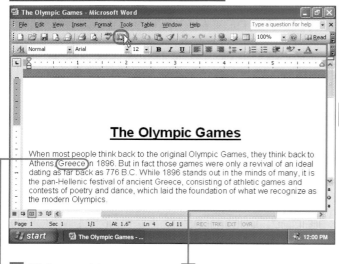

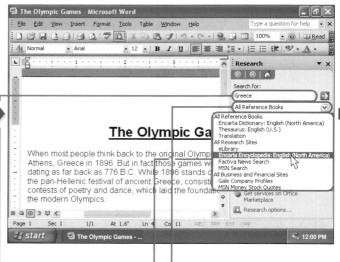

■ 1 Click a word in your document that you want to research.

■ 2 Click 🔍 to display the Research task pane.

■ The Research task pane appears.

■ This area displays the word you selected in step 1.

■ 3 Click this area to display a list of the resources you can use for your research.

■ 4 Click the resource you want to use to find information.

Note: In this example, we select Encarta Encyclopedia. The following screens depend on the resource you select.

What types of resources can I search using the Research task pane?

Reference Books

You can choose to look up terms in reference books, such as the Encarta Dictionary or a thesaurus. For information on using the thesaurus, see page 66.

Research Sites

You can research information online using eLibrary, Encarta Encyclopedia, Factiva News Search or MSN Search.

Business and Financial Sites

You can access company and stock market information through Gale Company Profiles or MSN Money Stock Quotes.

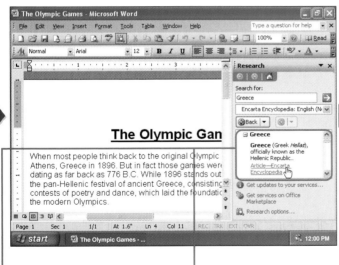 

■ The reference material appears in this area.

■ Each word that appears in **bold** in this area offers information about the word you specified in step 1.

■ Below each **bold** word, a short description of the available information and one or more links that you can choose appear.

5 Click a link to view the information.

■ A Web browser window opens and displays the information you selected.

■ The Research task pane also appears in the Web browser window.

■ To research a different word at any time, double-click this area and type the word. Then press the `Enter` key.

6 To return to your document, click ⊠.

INSERT SYMBOLS

You can insert symbols that do not appear on your keyboard into your document.

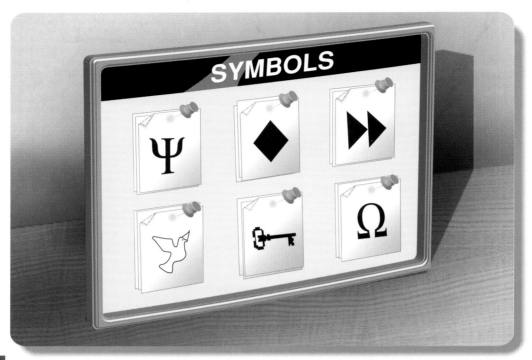

INSERT SYMBOLS

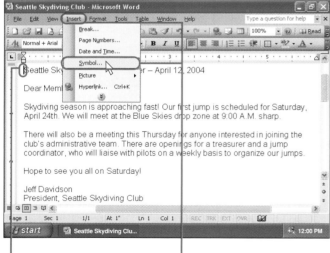

1 Click the location in your document where you want a symbol to appear.

2 Click **Insert**.

3 Click **Symbol**.

■ The Symbol dialog box appears, displaying the symbols for the current font.

4 To display the symbols for another font, click ⌄ in this area.

5 Click the font that provides the symbols you want to display.

How can I quickly insert a symbol I recently used?

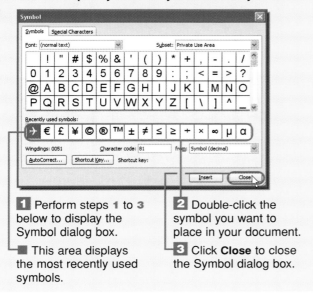

1 Perform steps **1** to **3** below to display the Symbol dialog box.

■ This area displays the most recently used symbols.

2 Double-click the symbol you want to place in your document.

3 Click **Close** to close the Symbol dialog box.

Is there another way to enter symbols in my document?

When you type one of the following sets of characters, Word automatically replaces the characters with a symbol.

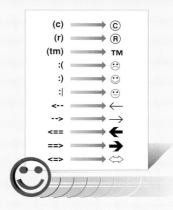

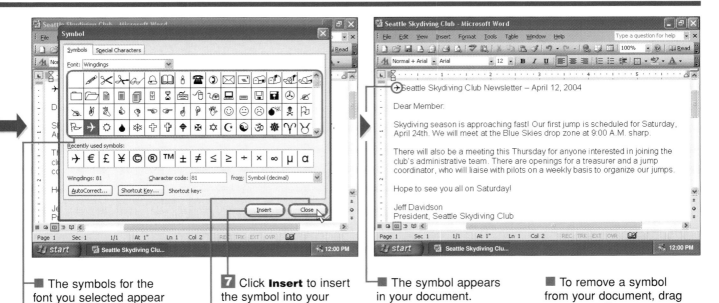

■ The symbols for the font you selected appear in this area.

6 Click the symbol you want to place in your document.

7 Click **Insert** to insert the symbol into your document.

8 Click **Close** to close the Symbol dialog box.

■ The symbol appears in your document.

■ To remove a symbol from your document, drag the mouse I over the symbol until you highlight the symbol and then press the Delete key.

ADD A COMMENT

You can add a comment to text in your document. A comment can be a note, explanation or reminder about information you need to verify later.

Comment: Verify date

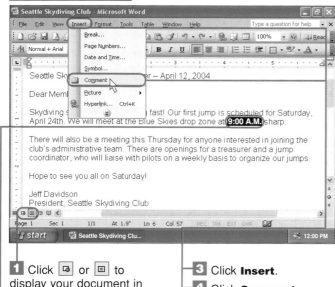

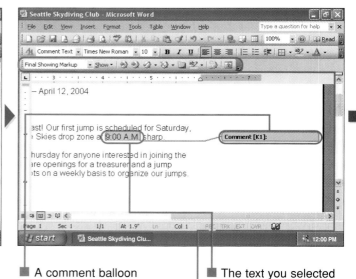

1 Click 🖼 or 🗐 to display your document in the Web Layout or Print Layout view.

2 Select the text you want to add a comment to. To select text, see page 8.

3 Click **Insert**.

4 Click **Comment**.

Note: If Comment does not appear on the menu, position the mouse ᐅ over the bottom of the menu to display the menu option.

■ A comment balloon appears in the right margin of your document.

Note: You may need to use the scroll bar to view the comment balloon.

■ The text you selected displays a color highlight. Colored brackets also appear around the text.

■ The Reviewing toolbar appears.

Can I edit a comment?

You can edit a comment to update the information in the comment. Click the comment balloon containing the comment you want to edit. You can then edit the text as you would edit any text in a document. To edit text, see page 50. When you finish editing the comment, click outside the comment balloon.

How do I view a comment in the Normal or Outline view?

In the Normal and Outline views, text you have added a comment to displays a colored highlight and is enclosed in colored brackets. To view the comment, position the mouse I over the text. After a few seconds, the comment will appear in a colored box. For more information on the document views, see page 36.

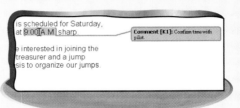

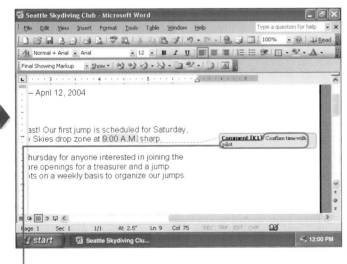

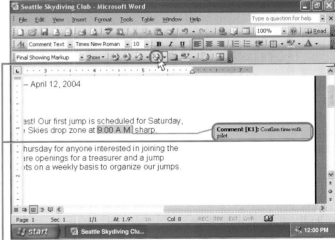

5 Type the comment you want to add.

6 When you finish typing the comment, click outside the comment balloon.

Note: You can also perform steps 1 to 6 to add a comment to a document displayed in the Reading Layout view. For information on the Reading Layout view, see page 44.

DELETE A COMMENT

1 Click the comment balloon containing the comment you want to delete.

2 Click [icon] to delete the comment.

■ Word deletes the comment balloon and removes the color highlight and brackets from the text in your document.

■ When you finish working with your comments, you can hide the Reviewing toolbar. To hide a toolbar, see page 39.

TRACK CHANGES

Word can keep track of the editing and formatting changes that are made to your document. Tracking changes is useful when multiple people are working with the same document.

Multiple people can work with a document you store on your network. Word will keep track of the changes you make to the document, as well as the changes that other people make.

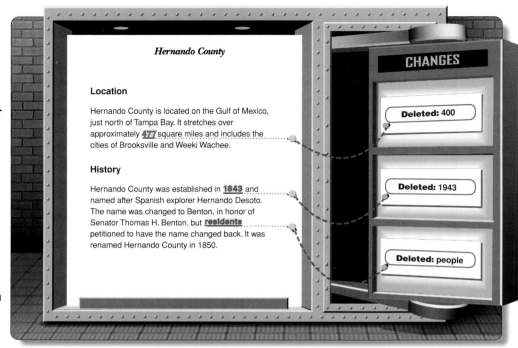

TRACK CHANGES

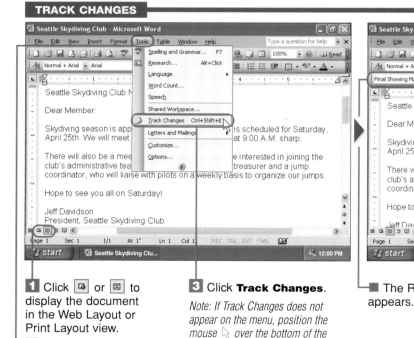

1 Click ⬜ or ⬜ to display the document in the Web Layout or Print Layout view.

2 Click **Tools**.

3 Click **Track Changes**.

Note: If Track Changes does not appear on the menu, position the mouse ⬦ over the bottom of the menu to display the menu option.

■ The Reviewing toolbar appears.

■ When Word tracks changes, this area displays **TRK** in bold.

4 You can now make changes to the document you want Word to track.

The balloons do not appear in the margin of the document. What is wrong?

The balloons appear in the margin of a document only when the document is displayed in the Print Layout, Web Layout or Reading Layout view. When the document is displayed in the Normal or Outline view, deleted text appears in the body of the document, crossed out and in color. Formatted text displays the formatting. For information on the views, see page 36.

Will the tracked changes appear on a printed page?

Yes. When you print a document that displays tracked changes, Word may automatically shrink the text in the document to fit the tracked changes on the printed page.

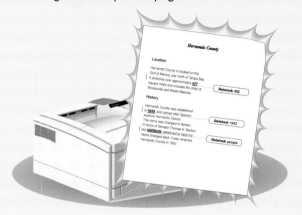

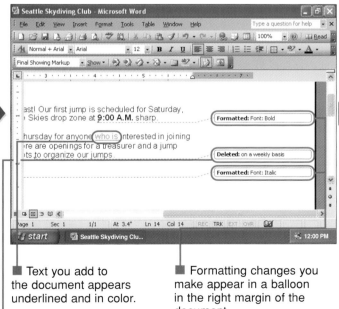

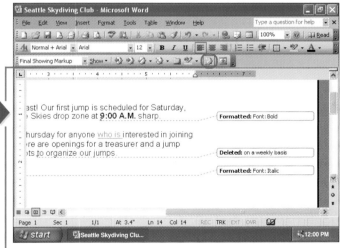

■ Text you add to the document appears underlined and in color.

■ Text you delete from the document appears in a balloon in the right margin of the document.

■ Formatting changes you make appear in a balloon in the right margin of the document.

Note: You may need to use the scroll bar to view the balloons.

■ A vertical line appears in the left margin beside text that contains a tracked change.

■ To stop tracking changes in the document, click 🗐.

■ You can now review the tracked changes in the document. To review tracked changes, see page 80.

REVIEW TRACKED CHANGES

You can review the tracked changes in a document and choose whether to accept or reject each change.

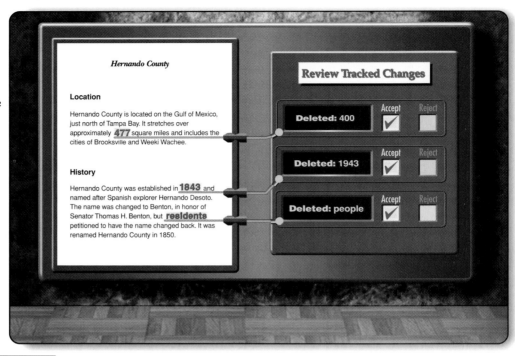

REVIEW TRACKED CHANGES

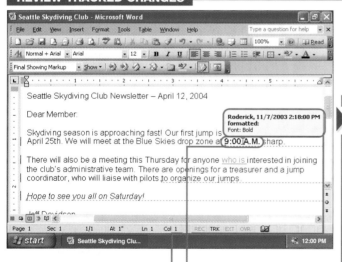

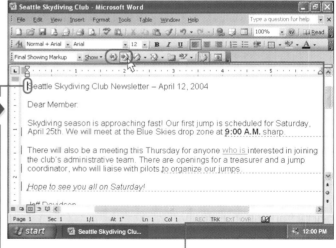

1 Open the document you want to review tracked changes for. To open a document, see page 24.

■ Word displays the changes that each person made in a different color.

2 To display information about a change, position the mouse I over the change.

■ After a few seconds, a colored box appears, displaying the name of the person who made the change and the date and time the change was made.

3 Click at the beginning of the document.

4 Click one of the following buttons to move to a tracked change in the document.

➡ Previous

➡ Next

How can I accept all the changes in a document at once?

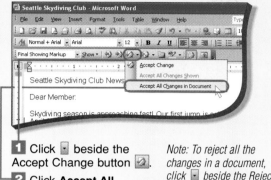

1 Click ⊡ beside the Accept Change button 🔲.

2 Click **Accept All Changes in Document**.

■ Word will accept all the changes in the document and stop tracking the changes.

*Note: To reject all the changes in a document, click ⊡ beside the Reject Change button (🔲) and then click **Reject All Changes in Document**.*

The tracked changes do not appear in my document. How do I display the changes?

■ You can repeat steps **1** and **2** to hide the tracked changes at any time. Hiding tracked changes allows you to review the document uncluttered with changes.

1 Click **View**.

2 Click **Markup**.

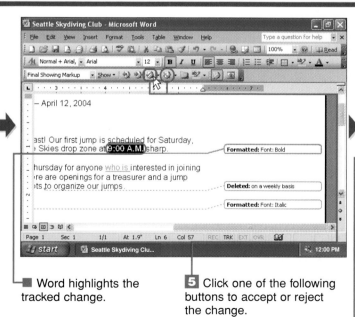

■ Word highlights the tracked change.

5 Click one of the following buttons to accept or reject the change.

🔲 Accept Change

🔲 Reject Change

■ Word accepts or rejects the change and stops tracking the change.

6 Repeat steps **4** and **5** until this dialog box appears.

7 Click **OK** to close the dialog box.

■ When you finish reviewing tracked changes, you can hide the Reviewing toolbar. To hide a toolbar, see page 39.

TRANSLATE TEXT

You can translate
a word in your
document from
one language to
another.

Word's translation
feature offers only
basic translation
services. If you need to
translate important
information or a large
amount of text, you
may want to hire a
professional translator.

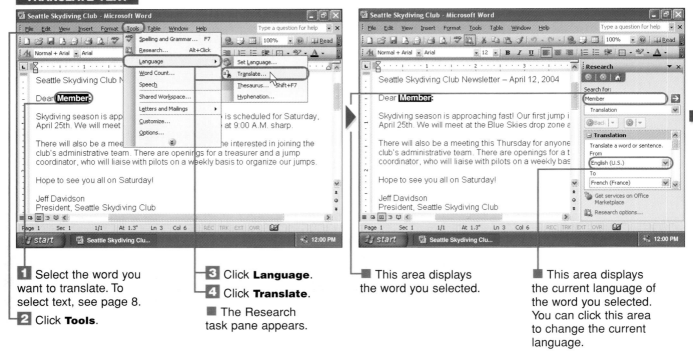

1 Select the word you
want to translate. To
select text, see page 8.

2 Click **Tools**.

3 Click **Language**.

4 Click **Translate**.

■ The Research
task pane appears.

■ This area displays
the word you selected.

■ This area displays
the current language of
the word you selected.
You can click this area
to change the current
language.

82

How can I translate my entire document?

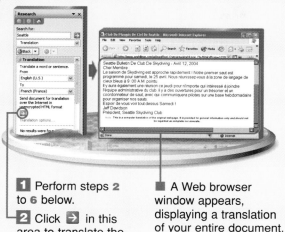

1 Perform steps **2** to **6** below.

2 Click ➡ in this area to translate the entire document.

■ A Web browser window appears, displaying a translation of your entire document.

Note: The translation is computer-generated and may contain errors.

 Is there a faster way to display the Research task pane so I can translate text?

Yes. Select the word that you want to translate in your document. Then press and hold down the **Alt** key as you click the word you selected to display the Research task pane. You can then perform steps **5** to **7** below to translate the word.

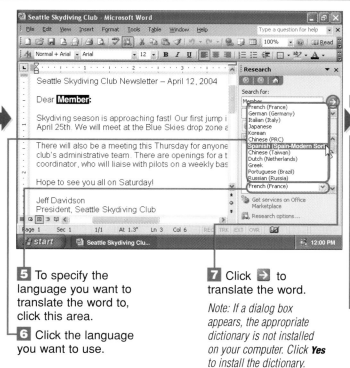

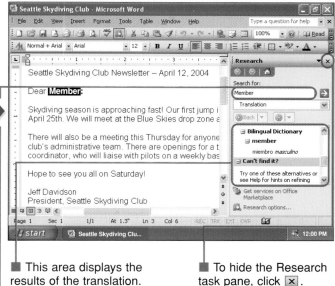

5 To specify the language you want to translate the word to, click this area.

6 Click the language you want to use.

7 Click ➡ to translate the word.

*Note: If a dialog box appears, the appropriate dictionary is not installed on your computer. Click **Yes** to install the dictionary.*

■ This area displays the results of the translation.

■ To translate another word at any time, drag the mouse I over the text in this area and then type the word. Then press the **Enter** key.

■ To hide the Research task pane, click ✕.

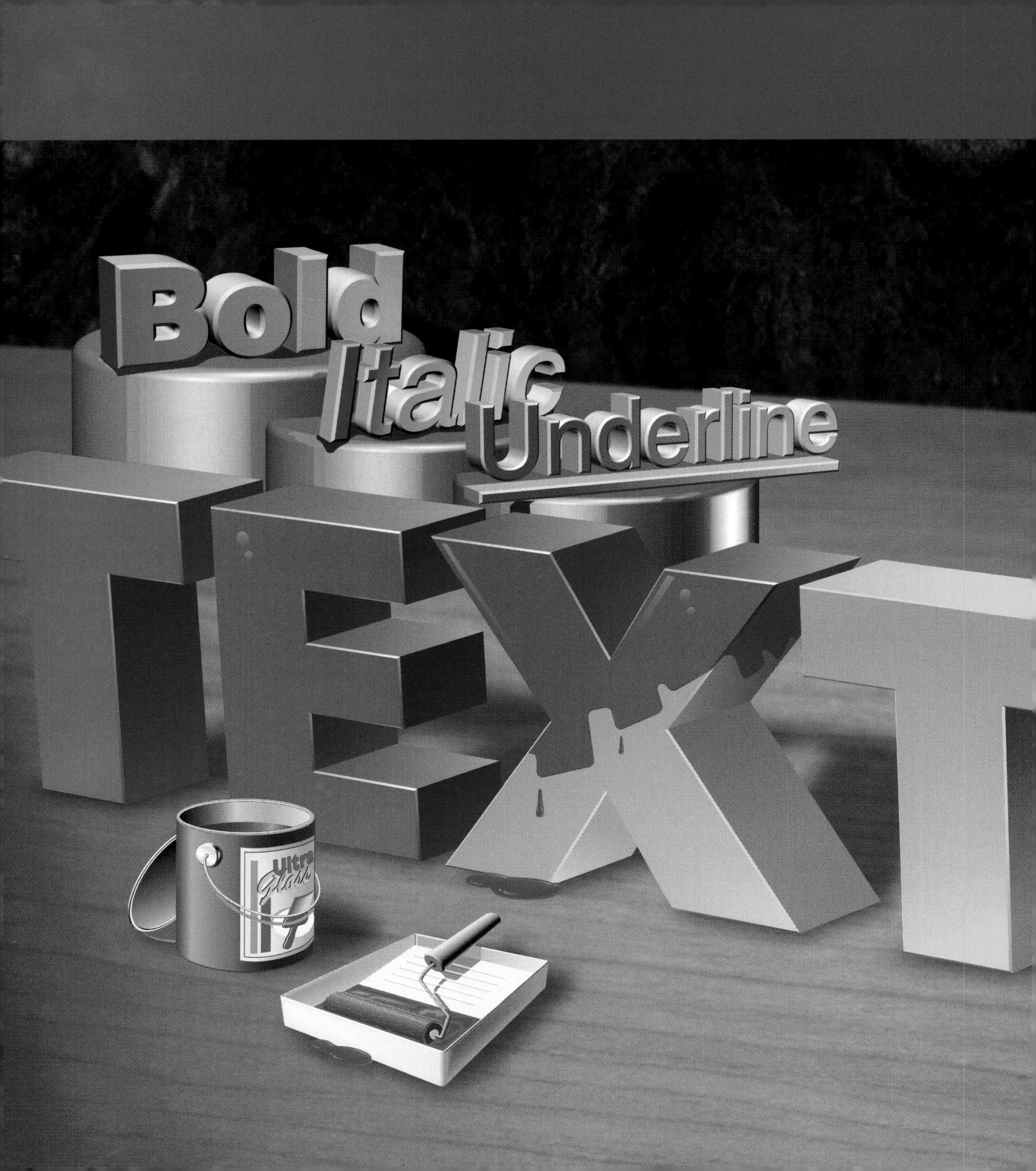
Bold
Italic
Underline
TEXT
Ultra

CHAPTER 5

Format Text

Would you like to emphasize information in your document and enhance the appearance of text? Read this chapter to learn how.

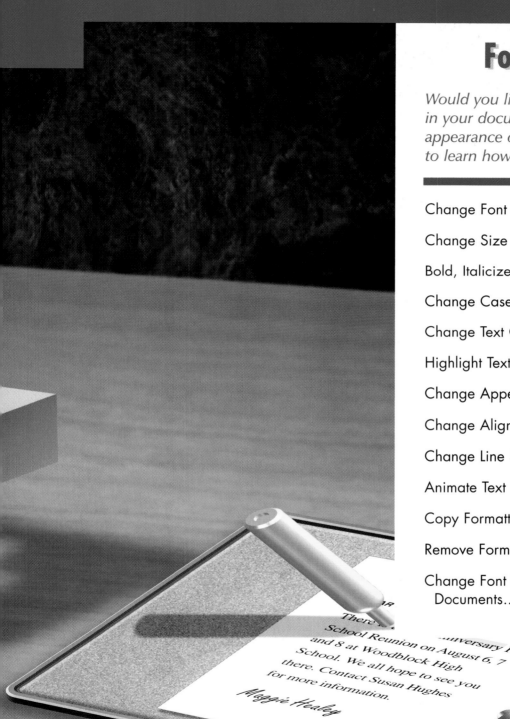

CHANGE FONT OF TEXT

You can change the font of text to enhance the appearance of your document.

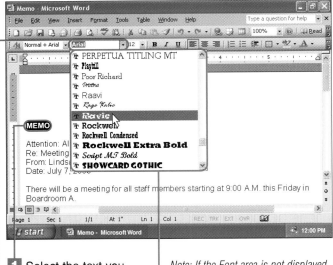

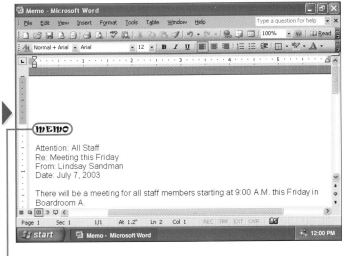

1 Select the text you want to change to a different font. To select text, see page 8.

2 Click ▼ in this area to display a list of the available fonts.

Note: If the Font area is not displayed, click ▯ *on the Formatting toolbar to display the area.*

3 Click the font you want to use.

Note: Word displays the fonts you have most recently used at the top of the list.

■ The text you selected changes to the new font.

■ To deselect text, click outside the selected area.

CHANGE SIZE OF TEXT

You can increase or decrease the size of text in your document.

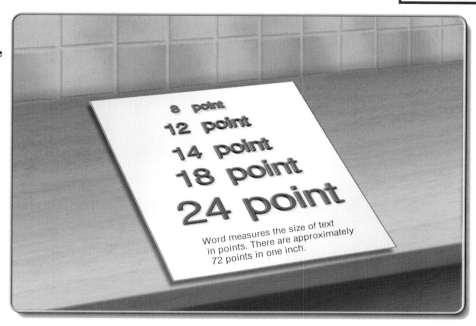

Word measures the size of text in points. There are approximately 72 points in one inch.

Larger text is easier to read, but smaller text allows you to fit more information on a page.

CHANGE SIZE OF TEXT

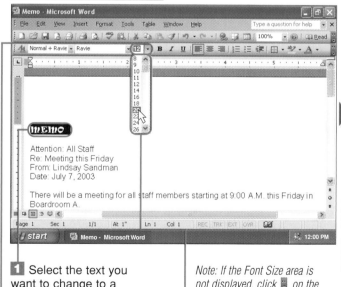

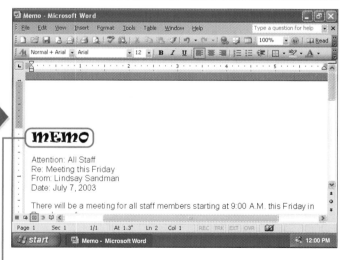

1 Select the text you want to change to a new size. To select text, see page 8.

2 Click ▾ in this area to display a list of the available sizes.

Note: If the Font Size area is not displayed, click ▾ on the Formatting toolbar to display the area.

3 Click the size you want to use.

■ The text you selected changes to the new size.

■ To deselect text, click outside the selected area.

BOLD, ITALICIZE OR UNDERLINE TEXT

You can bold, italicize or underline text to emphasize information in your document.

You can use one feature at a time or any combination of the three features to change the style of text.

BOLD, ITALICIZE OR UNDERLINE TEXT

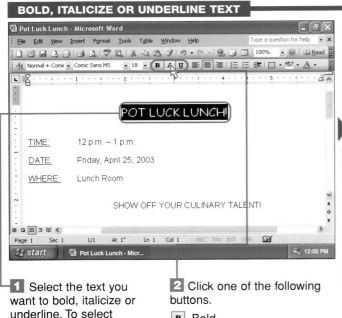

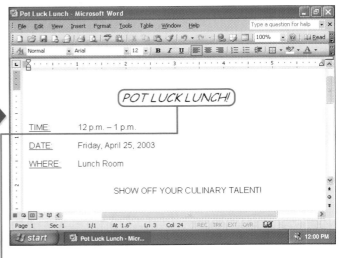

1 Select the text you want to bold, italicize or underline. To select text, see page 8.

2 Click one of the following buttons.

B Bold

I Italic

U Underline

Note: If the button you want is not displayed, click on the Formatting toolbar to display the button.

■ The text you selected appears in the new style.

■ To deselect text, click outside the selected area.

■ To remove a bold, italic or underline style, repeat steps **1** and **2**.

CHANGE CASE OF TEXT

You can change the case of text in your document without retyping the text. Word offers five case styles for you to choose from.

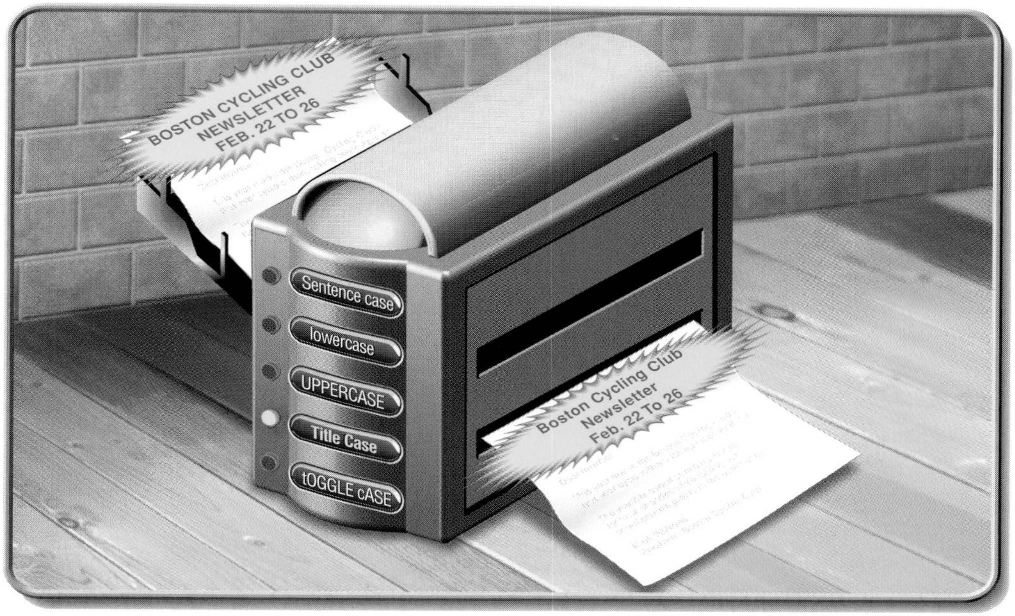

CHANGE CASE OF TEXT

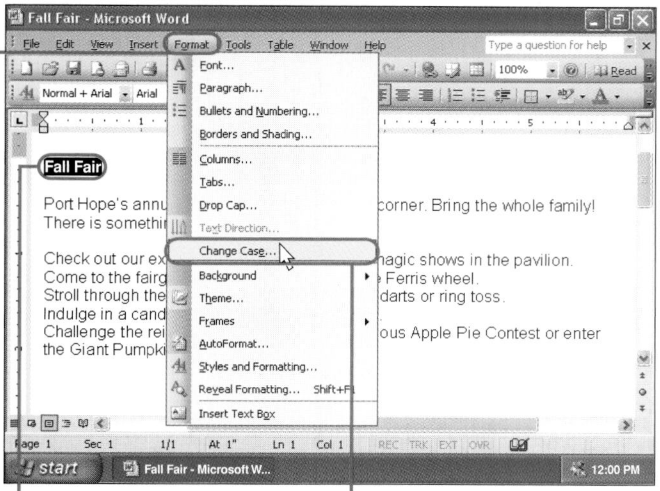

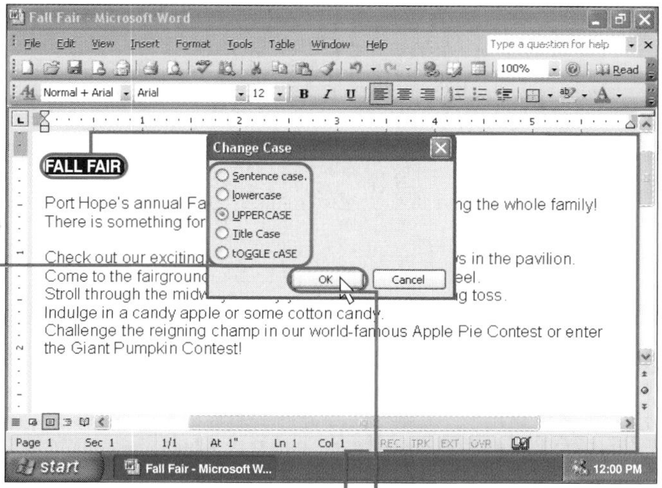

1 Select the text you want to change to a new case style. To select text, see page 8.

2 Click **Format**.

3 Click **Change Case**.

Note: If Change Case does not appear on the menu, position the mouse over the bottom of the menu to display the menu option.

■ The Change Case dialog box appears.

4 Click the case style you want to use (○ changes to ◉).

5 Click **OK** to confirm your selection.

■ The text you selected changes to the new case style.

■ To deselect text, click outside the selected area.

CHANGE TEXT COLOR

You can change the color of text to draw attention to headings or important information in your document.

Keep in mind that when you print a document that contains colored text on a black-and-white printer, the colored text will appear in shades of gray.

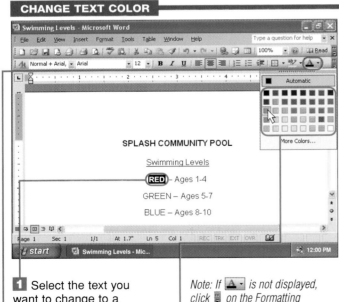

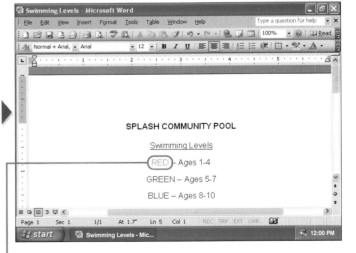

1 Select the text you want to change to a different color. To select text, see page 8.

2 Click ▾ in this area to display the available colors.

Note: If ▲▾ is not displayed, click ▸ on the Formatting toolbar to display the button.

3 Click the color you want to use.

■ The text you selected appears in the new color.

■ To deselect text, click outside the selected area.

■ To return text to its original color, repeat steps **1** to **3**, selecting **Automatic** in step **3**.

You can highlight text that you want to stand out in your document. Highlighting text is useful for marking information you want to review or verify later.

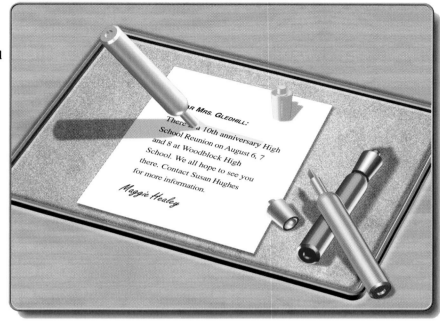

If you plan to print your document on a black-and-white printer, use a light highlight color so you will be able to easily read the printed text.

HIGHLIGHT TEXT

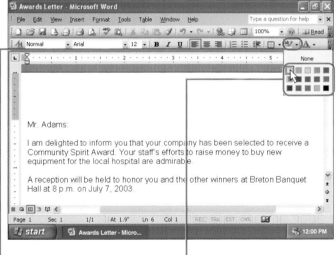

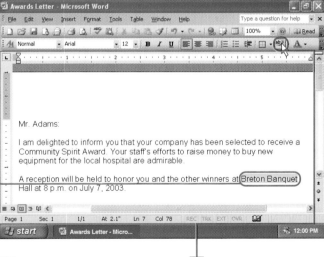

1 Click ⬛ in this area to display the available highlight colors.

Note: If ⬛ *is not displayed, click* ⬛ *on the Formatting toolbar to display the button.*

2 Click the highlight color you want to use.

■ The mouse I changes to ⬛ when over your document.

3 Select each area of text you want to highlight. To select text, see page 8.

■ The text you select appears highlighted.

4 When you finish highlighting text, click ⬛ or press the **Esc** key.

■ To remove a highlight from text, repeat steps **1** to **4**, selecting **None** in step **2**.

CHANGE APPEARANCE OF TEXT

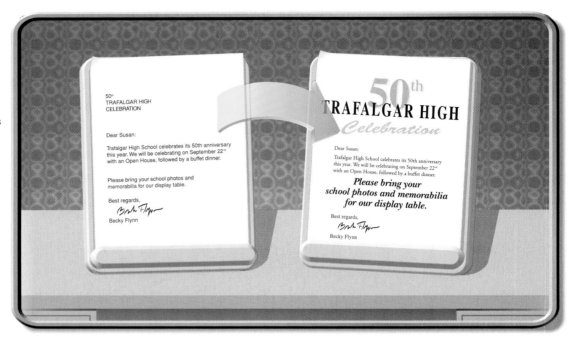

You can make text in your document look more attractive by using various fonts, styles, sizes, effects and colors.

CHANGE APPEARANCE OF TEXT

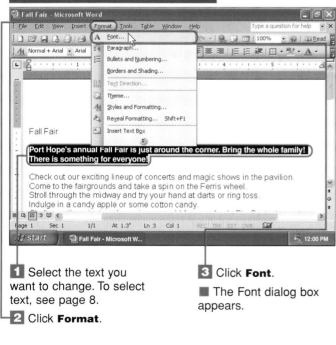

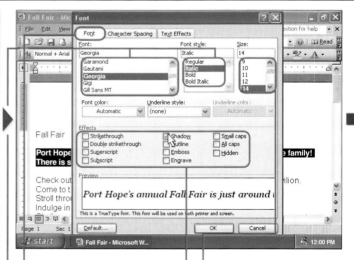

1 Select the text you want to change. To select text, see page 8.

2 Click **Format**.

3 Click **Font**.

■ The Font dialog box appears.

4 Click the **Font** tab.

5 To select a font for the text, click the font you want to use.

6 To select a style for the text, click the style you want to use.

7 To select a size for the text, click the size you want to use.

8 To select effects for the text, click each effect you want to use (☐ changes to ☑).

What determines which fonts are available on my computer?

The fonts available on your computer depend on the programs installed on your computer, the setup of your computer and your printer. You can obtain additional fonts at computer stores and on the Internet.

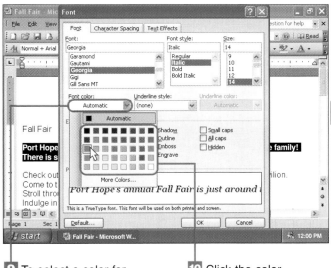

What effects can I add to text in my document?

Word offers many effects that you can use to change the appearance of text in your document.

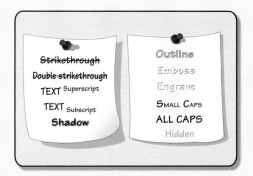

9 To select a color for the text, click this area.

10 Click the color you want to use.

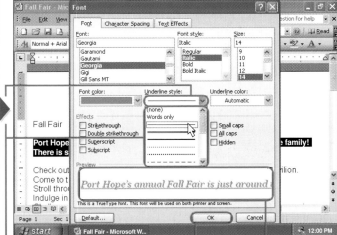

11 To select an underline style for the text, click this area.

12 Click the underline style you want to use.

■ This area displays a preview of how the text will appear in your document.

13 Click **OK** to apply your changes to the text you selected.

CHANGE ALIGNMENT OF TEXT

You can enhance the appearance of your document by aligning text in different ways.

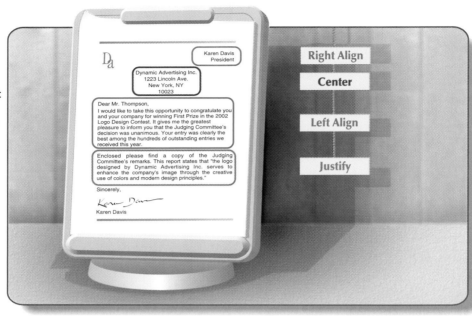

By default, Word aligns text along the left margin.

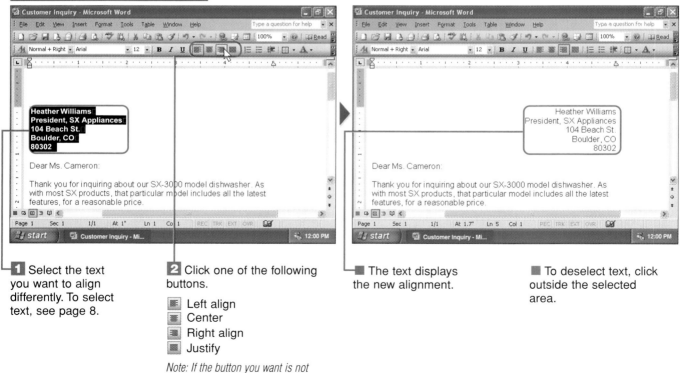

1 Select the text you want to align differently. To select text, see page 8.

2 Click one of the following buttons.

- ▤ Left align
- ▤ Center
- ▤ Right align
- ▤ Justify

Note: If the button you want is not displayed, click ⏷ on the Formatting toolbar to display the button.

■ The text displays the new alignment.

■ To deselect text, click outside the selected area.

CHANGE LINE SPACING

You can change the
amount of space
between the lines
of text in your
document.

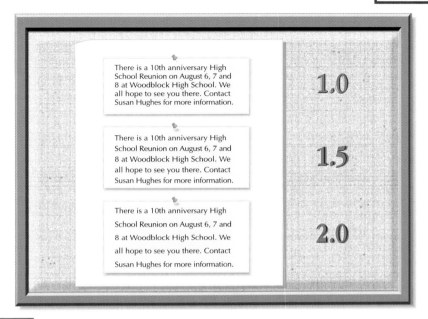

Changing the
line spacing
can make a
document
easier to
review and
edit.

CHANGE LINE SPACING

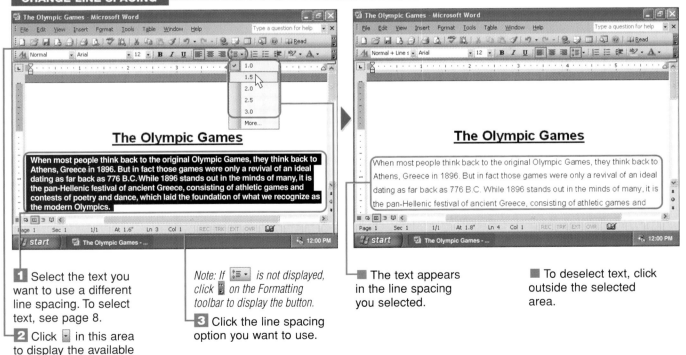

1 Select the text you
want to use a different
line spacing. To select
text, see page 8.

2 Click ⦿ in this area
to display the available
line spacing options.

*Note: If ⦿ is not displayed,
click ⦿ on the Formatting
toolbar to display the button.*

3 Click the line spacing
option you want to use.

■ The text appears
in the line spacing
you selected.

■ To deselect text, click
outside the selected
area.

ANIMATE TEXT

You can animate text in your document to make the text stand out. Animation effects are ideal for emphasizing text in a document that will be viewed on a computer screen.

An animation effect you add to your document will not appear when you print the document. For information on printing a document, see page 168.

ANIMATE TEXT

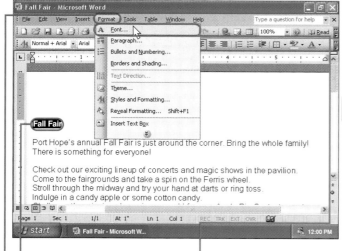

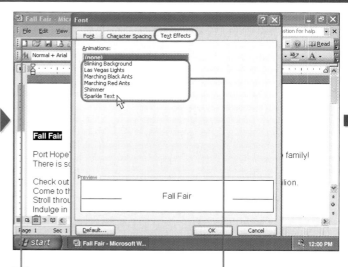

1 Select the text you want to animate. To select text, see page 8.

2 Click **Format**.

3 Click **Font**.

■ The Font dialog box appears.

4 Click the **Text Effects** tab.

5 Click the animation effect you want to use.

What types of animation effects does Word offer?

Word offers several animation effects that you can use to draw attention to text in your document.

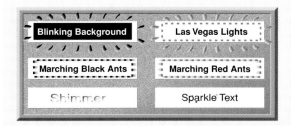

Blinking Background	Las Vegas Lights
Marching Black Ants	Marching Red Ants
Shimmer	Sparkle Text

Will I be able to view the animation effect when I display my document in a Web browser?

An animation effect you add to your document will not appear when you view the document in a Web browser window, even if you have saved the document as a Web page. For information on saving a document as a Web page, see page 294.

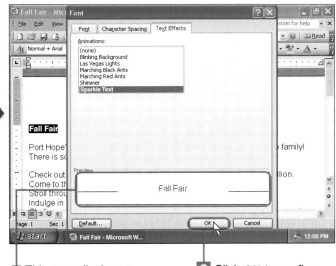

■ This area displays a preview of the animation effect.

6 Click **OK** to confirm your change.

■ The text you selected displays the animation effect.

■ To deselect text, click outside the selected area.

■ To remove an animation effect, repeat steps **1** to **6**, selecting **(none)** in step **5**.

COPY FORMATTING

You can copy the formatting of text to make one area of text in your document look exactly like another.

You may want to copy the formatting of text to make all the headings or important words in your document look the same. This will give the text in your document a consistent appearance.

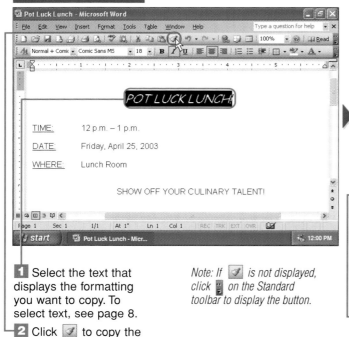

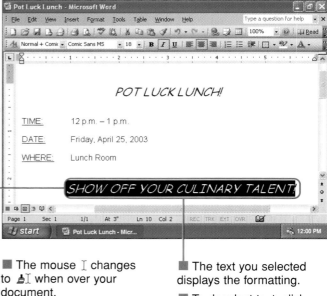

1 Select the text that displays the formatting you want to copy. To select text, see page 8.

2 Click  to copy the formatting of the text.

Note: If ✅ is not displayed, click ▾ on the Standard toolbar to display the button.

■ The mouse I changes to ▲I when over your document.

3 Select the text you want to display the same formatting.

■ The text you selected displays the formatting.

■ To deselect text, click outside the selected area.

You can remove
all the formatting
you have applied
to text in your
document.

REMOVE FORMATTING FROM TEXT

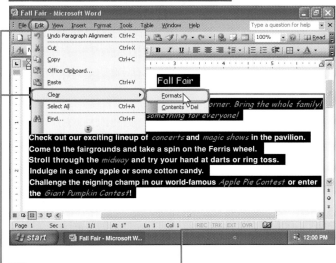

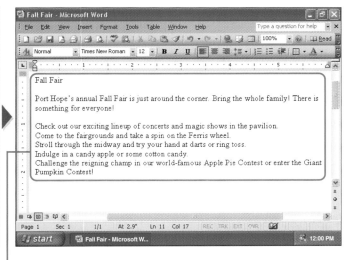

1 Select the text that displays the formatting you want to remove. To select text, see page 8.

2 Click **Edit**.

3 Click **Clear**.

Note: If Clear does not appear on the menu, position the mouse over the bottom of the menu to display the menu option.

4 Click **Formats**.

■ The formatting disappears from the text.

■ To deselect text, click outside the selected area.

You can change the font that Word uses for all new documents you create. This is useful when you want all your future documents to appear in a specific font.

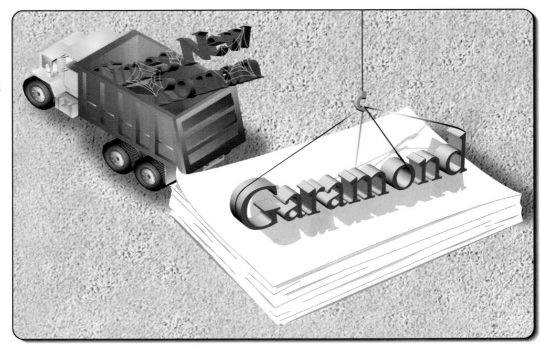

The font that Word uses for all new documents is called the default font.

CHANGE FONT FOR ALL NEW DOCUMENTS

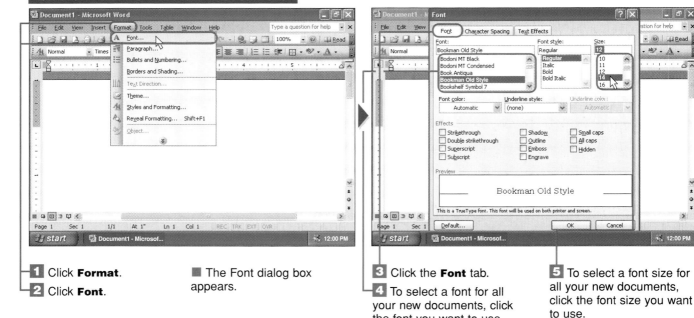

1 Click **Format**.

2 Click **Font**.

■ The Font dialog box appears.

3 Click the **Font** tab.

4 To select a font for all your new documents, click the font you want to use.

5 To select a font size for all your new documents, click the font size you want to use.

Will changing the font for all new documents affect the text in the documents I have already created?

No. Word will not change the font or size of text in documents you have already created. To change the font or size of text in existing documents, see page 92.

Can I base the default font on existing text in my document?

If your document contains text that displays the formatting you want to use for all new documents you create, you can use the text to set the default font. Select the text that displays the formatting you want to use. To select text, see page 8. Perform steps **1** and **2** below to display the Font dialog box and then skip to step **6** to set the formatting of the text you selected as the default font for all your new documents.

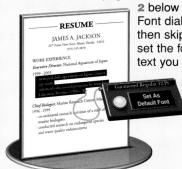

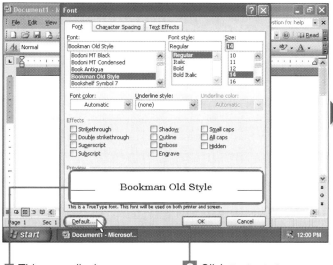

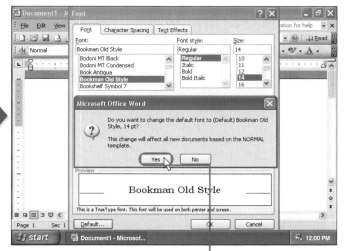

■ This area displays a preview of how the font will appear in all your new documents.

6 Click **Default** to use the font for all your new documents.

■ A dialog box appears, asking you to confirm the change.

7 Click **Yes** to confirm the change.

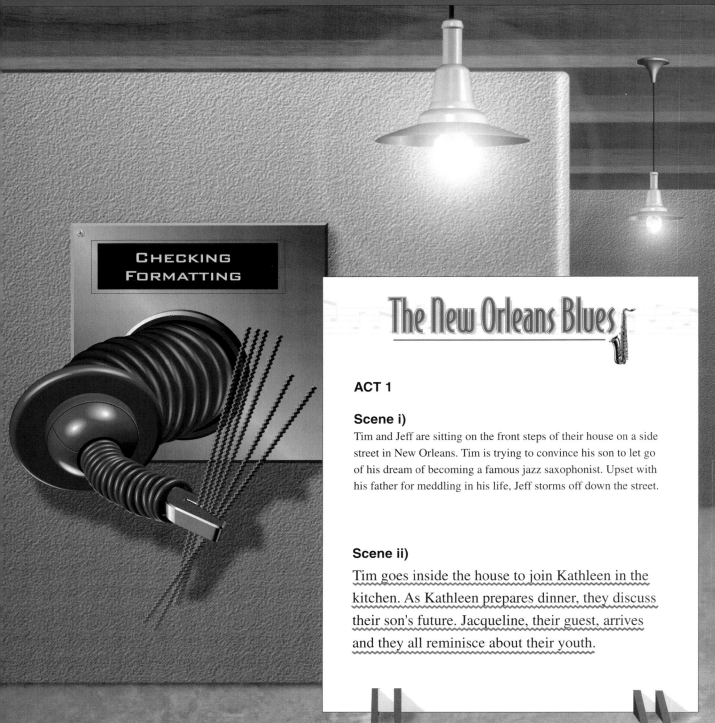

CHECKING FORMATTING

The New Orleans Blues

ACT 1

Scene i)

Tim and Jeff are sitting on the front steps of their house on a side street in New Orleans. Tim is trying to convince his son to let go of his dream of becoming a famous jazz saxophonist. Upset with his father for meddling in his life, Jeff storms off down the street.

Scene ii)

Tim goes inside the house to join Kathleen in the kitchen. As Kathleen prepares dinner, they discuss their son's future. Jacqueline, their guest, arrives and they all reminisce about their youth.

CHAPTER 6

Work With Formatting and Styles

Do you want to learn how to quickly apply formatting to text in a document? This chapter shows you how.

Act I

Act II

Formatting Differences

Arial	-->	Georgia
16 pt	-->	11 pt
No underline	-->	Underline
Blue Text	-->	Red Text

Plot Summary
ACT I

Scene I

Tim and Jeff are sitting on the front steps of their house on a side street in New Orleans. Tim is trying to convince his son to let go of his dream of becoming a famous jazz saxophonist. Upset with his father for meddling in his life, Jeff storms

REVIEW FORMATTING

Font:
 Arial
 10 pt
 Bold
 Font color: Red
Language:
 English

CHECK FORMATTING

You can have Word underline formatting inconsistencies in your document. You can then correct the inconsistencies to give the document a professional appearance.

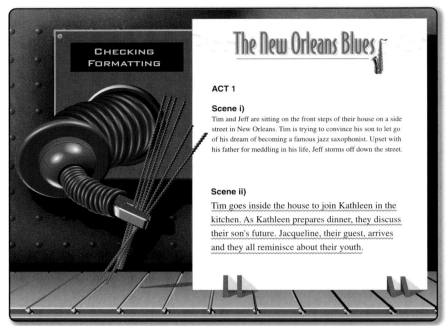

Word underlines formatting inconsistencies in blue.

CHECK FORMATTING

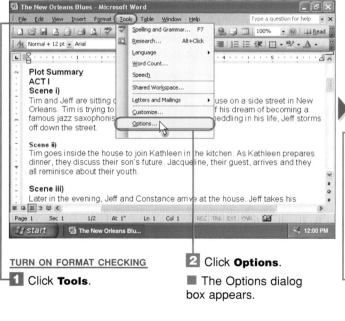

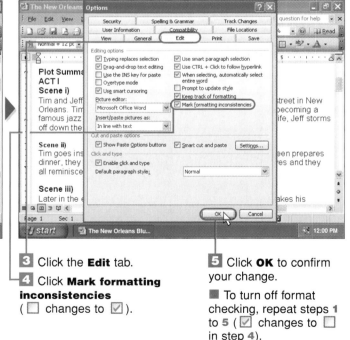

TURN ON FORMAT CHECKING

1 Click **Tools**.

2 Click **Options**.

■ The Options dialog box appears.

3 Click the **Edit** tab.

4 Click **Mark formatting inconsistencies** (☐ changes to ☑).

5 Click **OK** to confirm your change.

■ To turn off format checking, repeat steps **1** to **5** (☑ changes to ☐ in step **4**).

Why didn't Word underline all the formatting inconsistencies in my document?

Word only underlines inconsistent formatting that appears accidental, such as a heading that is slightly smaller than other headings in your document.

Is there another way I can check for inconsistent formatting in my document?

You can use the Reveal Formatting task pane to review details about the formatting applied to text in your document and compare the formatting of two areas of text. For more information on the Reveal Formatting task pane, see page 114.

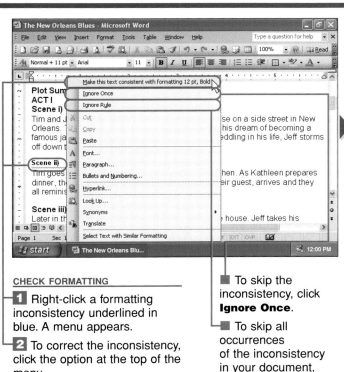

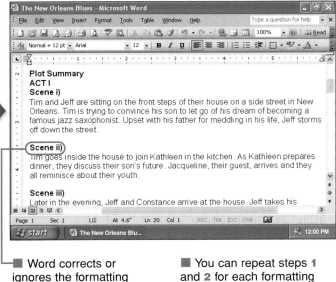

CHECK FORMATTING

1 Right-click a formatting inconsistency underlined in blue. A menu appears.

2 To correct the inconsistency, click the option at the top of the menu.

Note: The name of the option depends on the formatting inconsistency you selected.

■ To skip the inconsistency, click **Ignore Once**.

■ To skip all occurrences of the inconsistency in your document, click **Ignore Rule**.

■ Word corrects or ignores the formatting inconsistency.

■ The blue underline disappears from the text.

■ You can repeat steps **1** and **2** for each formatting inconsistency in your document.

APPLY FORMATTING

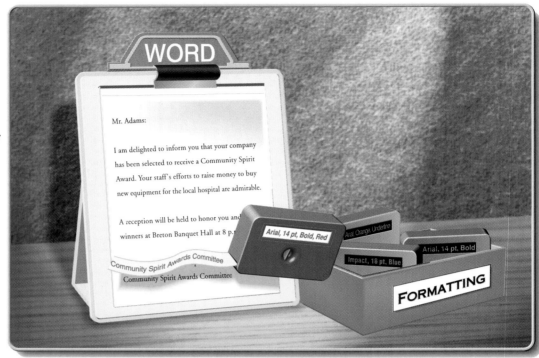

Word keeps track of the formatting you have applied to text in your document. You can apply the formatting to another area of text.

APPLY FORMATTING TO ONE AREA OF TEXT

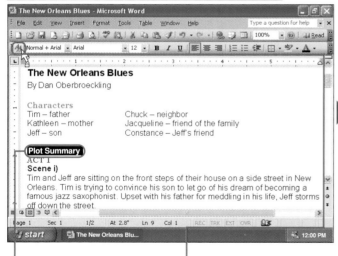

1 Select the text you want to apply formatting to. To select text, see page 8.

2 Click 🔄 to display the Styles and Formatting task pane.

Note: If 🔄 is not displayed, click ▾ on the Formatting toolbar to display the button.

■ The Styles and Formatting task pane appears.

■ This area displays the current formatting of the text you selected.

Is there another way to apply formatting to text in my document?

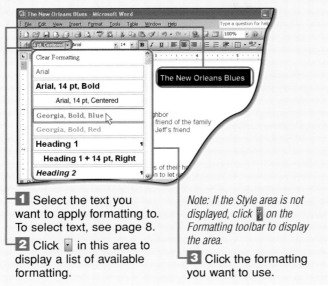

1 Select the text you want to apply formatting to. To select text, see page 8.

2 Click ⬝ in this area to display a list of available formatting.

Note: If the Style area is not displayed, click ⬝ on the Formatting toolbar to display the area.

3 Click the formatting you want to use.

Can I remove formatting I have applied to text?

You can remove formatting you have applied to text in your document. Perform steps **1** to **3** below, selecting **Clear Formatting** in step **3**.

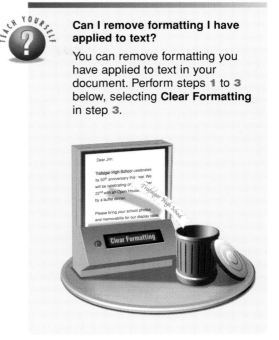

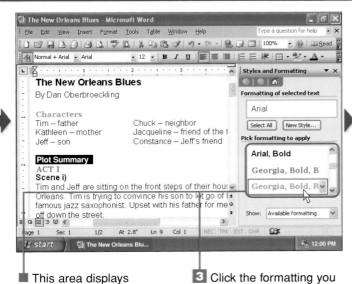

■ This area displays formatting you have used in your document.

Note: The area also displays styles included with Word and styles you have created. For information on styles, see pages 110 to 113.

3 Click the formatting you want to apply to the text.

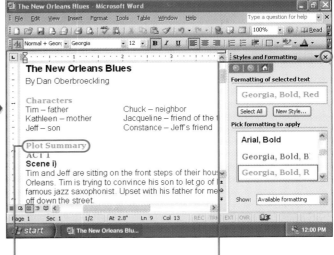

■ The text you selected displays the new formatting.

■ To deselect text, click outside the selected area.

■ To hide the Styles and Formatting task pane, click ✕.

CONTINUED

APPLY FORMATTING

You can instantly change the appearance of all the text in a document that displays the same formatting. This saves you time and keeps the appearance of text in your document consistent.

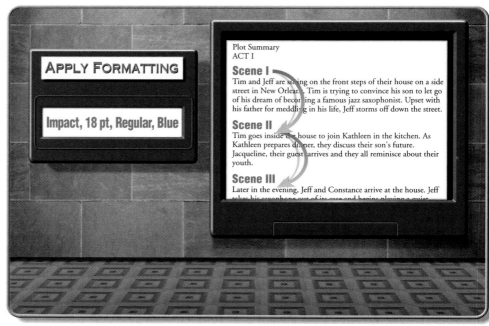

APPLY FORMATTING TO MANY AREAS OF TEXT

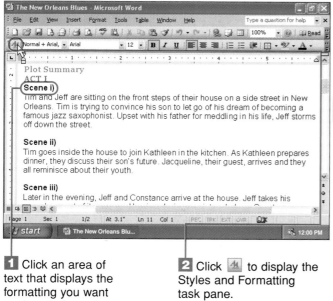

1 Click an area of text that displays the formatting you want to change throughout your document.

2 Click ▲ to display the Styles and Formatting task pane.

Note: If ▲ is not displayed, click ⁝ on the Formatting toolbar to display the button.

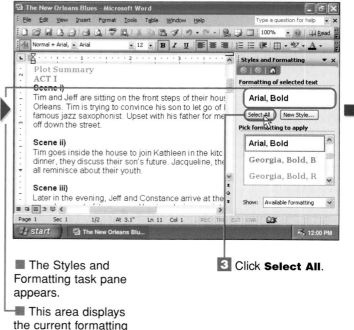

■ The Styles and Formatting task pane appears.

■ This area displays the current formatting of the text you selected.

3 Click **Select All**.

The Styles and Formatting task pane does not display the formatting I want to apply. What can I do?

Perform steps 1 to 3 below to select the areas of text you want to format. You can then format the text as you would format any text in a document. For example, you can change the font, size, color or alignment of the text. To format text, see pages 86 to 95.

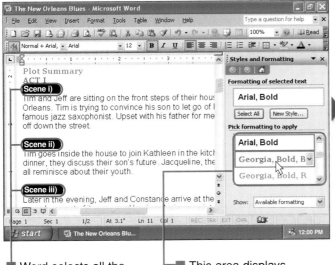

■ Word selects all the text in your document that displays the same formatting.

■ This area displays formatting you have used in your document.

Note: The area also displays styles included with Word and styles you have created. For information on styles, see pages 110 to 113.

4 Click the formatting you want to apply to the selected text.

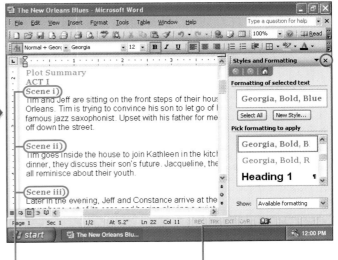

■ The selected text displays the new formatting.

■ To deselect text, click outside a selected area.

■ To hide the Styles and Formatting task pane, click ☒.

CREATE A STYLE

You can create a style to store formatting you like. You can then use the style to quickly apply formatting to text in your documents.

CREATE A STYLE

1 Click  to display the Styles and Formatting task pane.

Note: If is not displayed, click on the Formatting toolbar to display the button.

2 Click **New Style** to create a new style.

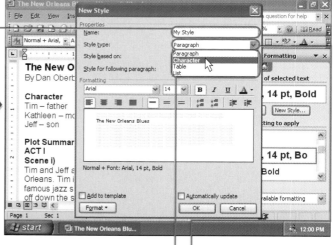

■ The New Style dialog box appears.

3 Type a name for the new style.

4 Click this area to select the type of style you want to create.

5 Click the type of style you want to create.

Note: For information on the types of styles, see the top of page 111.

What types of styles can I create?

Paragraph (¶)

A paragraph style includes formatting that changes the appearance of individual characters and entire paragraphs, such as text alignment and line spacing.

Character (a)

A character style includes formatting that changes the appearance of individual characters, such as font and text color.

Table (⊞)

A table style includes formatting that changes the appearance of tables, such as borders and shading. For information on tables, see pages 190 to 207.

List (≔)

A list style includes formatting that changes the appearance of numbers or bullets in a list, such as number or bullet styles and indenting. For information on lists, see page 120.

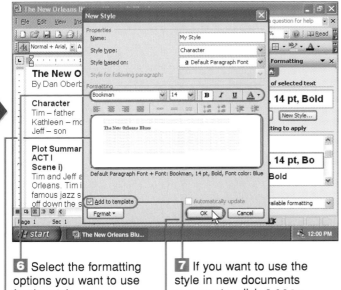

6 Select the formatting options you want to use for the style.

Note: The available formatting options depend on the type of style you selected.

■ This area displays a preview of the style.

7 If you want to use the style in new documents you create, click **Add to template** (☐ changes to ☑).

8 Click **OK** to create the style.

Note: To hide the Styles and Formatting task pane, repeat step 1.

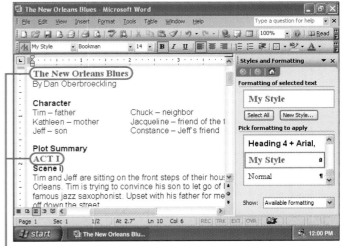

APPLY A STYLE

1 Select the text or list you want to apply a style to. To select text, see page 8.

■ To apply a style to a table, click the table.

2 Perform steps **2** and **3** starting on page 106 to apply the style.

CHANGE A STYLE

You can change a style you created. When you change a style, Word automatically changes all the text you formatted with the style.

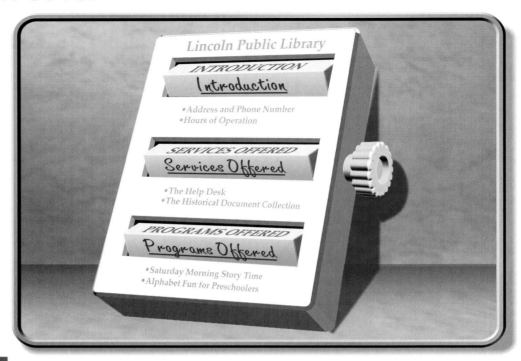

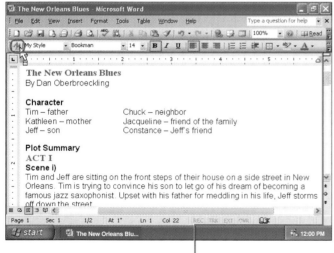

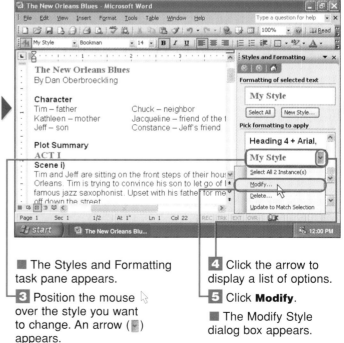

1 Open a document containing the style you want to change. To open a document, see page 24.

2 Click to display the Styles and Formatting task pane.

Note: If the button is not displayed, click on the Formatting toolbar to display the button.

■ The Styles and Formatting task pane appears.

3 Position the mouse over the style you want to change. An arrow appears.

4 Click the arrow to display a list of options.

5 Click **Modify**.

■ The Modify Style dialog box appears.

When would I want to change a style?

You may want to change an existing style to quickly change the appearance of a document. You can try several formats until the document appears the way you want.

Will changing a style affect documents I have already created?

No. When you change a style, Word will not change the appearance of text, lists or tables formatted with the style in documents you have already created.

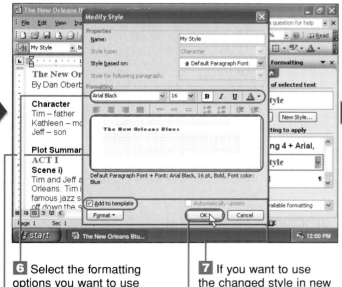

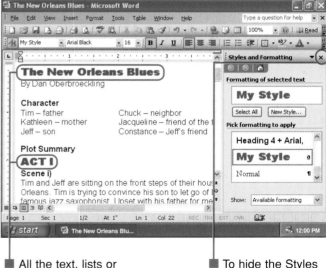

■■6 **Select the formatting options you want to use for the style.**

Note: The available formatting options depend on the type of style you are changing.

■ This area displays a preview of the style.

■■7 **If you want to use the changed style in new documents you create, click Add to template (☐ changes to ☑).**

■■8 **Click OK to change the style.**

■ All the text, lists or tables formatted with the style display the changes.

■ To hide the Styles and Formatting task pane, click ☒.

REVIEW FORMATTING

You can review details about the formatting applied to text in a document. This is useful when you want to determine exactly what formatting was applied to the text.

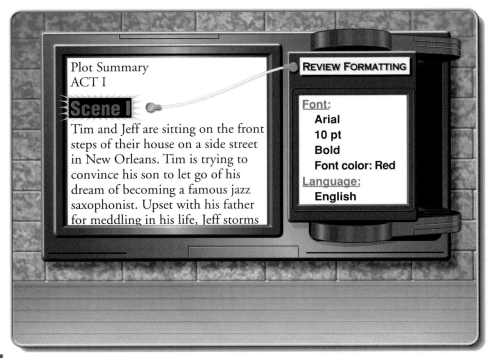

REVIEW FORMATTING

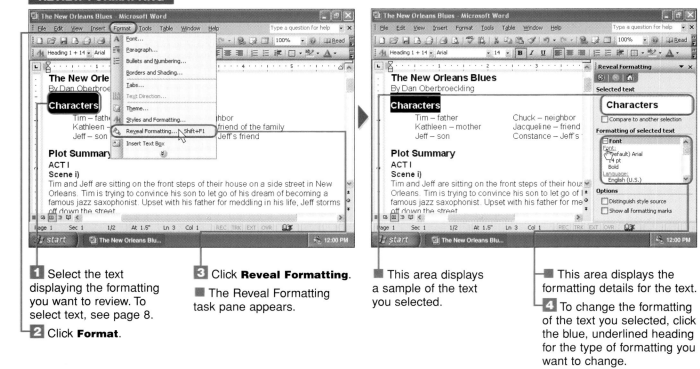

1 Select the text displaying the formatting you want to review. To select text, see page 8.

2 Click **Format**.

3 Click **Reveal Formatting**.

■ The Reveal Formatting task pane appears.

■ This area displays a sample of the text you selected.

■ This area displays the formatting details for the text.

4 To change the formatting of the text you selected, click the blue, underlined heading for the type of formatting you want to change.

What types of formatting can I review using the Reveal Formatting task pane?

The Reveal Formatting task pane allows you to review several types of formatting including font, paragraph and section formatting. For example, you can review paragraph formatting to determine the alignment of the paragraph or review section formatting to determine the margin settings for the section.

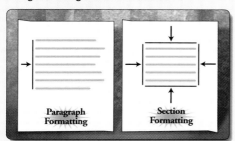

Paragraph Formatting

Section Formatting

When reviewing formatting, how can I display more details?

Each item that displays a plus sign (⊞) contains hidden details. To display the hidden details, click the plus sign (⊞) beside the item (⊞ changes to ⊟). To once again hide the details, click the minus sign (⊟) beside the item.

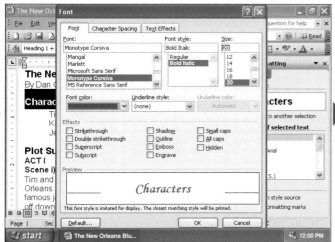

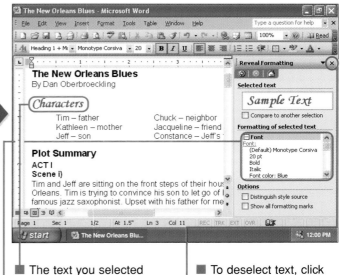

■ In this example, the Font dialog box appears.

Note: The dialog box that appears depends on the blue, underlined heading you selected.

5 Select the options you want in the dialog box to change the formatting of the text and then click **OK**.

Note: For information on the options available in the Font dialog box, see page 92.

■ The text you selected displays the formatting changes.

■ This area displays the new formatting details.

■ To deselect text, click outside the selected area.

■ To hide the Reveal Formatting task pane, click ×.

CONTINUED ▶

REVIEW FORMATTING

Word allows you to compare the formatting of two areas of text in a document. You can then match the formatting of the areas so they display the same formatting.

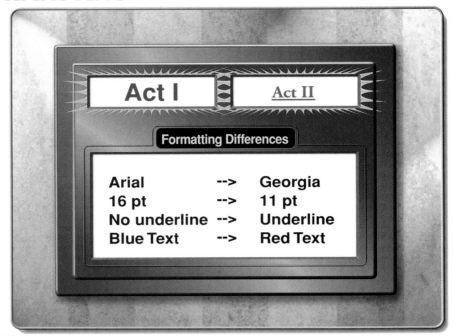

COMPARE FORMATTING

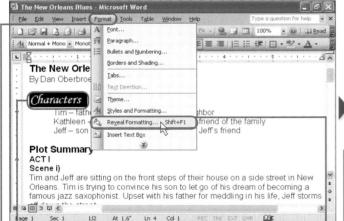

1 Select the text you want to compare to another area of text in your document. To select text, see page 8.

2 Click **Format**.

3 Click **Reveal Formatting**.

■ The Reveal Formatting task pane appears.

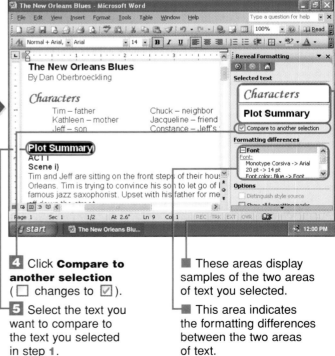

4 Click **Compare to another selection** (☐ changes to ☑).

5 Select the text you want to compare to the text you selected in step **1**.

■ These areas display samples of the two areas of text you selected.

■ This area indicates the formatting differences between the two areas of text.

Note: If there are no differences, the area displays the text **No formatting differences**.

When would I need to compare formatting?

You should compare formatting in a document that may contain inconsistent formatting. For example, when formatting a long document, you may have applied different formatting to different areas of the document. If you created a new document by copying text from other documents, the new document may display several different types of formatting.

How can I ensure that the formatting in my documents is consistent?

You can use the Styles and Formatting task pane to apply consistent formatting to text in your documents. For information on using the Styles and Formatting task pane, see pages 106 to 109.

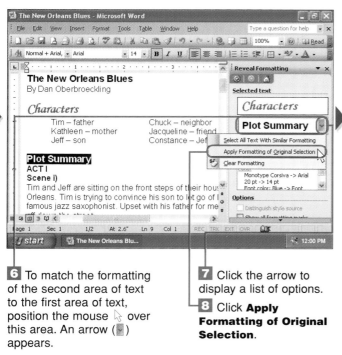

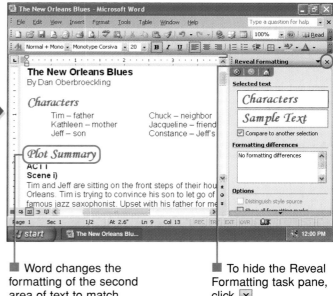

6 To match the formatting of the second area of text to the first area of text, position the mouse over this area. An arrow appears.

7 Click the arrow to display a list of options.

8 Click **Apply Formatting of Original Selection**.

■ Word changes the formatting of the second area of text to match the formatting of the first area of text.

■ To deselect text, click outside the selected area.

■ To hide the Reveal Formatting task pane, click ×.

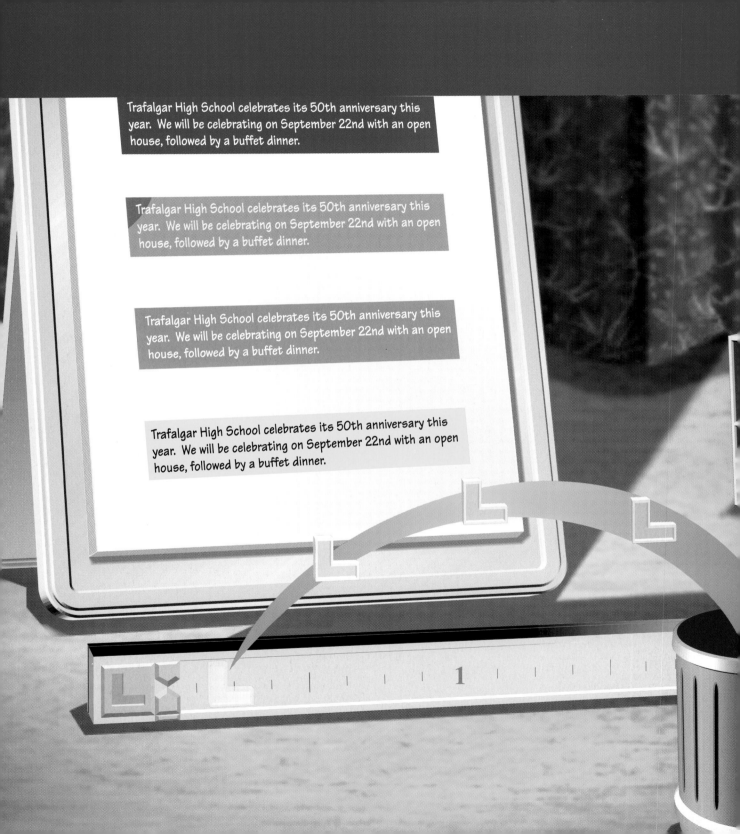

Trafalgar High School celebrates its 50th anniversary this year. We will be celebrating on September 22nd with an open house, followed by a buffet dinner.

Trafalgar High School celebrates its 50th anniversary this year. We will be celebrating on September 22nd with an open house, followed by a buffet dinner.

Trafalgar High School celebrates its 50th anniversary this year. We will be celebrating on September 22nd with an open house, followed by a buffet dinner.

Trafalgar High School celebrates its 50th anniversary this year. We will be celebrating on September 22nd with an open house, followed by a buffet dinner.

1

CHAPTER 7

Format Paragraphs

Do you want to create bulleted or numbered lists, indent paragraphs and add shading to text in your document? Learn how in this chapter.

CREATE A BULLETED OR NUMBERED LIST

You can separate items in a list by beginning each item with a bullet or number.

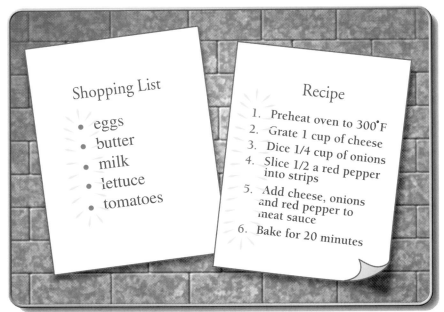

Shopping List

- eggs
- butter
- milk
- lettuce
- tomatoes

Recipe

1. Preheat oven to 300°F
2. Grate 1 cup of cheese
3. Dice 1/4 cup of onions
4. Slice 1/2 a red pepper into strips
5. Add cheese, onions and red pepper to meat sauce
6. Bake for 20 minutes

Bulleted lists are useful for items in no particular order, such as items in a shopping list.

Numbered lists are useful for items in a specific order, such as instructions in a recipe.

CREATE A BULLETED OR NUMBERED LIST

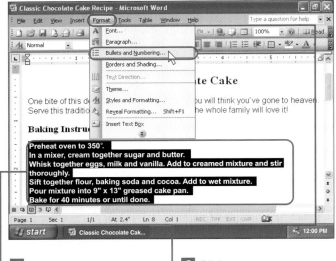

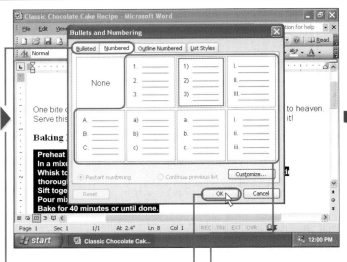

1 Select the text you want to display as a bulleted or numbered list. To select text, see page 8.

2 Click **Format**.

3 Click **Bullets and Numbering**.

■ The Bullets and Numbering dialog box appears.

4 Click the tab for the type of list you want to create.

5 Click the style you want to use.

6 Click **OK** to confirm your selection.

How can I create a bulleted or numbered list as I type?

1 Type ***** to create a bulleted list or type **1.** to create a numbered list. Then press the **Spacebar**.

2 Type the first item in the list and then press the **Enter** key. Word automatically adds a bullet or number for the next item.

3 Repeat step **2** for each item in the list.

4 To finish the list, press the **Enter** key twice.

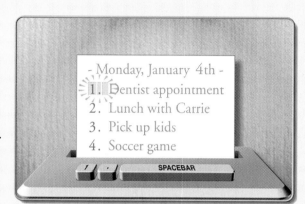

Note: When you create a bulleted or numbered list as you type, the AutoCorrect Options button ( ) appears. You can click this button and select **Undo Automatic Bullets/Numbering** to specify that you do not want Word to create a bulleted or numbered list in this instance.

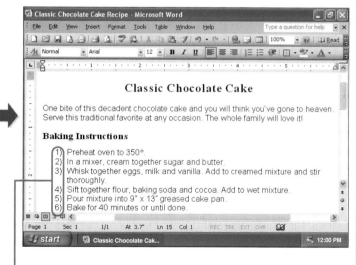

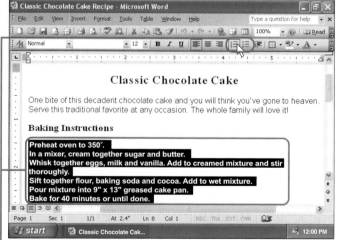

■ A bullet or number appears in front of each item in the list.

■ To deselect the text in the list, click outside the selected area.

■ To remove bullets or numbers from a list, repeat steps **1** to **6**, selecting **None** in step **5**.

USING THE TOOLBAR BUTTONS

1 Select the text you want to display as a list. To select text, see page 8.

2 Click one of the following buttons.

▤ Add numbers

▤ Add bullets

Note: If the button you want is not displayed, click on the Formatting toolbar to display the button.

INDENT PARAGRAPHS

You can indent text
to make paragraphs
in your document
stand out.

The spacious grounds of Foster City
Zoo were established in 1960 on 350 acres
of forest and farmland located five miles
west of Foster City, NY.

INDENT PARAGRAPHS

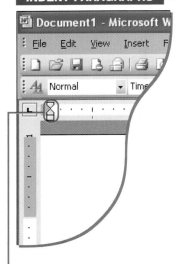

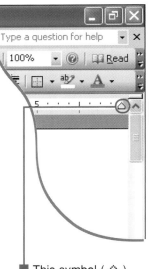

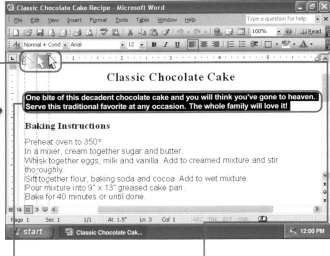

■ These symbols allow you
to indent the left edge of a
paragraph.

▽ Indent first line

△ Indent all but the first line

☐ Indent all lines

■ This symbol (△)
allows you to indent
the right edge of a
paragraph.

*Note: If the ruler is not
displayed, see page 38
to display the ruler.*

1 Select the paragraph(s)
you want to indent. To select
text, see page 8.

2 Position the mouse ℞
over the indent symbol you
want to use.

3 Drag the indent
symbol to a new position
on the ruler.

■ A dotted line shows
the new indent position.

What types of indents can I create?

First Line Indent

Indents only the first line of a paragraph. First line indents are often used to mark the beginning of paragraphs in letters and professional documents.

Hanging Indent

Indents all but the first line of a paragraph. Hanging indents are useful when you are creating a glossary or bibliography.

Indent Both Sides

Indenting both the left and right sides of a paragraph is useful when you want to set text, such as a quotation, apart from the rest of the text in your document.

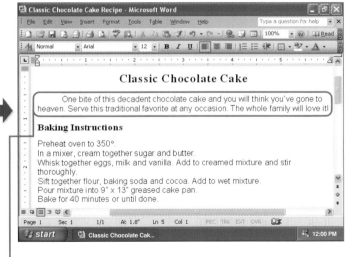

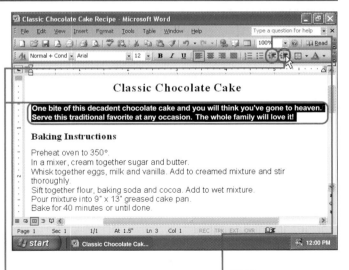

■ Word indents the paragraph(s) you selected.

■ To deselect text, click outside the selected area.

USING THE TOOLBAR BUTTONS

1 Select the paragraph(s) you want to indent. To select text, see page 8.

2 Click 🔳 to indent the left edge of the paragraph(s).

Note: If 🔳 is not displayed, click ┊ on the Formatting toolbar to display the button.

■ You can repeat step **2** to further indent the text.

■ To decrease the indent, click 🔳.

CHANGE TAB SETTINGS

You can use tabs to line up information in your document. Word offers several types of tabs that you can choose from.

Word automatically places a tab every 0.5 inches across a page.

You should use tabs instead of spaces to line up information. If you use spaces, the information may not be lined up when you print your document.

CHANGE TAB SETTINGS

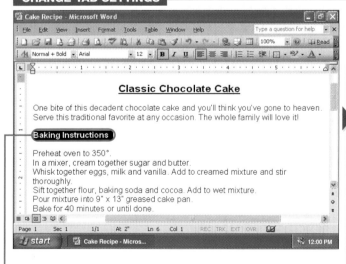

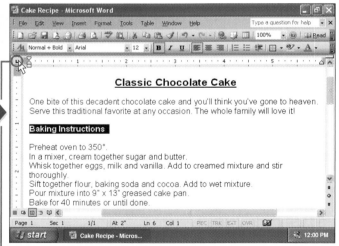

ADD A TAB

1 Select the text you want to use the new tab. To select text, see page 8.

■ To add a tab to text you are about to type, click the location in your document where you want to type the text.

2 Click this area until the type of tab you want to add appears.

⌊ Left tab

⌐ Center tab

⌐ Right tab

⌐ Decimal tab

Note: If the ruler is not displayed, see page 38 to display the ruler.

How do I move a tab?

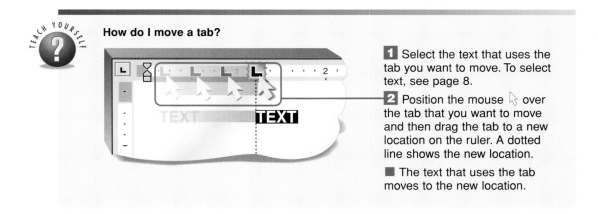

1 Select the text that uses the tab you want to move. To select text, see page 8.

2 Position the mouse ⊮ over the tab that you want to move and then drag the tab to a new location on the ruler. A dotted line shows the new location.

■ The text that uses the tab moves to the new location.

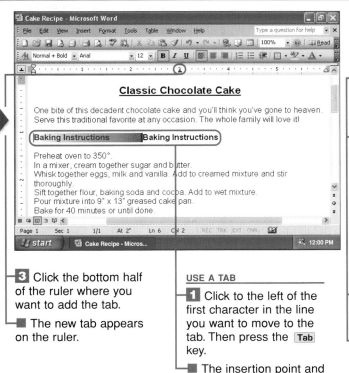

3 Click the bottom half of the ruler where you want to add the tab.

■ The new tab appears on the ruler.

USE A TAB

1 Click to the left of the first character in the line you want to move to the tab. Then press the `Tab` key.

■ The insertion point and the text that follows move to the tab you set.

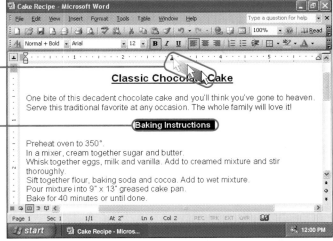

REMOVE A TAB

1 Select the text that uses the tab you want to remove. To select text, see page 8.

2 Position the mouse ⊮ over the tab you want to remove and then drag the tab downward off the ruler.

■ The tab disappears from the ruler.

■ To move the text back to the left margin, click to the left of the first character. Then press the `+Backspace` key.

CONTINUED

125

CHANGE TAB SETTINGS

You can insert a line
or row of dots, called
leader characters,
before a tab to
help lead the
eye from one
column of
information
to another.

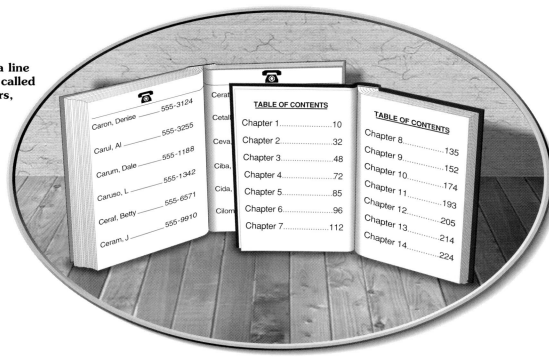

ADD A TAB WITH LEADER CHARACTERS

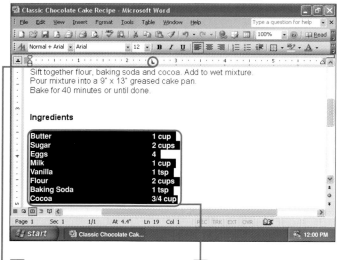

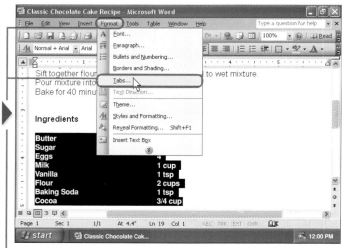

1 Add a tab to the text
you want to display leader
characters. To add a tab,
see page 124.

2 Select the text
containing the tab. To
select text, see page 8.

3 Click **Format**.

4 Click **Tabs**.

*Note: If Tabs does not appear on
the menu, position the mouse
over the bottom of the menu to
display the menu option.*

■ The Tabs dialog box
appears.

Why would I use leader characters?

Leader characters make information such as a table of contents or a list of telephone numbers easier to read.

Carson, S...... 555-5670
Hyland, M...... 555-2346
Inglis, K......... 555-4328
Kerr, D.......... 555-7621
Moore, S....... 555-3066
Schmidt, S.... 555-8087
Smith, M....... 555-5190
Taylor, D...... 555-3487
Trott, P........ 555-1729
Walker, B...... 555-5430

Leader characters are also used in forms to create areas where people can enter information.

JOB APPLICATION
Please enter information in the areas provided.
Last Name: _____
First Name: _____
Address: _____
_____
City/State: _____
Zip Code: _____
Phone No: _____

How do I remove the leader characters from my document?

To remove the leader characters, perform steps **2** to **7** below, selecting **None** in step **6**.

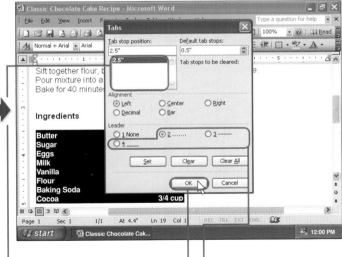

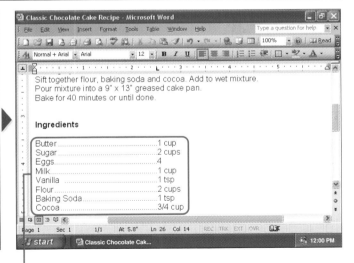

■ This area displays the positions of all the tabs for the text you selected.

5 Click the tab you want to display leader characters.

6 Click the type of leader character you want to use (○ changes to ◉).

7 Click **OK** to confirm your selections.

■ The text you selected displays the leader characters.

■ To deselect text, click outside the selected area.

CREATE A DROP CAP

You can create a large capital letter at the beginning of a paragraph to enhance the appearance of the paragraph.

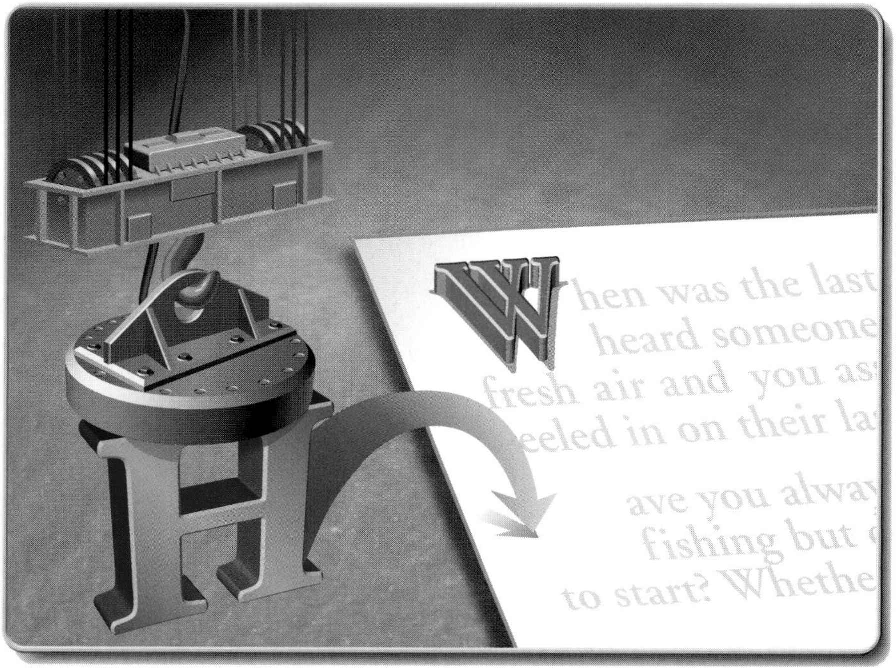

Word can properly display a drop cap only in the Print Layout and Web Layout views. To change the view of a document, see page 36.

CREATE A DROP CAP

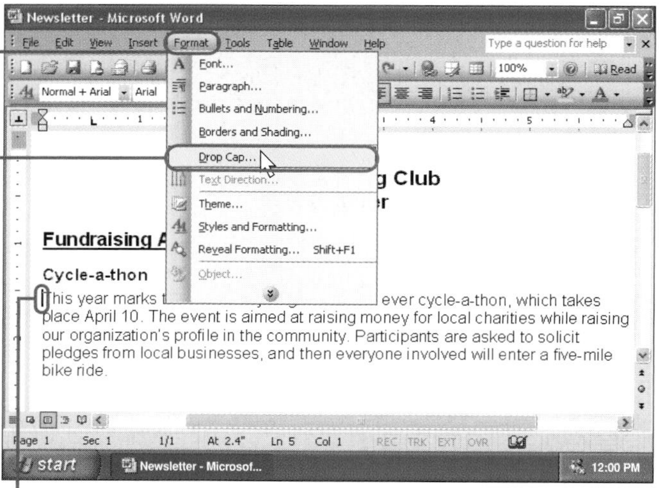

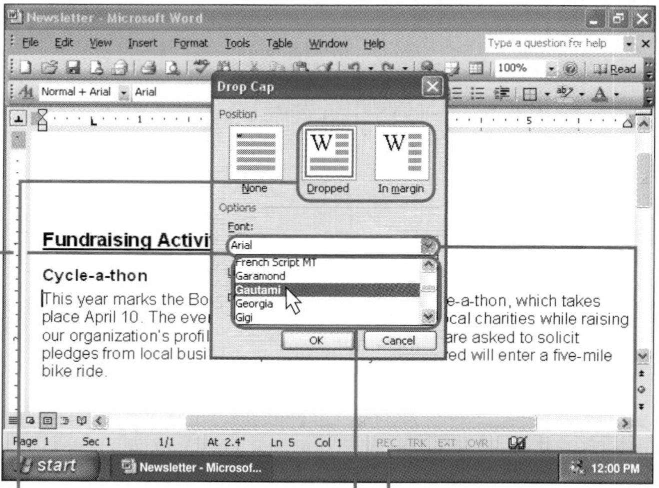

1 Click the paragraph you want to display a drop cap.

2 Click **Format**.

3 Click **Drop Cap**.

Note: If Drop Cap does not appear on the menu, position the mouse over the bottom of the menu to display the menu option.

■ The Drop Cap dialog box appears.

4 Click the type of drop cap you want to create.

Note: For information on the types of drop caps you can create, see the top of page 129.

■ This area displays the font the drop cap will display.

5 To select another font for the drop cap, click in this area.

6 Click the font you want the drop cap to display.

What types of drop caps can I create?

Dropped

Wraps text in the paragraph around the drop cap.

In margin

Moves the drop cap into the left margin of the document. For information on margins, see page 150.

Can I create a drop cap using more than one letter?

You can create a drop cap using several letters or an entire word at the beginning of a paragraph. Drag the mouse I over the letters or word you want to make a drop cap until you highlight the text. Then perform steps **2** to **8** below.

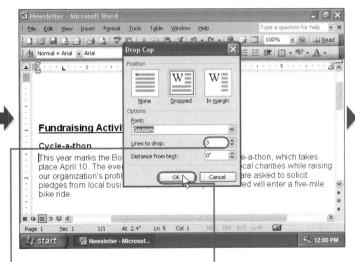

■ This area displays the number of lines that the drop cap will extend down from the first line of the paragraph.

7 To change the number of lines, double-click the number in this area and then type a new number.

8 Click **OK** to create the drop cap.

■ The drop cap appears in your document.

■ To deselect the drop cap, click outside the drop cap.

■ To remove a drop cap, repeat steps **1** to **4**, selecting **None** in step **4**. Then perform step **8**.

ADD A BORDER

You can add a border to text in your document to draw attention to important information.

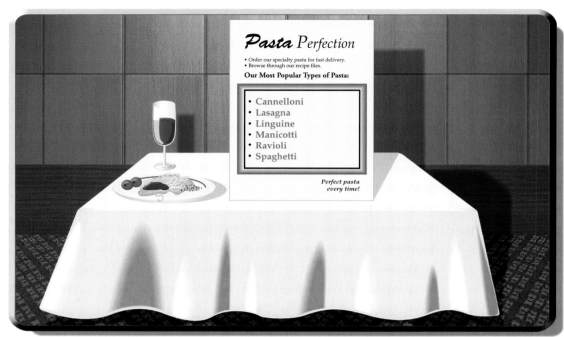

ADD A BORDER

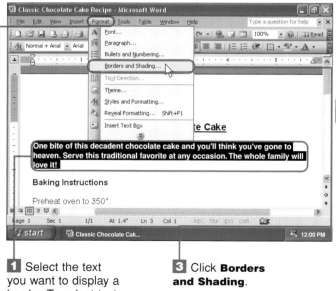

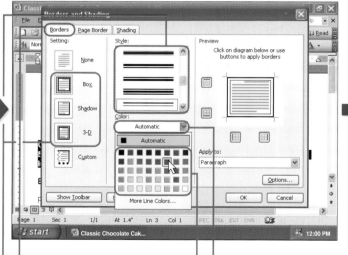

1 Select the text you want to display a border. To select text, see page 8.

2 Click **Format**.

3 Click **Borders and Shading**.

■ The Borders and Shading dialog box appears.

4 Click the **Borders** tab.

5 Click the type of border you want to add.

6 Click the line style you want to use for the border.

7 To select a color for the border, click this area.

8 Click the color you want to use.

How can I quickly add a border to text in my document?

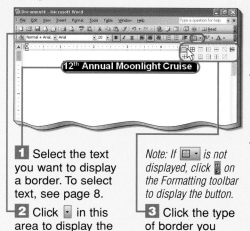

Note: If you changed the line style or color for a border since you last started Word, the new border will display the line style or color you selected.

1 Select the text you want to display a border. To select text, see page 8.

2 Click ⬝ in this area to display the available types of borders.

Note: If ⬚ ⬝ is not displayed, click ⬝ on the Formatting toolbar to display the button.

3 Click the type of border you want to add.

How can I quickly add a line across my page?

Type a set of characters shown in the chart below and then press the Enter key. Word will automatically add a line across your page.

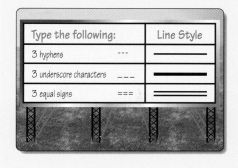

Type the following:		Line Style
3 hyphens	---	
3 underscore characters	___	
3 equal signs	===	

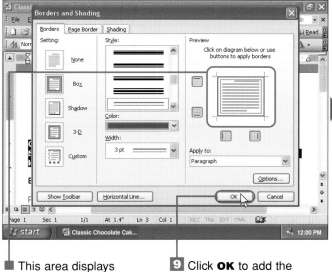

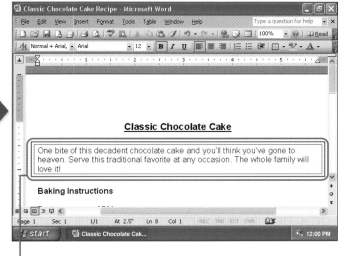

■ This area displays a preview of the border you selected.

9 Click **OK** to add the border to your document.

■ The text you selected displays the border.

■ To deselect text, click outside the selected area.

■ To remove a border, repeat steps **1** to **5**, selecting **None** in step **5**. Then perform step **9**.

ADD SHADING

You can add shading to your document to emphasize an area of text.

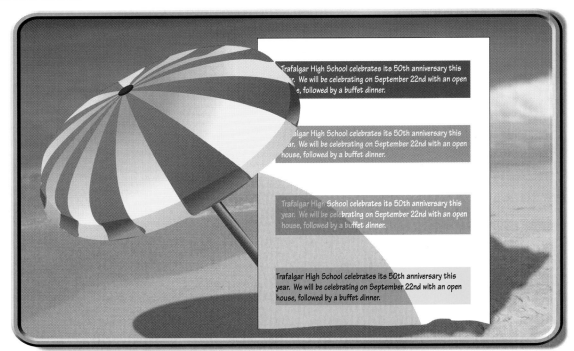

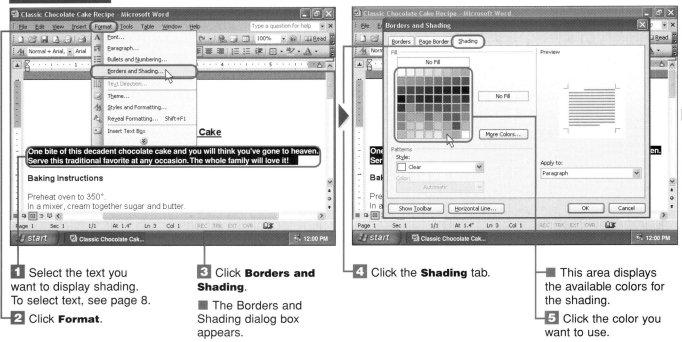

1 Select the text you want to display shading. To select text, see page 8.

2 Click **Format**.

3 Click **Borders and Shading**.

■ The Borders and Shading dialog box appears.

4 Click the **Shading** tab.

■ This area displays the available colors for the shading.

5 Click the color you want to use.

How will the shading I add to my document appear when I print the document?

When you print your document on a color printer, the shading will appear on the printed page as it appears on your screen. When you print your document on a black-and-white printer, any colored shading you added will appear as a shade of gray on the printed page.

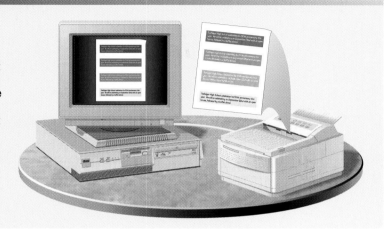

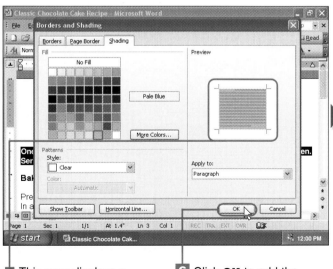

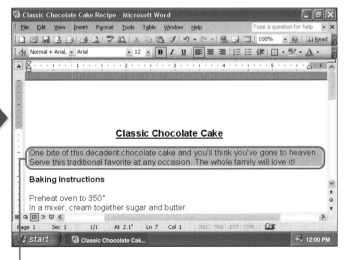

■ This area displays a preview of the shading you selected.

6 Click **OK** to add the shading to your document.

■ The text you selected displays the shading.

■ To deselect text, click outside the selected area.

■ To remove shading from your document, repeat steps **1** to **6**, selecting **No Fill** in step **5**.

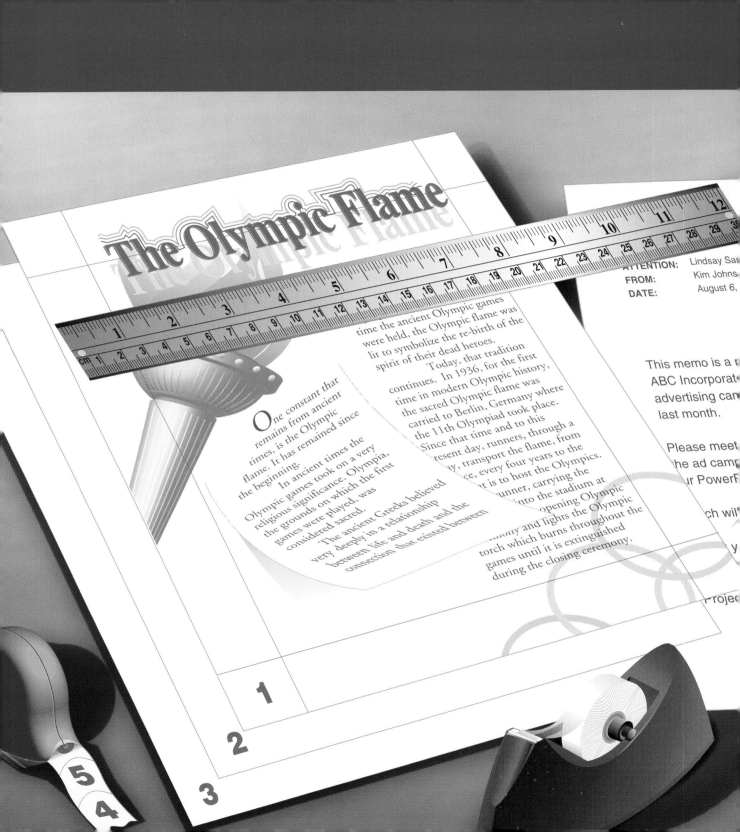

CHAPTER 8

Format Pages

Are you wondering how to change the appearance of pages in your document? In this chapter, you will learn how to add page numbers, change margins, create newspaper columns and more.

INSERT A PAGE BREAK

You can insert a page break to start a new page at a specific location in your document. A page break indicates where one page ends and another begins.

Inserting a page break is useful when you want a heading to appear at the top of a new page.

INSERT A PAGE BREAK

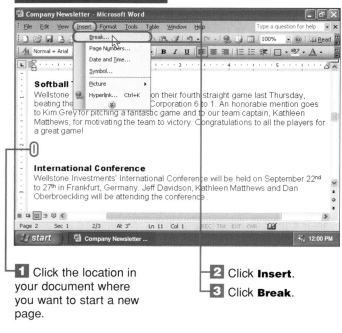

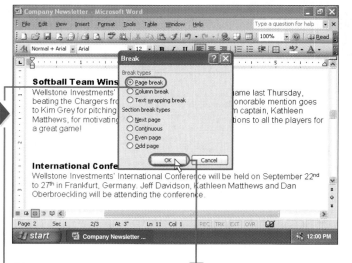

1 Click the location in your document where you want to start a new page.

2 Click **Insert**.

3 Click **Break**.

■ The Break dialog box appears.

4 Click this option to add a page break to your document (○ changes to ⊙).

5 Click **OK** to confirm your selection.

■ Word adds the page break to your document.

Will Word ever insert a page break automatically?

When you fill a page with information, Word automatically starts a new page by inserting a page break to start a new page. The length of the pages in your document is determined by the paper size and margin settings you are using. For information on margins, see page 150.

How can I quickly insert a page break?

1 Click the location in your document where you want to insert a page break.

2 Press and hold down the `Ctrl` key as you press the `Enter` key.

DELETE A PAGE BREAK

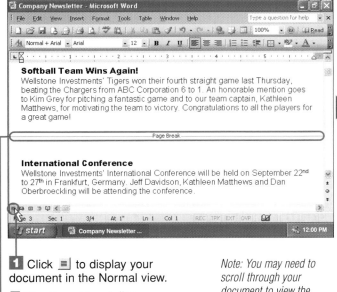

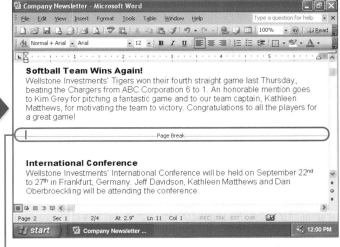

1 Click ≡ to display your document in the Normal view.

■ The **Page Break** line shows where one page ends and another begins. The line will not appear when you print your document.

Note: You may need to scroll through your document to view the line.

2 Click the **Page Break** line.

3 Press the `Delete` key to remove the page break.

INSERT A SECTION BREAK

You can insert section breaks to divide your document into sections.

Dividing your document into sections allows you to apply formatting to only part of your document. For example, you may want to vertically center text or change the margins for only part of your document.

INSERT A SECTION BREAK

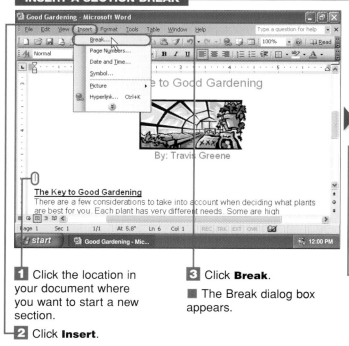

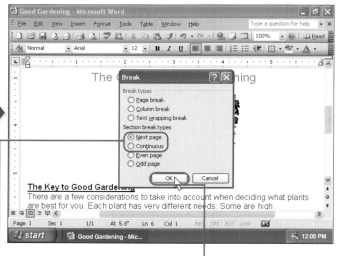

1 Click the location in your document where you want to start a new section.

2 Click **Insert**.

3 Click **Break**.

■ The Break dialog box appears.

4 Click the type of section break you want to add (○ changes to ◉).

Next page - Starts a new section on a new page.

Continuous - Starts a new section on the current page.

5 Click **OK** to confirm your selection.

■ Word adds the section break to your document.

138

Will the appearance of my document change when I delete a section break?

When you delete a section break, the text above the break assumes the appearance of the text below the break. For example, if you changed the margins for the text below a section break, the text above the break will also display the new margins when you delete the break.

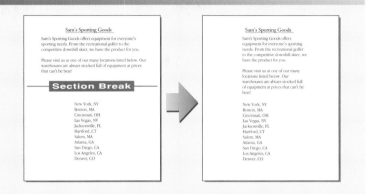

DELETE A SECTION BREAK

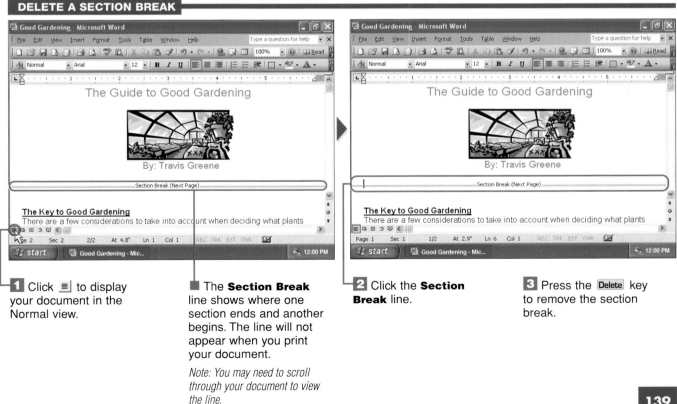

1 Click ≣ to display your document in the Normal view.

■ The **Section Break** line shows where one section ends and another begins. The line will not appear when you print your document.

Note: You may need to scroll through your document to view the line.

2 Click the **Section Break** line.

3 Press the Delete key to remove the section break.

ADD PAGE NUMBERS

You can have Word number the pages in your document. Numbering pages can help make a long document easier to organize when printed.

To view the page numbers on your screen, your document must be displayed in the Print Layout view. For information on changing the view of a document, see page 36.

ADD PAGE NUMBERS

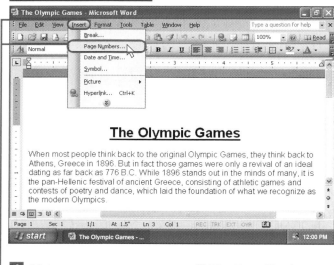

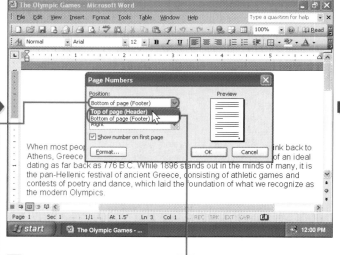

1 Click **Insert**.

2 Click **Page Numbers**.

■ The Page Numbers dialog box appears.

3 Click this area to select a position for the page numbers.

4 Click the position where you want the page numbers to appear.

How do I remove page numbers from my document?

Deleting a page number from your document's header or footer will remove all the page numbers from your document.

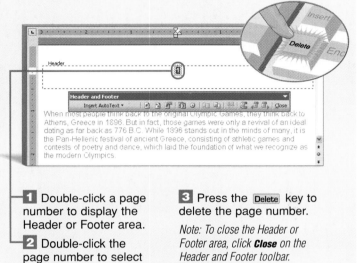

1 Double-click a page number to display the Header or Footer area.

2 Double-click the page number to select the number.

3 Press the Delete key to delete the page number.

*Note: To close the Header or Footer area, click **Close** on the Header and Footer toolbar.*

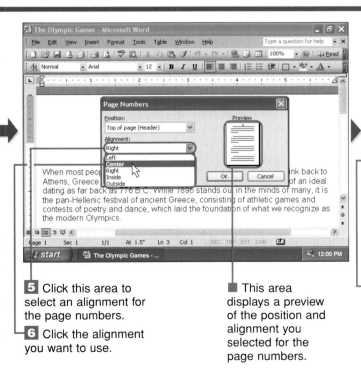

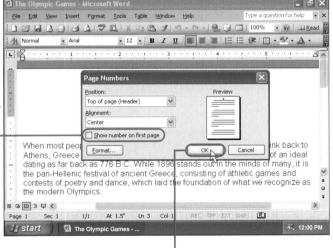

5 Click this area to select an alignment for the page numbers.

6 Click the alignment you want to use.

■ This area displays a preview of the position and alignment you selected for the page numbers.

7 If you want to hide the page number on the first page of your document, click this option (☑ changes to ☐).

Note: This option is useful if the first page in your document is a title page.

8 Click **OK** to add the page numbers to your document.

■ If you later make changes that affect the pages in your document, such as adding or removing text, Word will automatically adjust the page numbers for you.

ADD A HEADER OR FOOTER

You can add a header or footer to display additional information on each page of your document. A header or footer can contain information such as a chapter title, a page number or the current date.

A **header** appears at the top of each printed page.

A **footer** appears at the bottom of each printed page.

Word can display headers and footers only in the Print Layout view. To change the view of a document, see page 36.

ADD A HEADER OR FOOTER

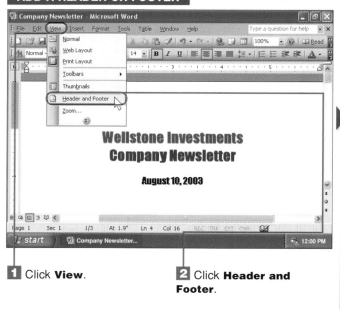

1 Click **View**.

2 Click **Header and Footer**.

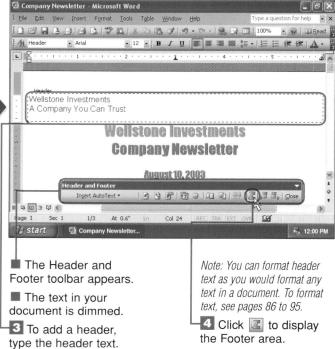

■ The Header and Footer toolbar appears.

■ The text in your document is dimmed.

3 To add a header, type the header text.

Note: You can format header text as you would format any text in a document. To format text, see pages 86 to 95.

4 Click ⬛ to display the Footer area.

Can I edit a header or footer?

Yes. Double-click the dimmed text for the header or footer you want to edit. You can then edit the header or footer text as you would edit any text in a document. To edit text, see page 50. When you finish editing header or footer text, perform step **6** below.

 How do I remove a header or footer from my document?

Double-click the dimmed text for the header or footer you want to remove. Drag the mouse I over the header or footer text until you highlight all the text. Then press the **Delete** key to remove the header or footer from your document. When you finish deleting header or footer text, perform step **6** below.

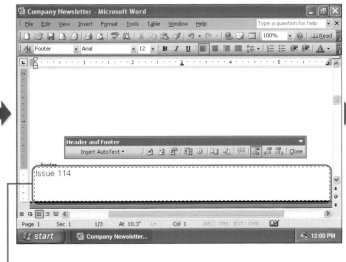

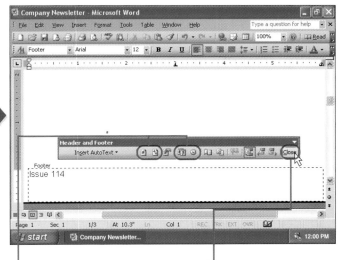

■ The Footer area appears.

Note: You can repeat step 4 to return to the Header area at any time.

5 To add a footer, type the footer text.

Note: You can format footer text as you would format any text in a document. To format text, see pages 86 to 95.

■ You can click one of the following buttons to quickly insert information into a header or footer.

🔲 Page number

🔲 Total number of pages

🔲 Date

🔲 Time

6 When you finish adding the header and footer to your document, click **Close**.

CONTINUED

143

ADD A HEADER OR FOOTER

You can add different headers and footers to different pages in your document.

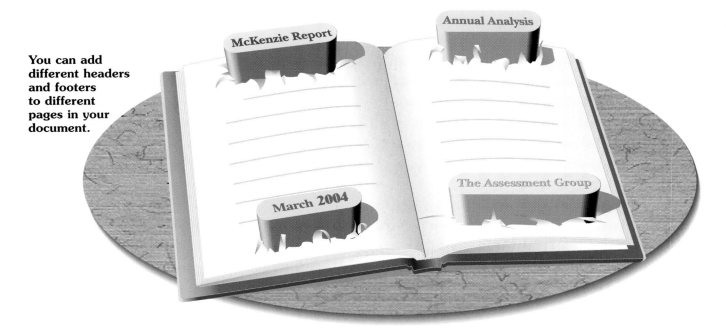

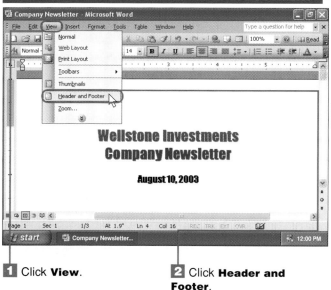

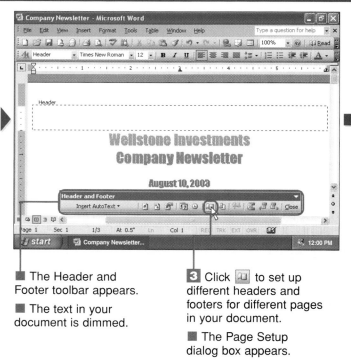

1 Click **View**.

2 Click **Header and Footer**.

■ The Header and Footer toolbar appears.

■ The text in your document is dimmed.

3 Click 🔲 to set up different headers and footers for different pages in your document.

■ The Page Setup dialog box appears.

What Header and Footer areas does Word provide?

Word offers the following Header and Footer areas. The Header and Footer areas available in your document depend on the options you select in steps **5** and **6** below.

First Page Header/Footer

The text you type in this area only appears on the first page of the document.

Note: If you do not want a header or footer on the first page, leave this area blank.

Header/Footer

The text you type in this area appears on all but the first page of the document.

Odd Page Header/Footer

The text you type in this area appears on each odd-numbered page in the document.

Even Page Header/Footer

The text you type in this area appears on each even-numbered page in the document.

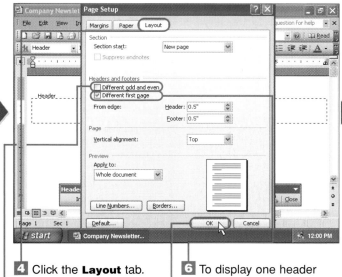

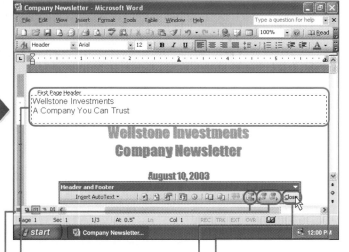

4 Click the **Layout** tab.

5 To display one header and footer on odd-numbered pages and a different header and footer on even-numbered pages, click this option (☐ changes to ☑).

6 To display one header and footer on the first page and a different header and footer on all the other pages, click this option (☐ changes to ☑).

7 Click **OK** to confirm your changes.

■ The first Header area appears.

■ You can click 🗐 to switch between the Header and Footer areas on the current page.

■ You can click 🗐 or 🗐 to display the previous or next Header or Footer area.

8 Type the header or footer text for each area.

9 When you have finished adding headers and footers to your document, click **Close**.

ADD FOOTNOTES OR ENDNOTES

You can add a footnote or endnote to provide additional information about text in your document. Footnotes and endnotes can provide information such as an explanation, comment or reference.

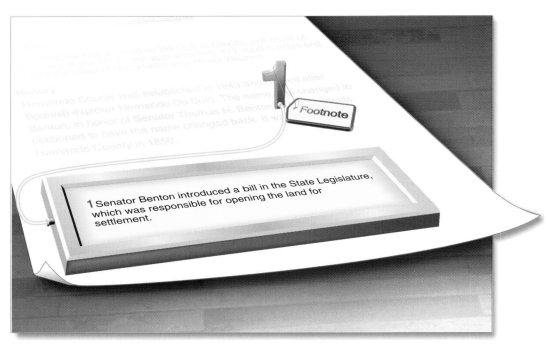

Word displays footnotes and endnotes as they will appear on a printed page in the Print Layout view. For information on the views, see page 36.

ADD FOOTNOTES OR ENDNOTES

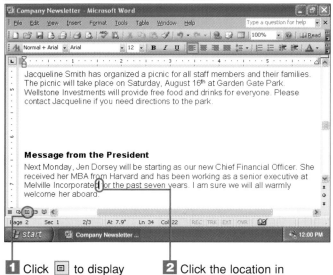

1 Click 🔲 to display your document in the Print Layout view.

2 Click the location in your document where you want the number for the footnote or endnote to appear.

Note: The footnote or endnote number will appear where the insertion point flashes on your screen.

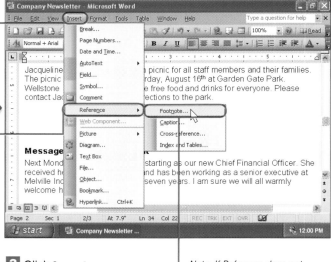

3 Click **Insert**.

4 Click **Reference**.

5 Click **Footnote**.

Note: If Reference does not appear on the menu, position the mouse ☟ over the bottom of the menu to display the menu option.

What is the difference between footnotes and endnotes?

Footnotes

By default, footnotes in a document are indicated by numbers (example: 1, 2, 3). The text for a footnote appears on the bottom of the page that displays the footnote number.

Endnotes

By default, endnotes in a document are indicated by lowercase roman numerals (example: i, ii, iii). The text for all the endnotes in a document appears at the end of the document.

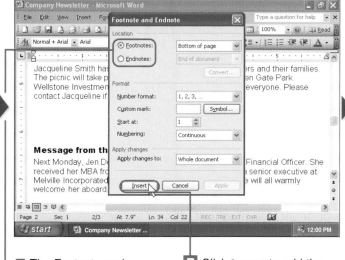

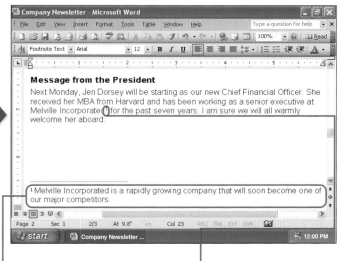

■ The Footnote and Endnote dialog box appears.

6 Click **Footnotes** or **Endnotes** to specify the type of note you want to add (○ changes to ⊙).

7 Click **Insert** to add the note to your document.

■ Word displays the footnote or endnote area.

8 Type the text for the footnote or endnote. You can format the text as you would format any text in a document. To format text, see pages 86 to 95.

■ The number for the footnote or endnote appears in your document.

Note: You may need to scroll through your document to view the number.

CONTINUED ▶

ADD FOOTNOTES OR ENDNOTES

You can view and edit a footnote or endnote you added to your document. You can also delete a footnote or endnote you no longer need.

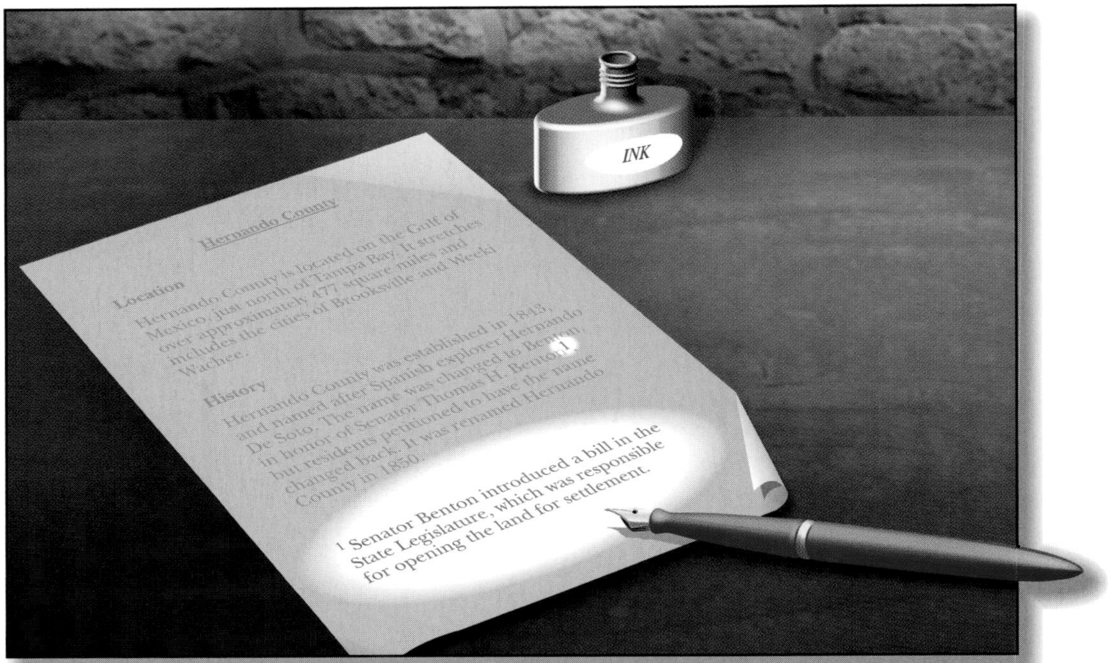

VIEW FOOTNOTES OR ENDNOTES

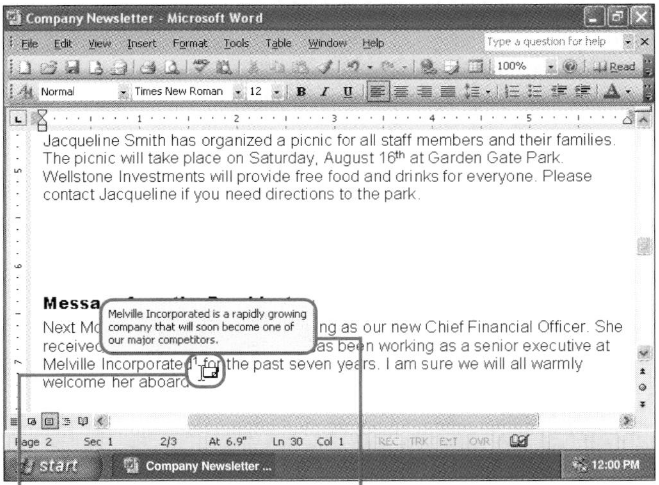

1 To view the text for a footnote or endnote, position the mouse I over the footnote or endnote number in your document (I changes to).

■ A yellow box appears, displaying the text for the footnote or endnote.

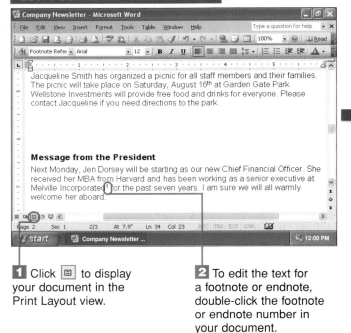

EDIT FOOTNOTES OR ENDNOTES

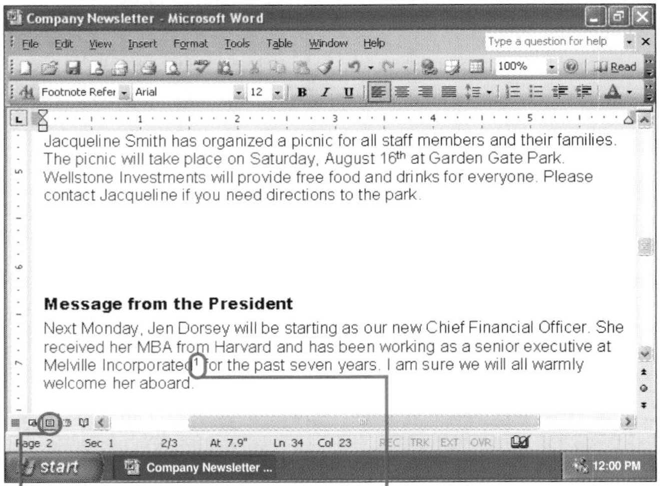

1 Click to display your document in the Print Layout view.

2 To edit the text for a footnote or endnote, double-click the footnote or endnote number in your document.

How can I print endnotes on a separate page?

Word automatically prints endnotes after the last line in your document. To print endnotes on a separate page, you need to insert a page break directly above the endnote area. To insert a page break, see page 136.

Can I copy a footnote or endnote?

Yes. Copying a footnote or endnote is useful when you want to provide the same comment or reference for several areas of text.

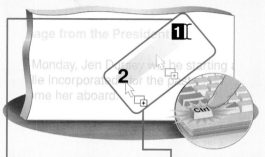

1 To copy a note, drag the mouse I over the footnote or endnote number until you highlight the number.

2 Press and hold down the Ctrl key as you drag the number to a new location.

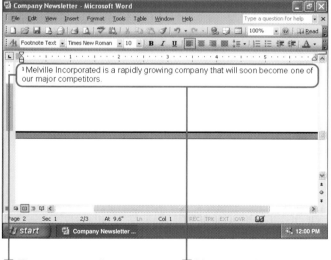

■ The corresponding footnote or endnote area appears.

■ You can edit the text for a footnote or endnote as you would edit any text in a document. To edit text, see page 50.

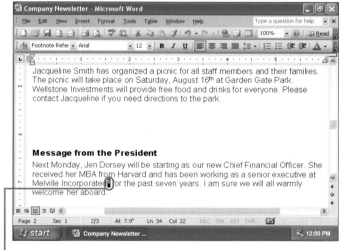

DELETE FOOTNOTES OR ENDNOTES

1 Drag the mouse I over the number for the footnote or endnote you want to delete until you highlight the number.

2 Press the Delete key.

■ The footnote or endnote disappears from your document.

■ Word automatically renumbers the remaining footnotes or endnotes in your document.

CHANGE MARGINS

You can change the margins in your document to suit your needs. A margin is the amount of space between the text in your document and the edge of your paper.

Word automatically sets the top and bottom margins to 1 inch and the left and right margins to 1.25 inches.

Changing the margins allows you to fit more or less information on a page and can help you accommodate letterhead and other specialty paper.

CHANGE MARGINS

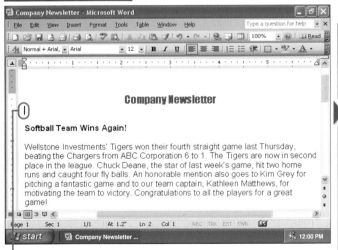

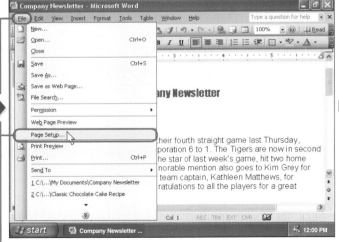

1 Click anywhere in the document or section where you want to change the margins.

Note: To change the margins for only part of your document, you must divide the document into sections. To divide a document into sections, see page 138.

2 Click **File**.

3 Click **Page Setup**.

■ The Page Setup dialog box appears.

Is there another way to change the margins for my document?

Yes. In the Print Layout view, margins are shown in gray on the ruler. To change a margin, position the mouse over the edge of the margin (↳ changes to ↔ or ↕) and then drag the margin to a new location on the ruler.

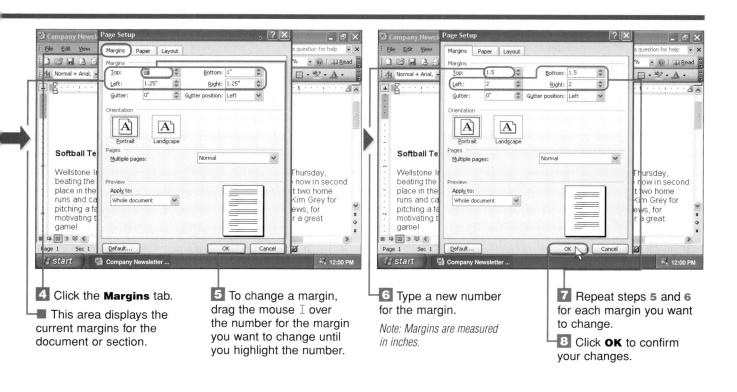

4 Click the **Margins** tab.

■ This area displays the current margins for the document or section.

5 To change a margin, drag the mouse I over the number for the margin you want to change until you highlight the number.

6 Type a new number for the margin.

Note: Margins are measured in inches.

7 Repeat steps **5** and **6** for each margin you want to change.

8 Click **OK** to confirm your changes.

CENTER TEXT ON A PAGE

You can vertically center the text on each page in your document. Vertically centering text is useful when creating title pages and short memos.

GLOBAL REPORT
Helping the Third World Countries

By: Cathy Best, MBA
University of Washington

When you vertically center text on a page, Word centers the text between the top and bottom margins of the page. For information on margins, see page 150.

To view text vertically centered on a page, you can display the document in the Print Layout view. To change the view of a document, see page 36.

CENTER TEXT ON A PAGE

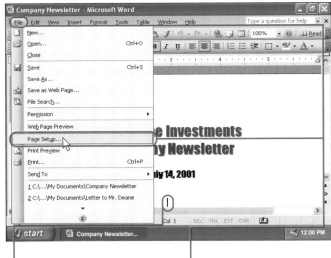

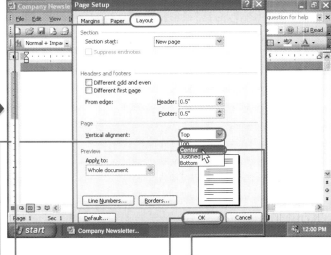

1 Click anywhere in the document or section you want to vertically center.

Note: To vertically center only some of the text in a document, you must divide the document into sections. For more information, see page 138.

2 Click **File**.

3 Click **Page Setup**.

■ The Page Setup dialog box appears.

4 Click the **Layout** tab.

5 Click this area to display the vertical alignment options.

6 Click **Center** to vertically center the text on the page.

7 Click **OK** to confirm the change.

■ To remove the centering, repeat steps **1** to **7**, except select **Top** in step **6**.

You can change the
orientation of pages
in your document.
The page orientation
determines the
direction information
prints on a page.

Portrait
Portrait is the
standard page
orientation and
is used to print
most documents,
such as letters,
memos and
reports.

Landscape
Landscape prints
information across
the long side of a
page and is often
used to print
certificates and
tables.

CHANGE PAGE ORIENTATION

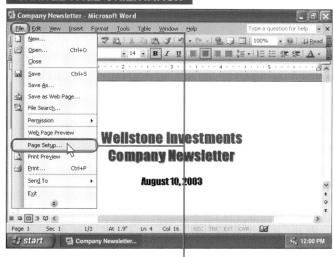

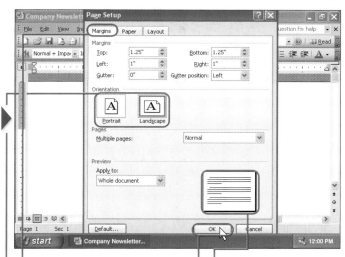

1 Click anywhere in the
document or section you
want to change to a different
page orientation.

*Note: To change the page orientation
for only part of your document,
you must divide the document into
sections. To divide a document
into sections, see page 138.*

2 Click **File**.

3 Click **Page Setup**.

■ The Page Setup
dialog box appears.

4 Click the **Margins** tab.

5 Click the page orientation
you want to use.

■ This area displays
a preview of how your
document will appear.

6 Click **OK** to confirm
your change.

CONTROL PAGE BREAKS

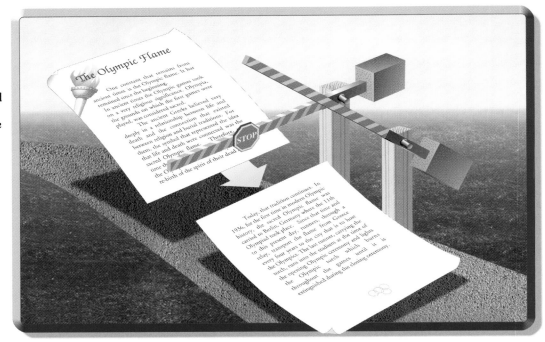

You can control the page breaks in a long document to tell Word how you want text to flow from one page to the next.

When you fill a page with information, Word automatically inserts a page break to start a new page.

CONTROL PAGE BREAKS

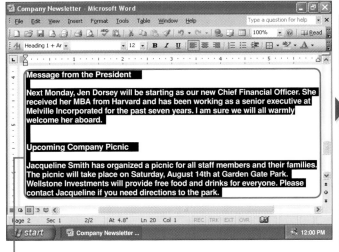

1 Select the paragraphs you want to control page breaks for. To select text, see page 8.

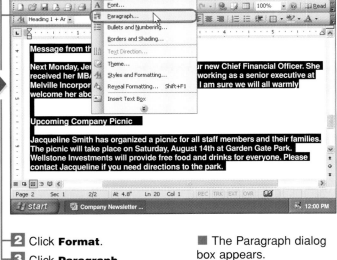

2 Click **Format**.

3 Click **Paragraph**.

■ The Paragraph dialog box appears.

What page break options can I choose?

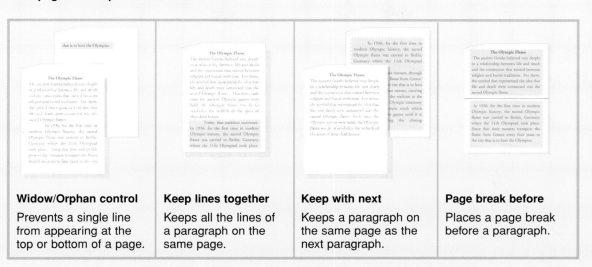

Widow/Orphan control

Prevents a single line from appearing at the top or bottom of a page.

Keep lines together

Keeps all the lines of a paragraph on the same page.

Keep with next

Keeps a paragraph on the same page as the next paragraph.

Page break before

Places a page break before a paragraph.

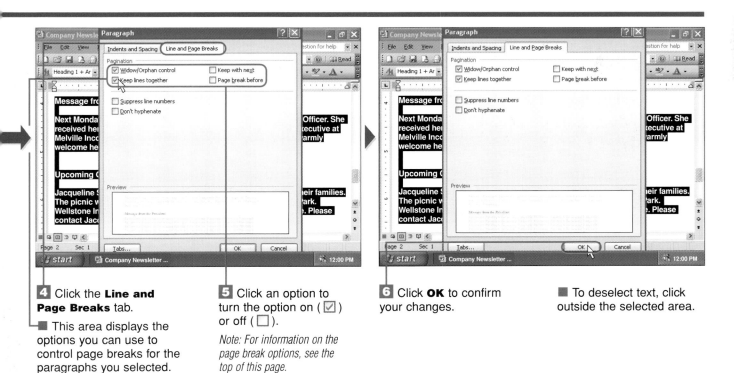

4 Click the **Line and Page Breaks** tab.

■ This area displays the options you can use to control page breaks for the paragraphs you selected.

5 Click an option to turn the option on (☑) or off (☐).

Note: For information on the page break options, see the top of this page.

6 Click **OK** to confirm your changes.

■ To deselect text, click outside the selected area.

ADD A WATERMARK

You can add a watermark to your document to display a faint picture or text behind the information in the document. A watermark can add interest to or identify the status of a document.

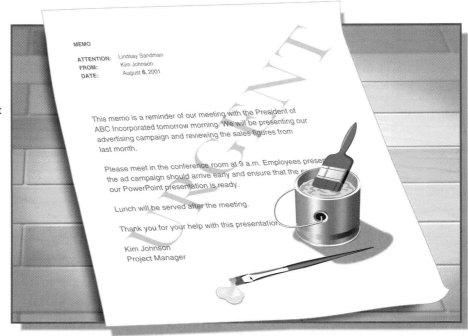

Word can display watermarks only in the Print Layout view. To change the view of a document, see page 36.

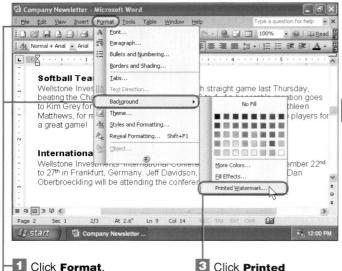

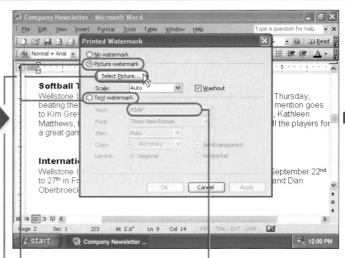

1 Click **Format**.

2 Click **Background**.

Note: If Background does not appear on the menu, position the mouse ▷ over the bottom of the menu to display the menu option.

3 Click **Printed Watermark**.

■ The Printed Watermark dialog box appears.

4 Click an option to specify the type of watermark you want to add (○ changes to ⊙).

5 If you selected Picture watermark in step **4**, click **Select Picture** to locate the picture you want to use.

■ If you selected Text watermark in step **4**, double-click the text in this area and then type the text you want to use. Then skip to step **8**.

Does Word provide any text watermarks that I can use?

Yes. Word provides several text watermarks including ASAP, CONFIDENTIAL, PERSONAL and URGENT, that you can add to your document.

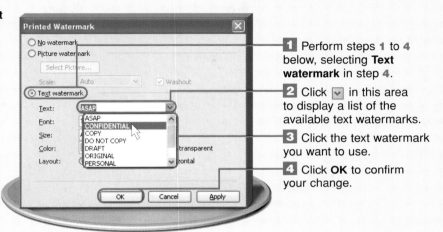

1 Perform steps **1** to **4** below, selecting **Text watermark** in step **4**.

2 Click ☑ in this area to display a list of the available text watermarks.

3 Click the text watermark you want to use.

4 Click **OK** to confirm your change.

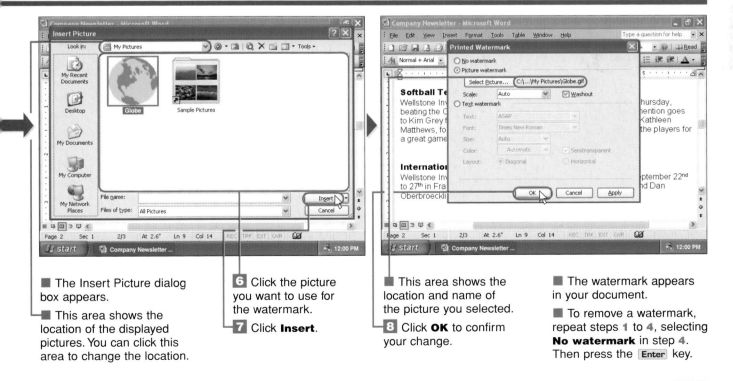

■ The Insert Picture dialog box appears.

■ This area shows the location of the displayed pictures. You can click this area to change the location.

6 Click the picture you want to use for the watermark.

7 Click **Insert**.

■ This area shows the location and name of the picture you selected.

8 Click **OK** to confirm your change.

■ The watermark appears in your document.

■ To remove a watermark, repeat steps **1** to **4**, selecting **No watermark** in step **4**. Then press the Enter key.

ADD A PAGE BORDER

You can place a border around each page of your document to enhance the appearance of the document.

Line Borders

You can use a line border for certificates and title pages.

Art Borders

You can use a colorful art border to enhance invitations and newsletters.

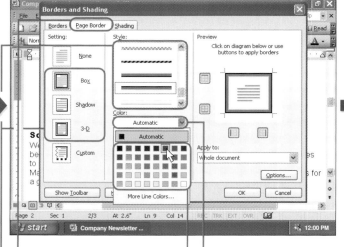

ADD A LINE BORDER

1 Click **Format**.

2 Click **Borders and Shading**.

■ The Borders and Shading dialog box appears.

3 Click the **Page Border** tab.

4 Click the type of line border you want to add.

5 Click the line style you want to use for the border.

6 To select a color for the border, click this area.

7 Click the color you want to use.

Why does a dialog box appear when I try to add an art border to my document?

A dialog box appears if the art borders are not installed on your computer. Click **Yes** to install the art borders.

Why does the page border disappear when I change the view of my document?

Word can display page borders only in the Print Layout view. To change the view of a document, see page 36.

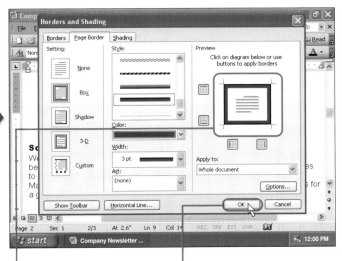

■ This area displays a preview of the border you selected.

8 Click **OK** to add the border to your document.

■ To remove a line border, repeat steps **1** to **4**, selecting **None** in step **4**. Then perform step **8**.

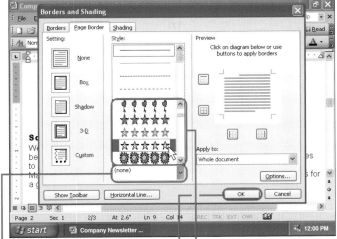

ADD AN ART BORDER

1 Perform steps **1** to **3** on page 158.

2 Click this area to display the available art borders.

Note: If a dialog box appears, see the top of this page.

3 Click the art border you want to use.

4 Click **OK**.

■ To remove an art border, perform steps **1** to **4** on page 158, selecting **None** in step **4**. Then perform step **8**.

APPLY A THEME

Word offers many ready-to-use designs, called themes, that you can use to give your document a new appearance.

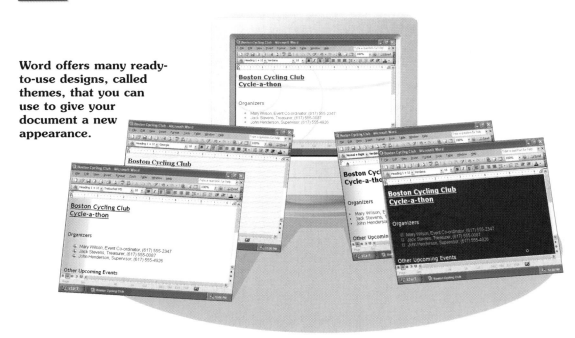

Themes are ideal for documents that will be viewed on the Internet or on your computer screen. Word can display themes only in the Print Layout, Web Layout and Reading Layout views. To change the view of a document, see page 36.

APPLY A THEME

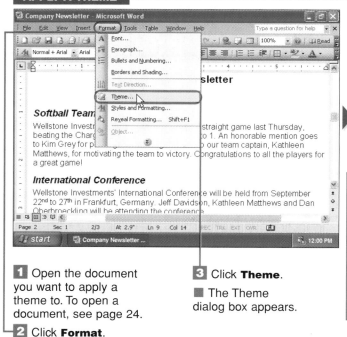

1 Open the document you want to apply a theme to. To open a document, see page 24.

2 Click **Format**.

3 Click **Theme**.

■ The Theme dialog box appears.

■ This area displays a list of the available themes.

4 Click a theme you want to apply to your document.

■ This area displays a sample of the theme you selected.

*Note: If a sample of the theme does not appear, the theme is not installed on your computer. Click **Install** to install the theme.*

What are some of the elements that a theme will affect in my document?

When you apply a theme to your document, the theme may affect elements such as the background color or graphics, headings and body text, hyperlink colors, horizontal lines and table border colors.

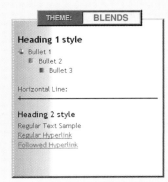

The background design is not displayed when I print my document. What is wrong?

The themes offered by Word are designed for documents that will be viewed on the computer screen. Some theme elements, such as the background design, will not appear when you print the document.

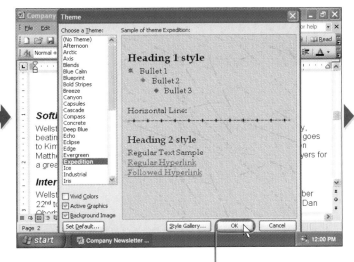

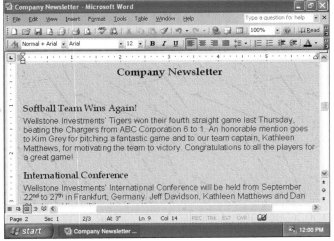

■ Repeat step **4** until the theme you want to use appears.

5 Click **OK** to apply the theme to your document.

■ Your document displays the theme you selected.

■ To remove a theme, repeat steps **1** to **5**, selecting **(No Theme)** in step **4**.

CREATE NEWSPAPER COLUMNS

You can display text in columns like those found in a newspaper. Creating columns is useful in documents such as newsletters and brochures.

CREATE NEWSPAPER COLUMNS

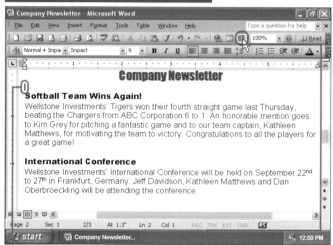

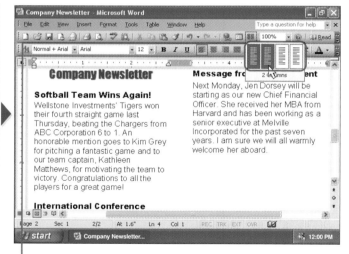

1 Click anywhere in the document or section you want to display in newspaper columns.

Note: To create newspaper columns for only part of your document, you must divide the document into sections. To divide a document into sections, see page 138.

2 Click ▦ to create newspaper columns.

Note: If ▦ is not displayed, click ⁝ on the Standard toolbar to display the button.

3 Drag the mouse ⬚ until you highlight the number of columns you want to create.

■ The text in the document or section appears in newspaper columns.

■ Word will fill one column with text before starting a new column.

■ To remove newspaper columns, repeat steps **1** to **3**, selecting one column in step **3**.

Why do the newspaper columns disappear when I change the view of my document?

Word can display newspaper columns side by side only in the Print Layout view. To change the view of a document, see page 36.

How do I remove a column break?

If you want to move text back to the previous column, you can remove a column break.

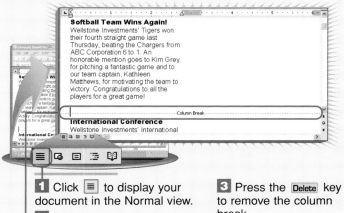

1 Click 📄 to display your document in the Normal view.

2 Click the **Column Break** line.

3 Press the Delete key to remove the column break.

INSERT A COLUMN BREAK

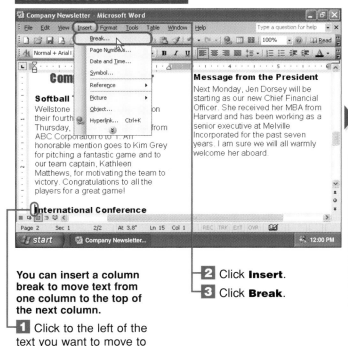

You can insert a column break to move text from one column to the top of the next column.

1 Click to the left of the text you want to move to the next column.

2 Click **Insert**.

3 Click **Break**.

■ The Break dialog box appears.

4 Click this option to add a column break (○ changes to ⊙).

5 Click **OK** to confirm your selection.

■ Word moves the text after the insertion point to the top of the next column.

CHAPTER 9

Print Documents

Are you ready to print your document? In this chapter, you will learn how to print documents, envelopes and labels.

PREVIEW A DOCUMENT BEFORE PRINTING

You can use the Print Preview feature to see how your document will look when printed.

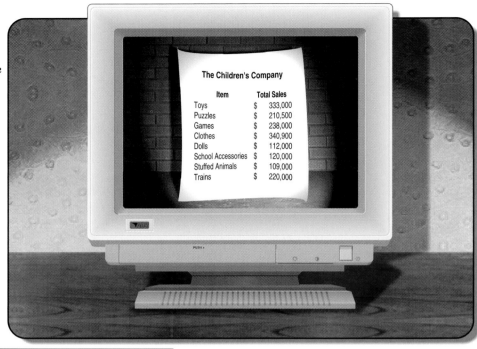

The Print Preview feature allows you to confirm that the document will print the way you want.

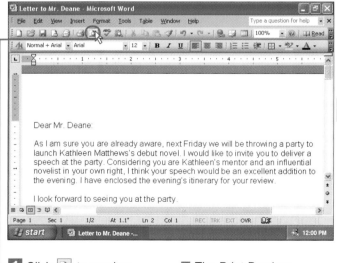

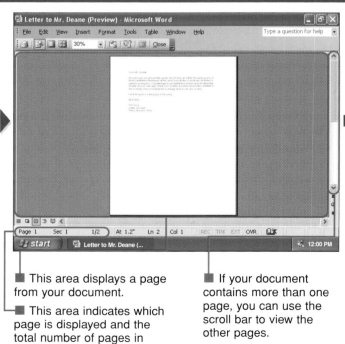

■ **1** Click 🔍 to preview your document before printing.

Note: If 🔍 is not displayed, click ⁞ on the Standard toolbar to display the button.

■ The Print Preview window appears.

■ This area displays a page from your document.

■ This area indicates which page is displayed and the total number of pages in your document.

■ If your document contains more than one page, you can use the scroll bar to view the other pages.

Can I edit my document in the Print Preview window?

Yes. If the mouse pointer looks like I when over your document, you can edit the document. If the mouse pointer looks like ⊕ or ⊖ when over your document, you can enlarge or reduce the size of the page displayed on your screen. To change the appearance of the mouse pointer, click the Magnifier button ( ).

Can I shrink the text in my document to fit on one less page?

If the last page in your document contains only a few lines of text, Word can shrink the text in your document to fit on one less page. In the Print Preview window, click the Shrink to Fit button ( ) to shrink the text in your document.

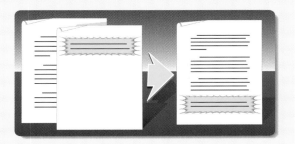

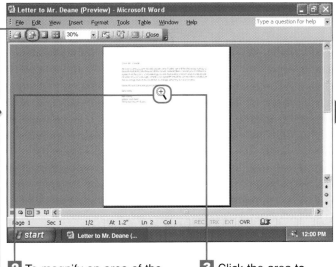

2 To magnify an area of the page, position the mouse over the area you want to magnify (changes to ⊕).

■ If the mouse pointer looks like I when over the page, click .

3 Click the area to magnify the area.

■ A magnified view of the area appears.

4 To once again display the entire page, click anywhere on the page.

5 When you finish previewing your document, click **Close** to close the Print Preview window.

PRINT A DOCUMENT

You can produce a paper copy of the document displayed on your screen.

Before printing your document, make sure the printer is turned on and contains an adequate supply of paper.

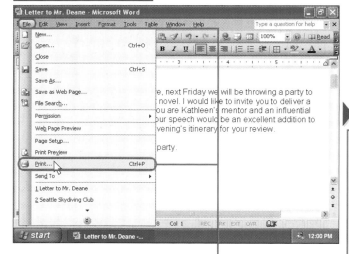

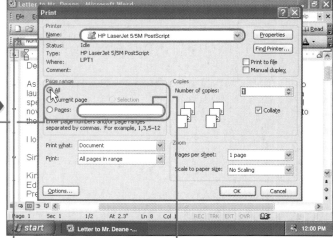

1 Click anywhere in the document or page you want to print.

■ To print only some of the text in the document, select the text you want to print. To select text, see page 8.

2 Click **File**.

3 Click **Print**.

■ The Print dialog box appears.

■ This area displays the printer that will print your document. You can click this area to select a different printer.

4 Click the print option you want to use (○ changes to ●).

Note: For more information on the print options, see the top of page 169.

■ If you selected **Pages** in step **4**, type the pages you want to print in this area (example: 1,3,5 or 2-4).

168

Which print option should I use?

All

Prints every page in the document.

Current page

Prints the page containing the insertion point.

Pages

Prints the pages you specify.

Selection

Prints the text you selected.

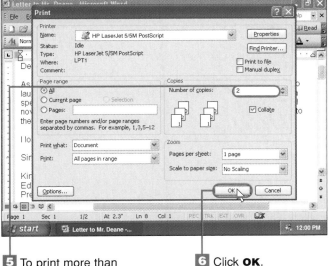

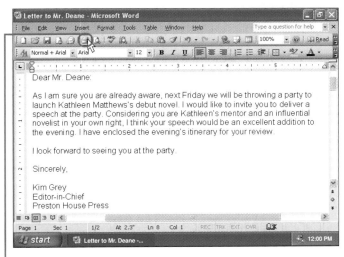

5 To print more than one copy of the document, double-click the number in this area and then type the number of copies you want to print.

6 Click **OK**.

QUICKLY PRINT ENTIRE DOCUMENT

1 Click 🖨 to quickly print your entire document.

Note: If 🖨 is not displayed, click ⁝ on the Standard toolbar to display the button.

PRINT AN ENVELOPE

You can use Word to print a delivery address and return address on an envelope.

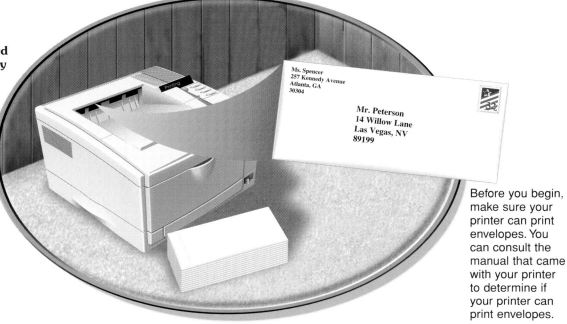

Before you begin, make sure your printer can print envelopes. You can consult the manual that came with your printer to determine if your printer can print envelopes.

PRINT AN ENVELOPE

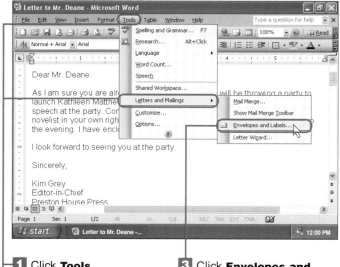

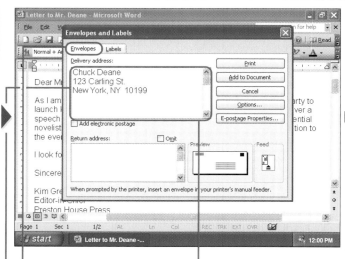

1 Click **Tools**.

2 Click **Letters and Mailings**.

3 Click **Envelopes and Labels**.

■ The Envelopes and Labels dialog box appears.

4 Click the **Envelopes** tab.

■ This area displays the delivery address. If Word finds an address in your document, Word will enter the address for you.

5 To enter a delivery address, click this area. Then type the delivery address.

Note: To remove any existing text before typing a delivery address, drag the mouse I over the text until you highlight the text. Then press the Delete *key.*

When would I omit the return address from an envelope?

You would omit the return address if your envelope already displays a return address. Company stationery often displays a return address.

Can I make an envelope part of my document?

Yes. To make an envelope part of your document, perform steps **1** to **9** below, except click the **Add to Document** button in step **8**. The envelope appears before the first page in your document. You can edit, format, save and print the envelope as part of your document.

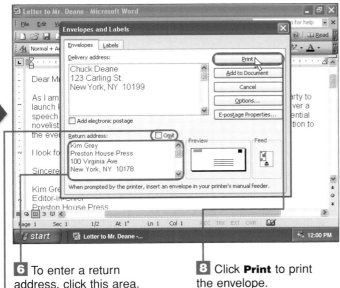

6 To enter a return address, click this area. Then type the return address.

7 If you do not want to print a return address, click **Omit** (☐ changes to ☑).

8 Click **Print** to print the envelope.

■ This dialog box appears if you entered a return address.

9 To save the return address, click **Yes**.

■ If you save the return address, the address will appear as the return address each time you print an envelope. This saves you from having to retype the address.

PRINT LABELS

You can use Word to print labels. Labels are useful for addressing envelopes, creating name tags, labeling file folders and more.

PRINT LABELS

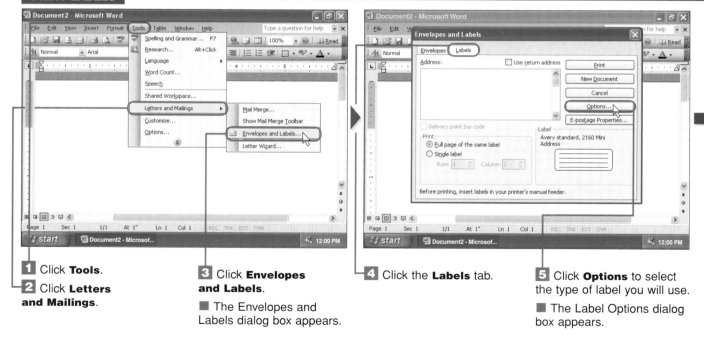

1 Click **Tools**.

2 Click **Letters and Mailings**.

3 Click **Envelopes and Labels**.

■ The Envelopes and Labels dialog box appears.

4 Click the **Labels** tab.

5 Click **Options** to select the type of label you will use.

■ The Label Options dialog box appears.

What types of printers can I use to print labels?

Word can set up labels to print on dot matrix, laser and ink jet printers. If you are not sure which type of printer you have, you can consult the documentation included with the printer.

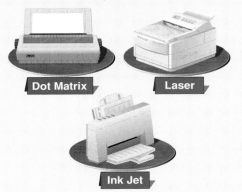

Dot Matrix

Laser

Ink Jet

Which label product and type should I choose?

You can check your label packaging to determine which label product and type you should choose when printing labels.

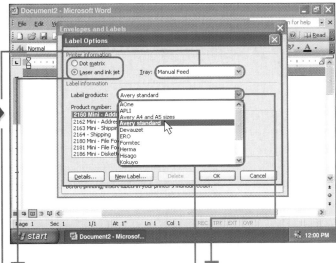

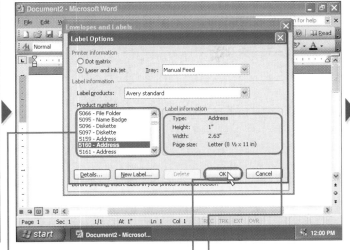

6 Click an option to specify the type of printer you will use to print the labels (○ changes to ◉).

■ This area displays the printer tray that will contain the labels. You can click this area to specify a different tray.

7 Click this area to display a list of the available label products.

8 Click the label product you will use.

■ This area displays the types of labels available for the label product you selected.

9 Click the type of label you will use.

■ This area displays information about the type of label you selected.

10 Click **OK** to confirm your selections.

CONTINUED

PRINT LABELS

After you specify the type of label you will use, Word can add the labels to a new document. You can then enter the information you want to appear on each label.

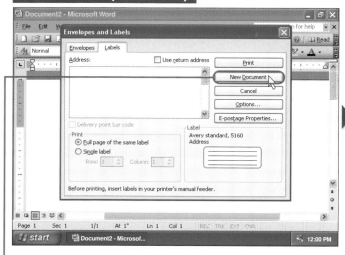

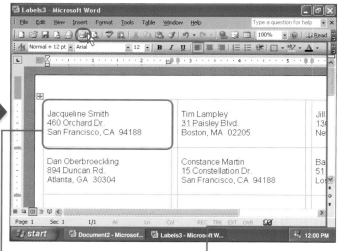

11 Click **New Document** to add the labels to a new document.

■ The labels appear in a new document.

12 Click a label where you want to enter text and then type the text. Repeat this step for each label.

Note: You can format the text on the labels as you would format any text in a document. To format text, see pages 86 to 95.

13 Click 🖨 to print the labels.

Should I save the labels I created?

If you want to be able to edit and print the labels in the future, you should save the labels you created. To save the document containing the labels, see page 20.

Can I quickly create a label for each person on my mailing list?

You can use the Mail Merge Wizard included with Word to quickly create a label for each person on your mailing list. For information on using the Mail Merge Wizard to create labels, see page 268.

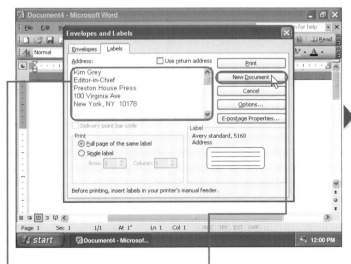

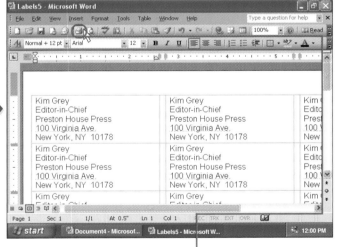

PRINT THE SAME INFORMATION ON EVERY LABEL

1 Perform steps **1** to **10**, starting on page 172.

2 Click this area and then type the information you want to appear on every label.

3 Click **New Document** to add the labels to a new document.

■ The labels appear in a new document. Each label displays the same information.

4 Click 🖨 to print the labels.

CHANGE PAPER SIZE AND SOURCE

Word sets each page in your document to print on letter-sized paper. If you want to use a different paper size, you can change this setting. You can also change the location where Word will look for the paper to print your document.

CHANGE PAPER SIZE AND SOURCE

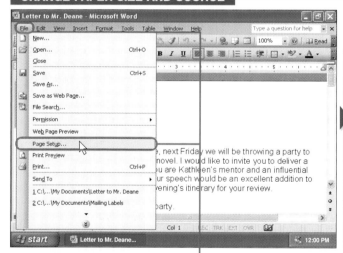

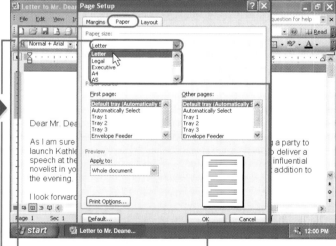

1 Click anywhere in the document or section you want to print using a different paper size or source.

Note: To change the paper size or source for only part of your document, you must divide the document into sections. To divide a document into sections, see page 138.

2 Click **File**.

3 Click **Page Setup**.

■ The Page Setup dialog box appears.

4 Click the **Paper** tab.

5 To change the paper size, click this area to display a list of the paper sizes your printer supports.

6 Click the paper size you want to use.

What paper sizes can I use?

The available paper sizes depend on the printer you are using. Most printers can print on letter-sized and legal-sized paper. You can consult the manual that came with your printer to determine which paper sizes the printer can use.

Why would I change the paper source?

Changing the paper source is useful if your printer stores letterhead in one location and plain paper in another location. You can print the first page of your document on letterhead and print the rest of the document on plain paper.

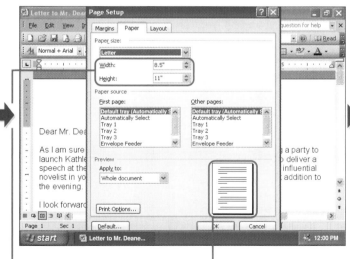

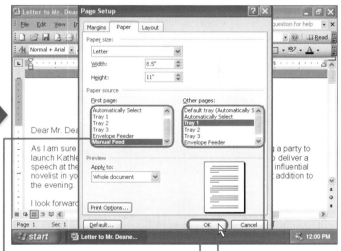

■ This area displays the width and height of the paper size you selected.

■ This area displays a preview of the paper size you selected.

7 To change the paper source, click the location of the paper you want to use for the first page of the document or section in this area.

Note: The available paper source options depend on your printer.

8 Click the location of the paper you want to use for the other pages of the document or section in this area.

9 Click **OK** to confirm your changes.

WORD

Dear Randy:

I just wanted to thank you for arranging my retirement party last weekend. It was a big surprise to see everyone from work gathered at my house Saturday morning!

Meeting Agenda

1 Call the meeting to order. Ensure all members are present.

Boston Cycling Club
Newsletter - Apr. 12 to 19

Dear Member:

CHAPTER 10

Work With Multiple Documents

Do you want to work with more than one document at a time? This chapter teaches you how to switch between documents, move or copy text between documents and more.

CREATE A NEW DOCUMENT

You can create a new document to start writing a new letter, memo or report.

Each document is like a separate piece of paper. Creating a new document is like placing a new piece of paper on your screen.

CREATE A NEW DOCUMENT

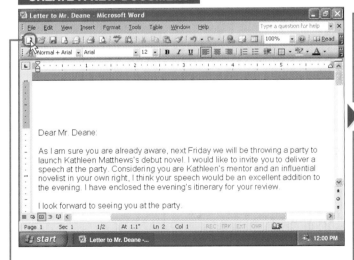

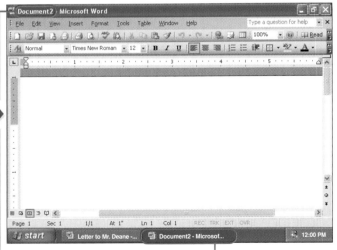

1 Click 🗋 to create a new document.

Note: If 🗋 is not displayed, click 🔽 on the Standard toolbar to display the button.

■ The new document appears. The previous document is now hidden behind the new document.

■ Word gives the new document a temporary name, such as Document2, until you save the document. To save a document, see page 20.

■ A button for the new document appears on the taskbar.

SWITCH BETWEEN DOCUMENTS

You can have several
documents open at
once. Word allows
you to easily switch
from one open
document to another.

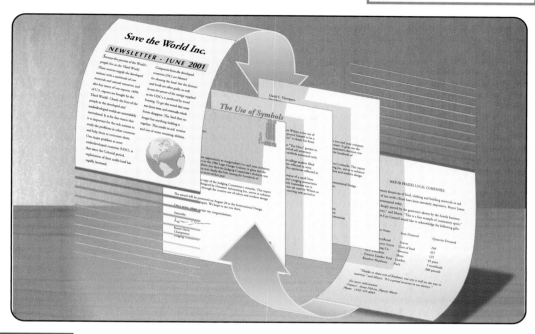

SWITCH BETWEEN DOCUMENTS

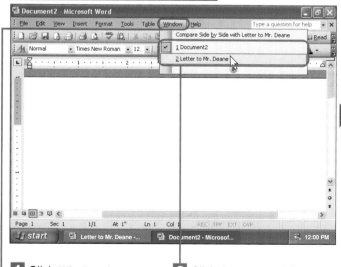

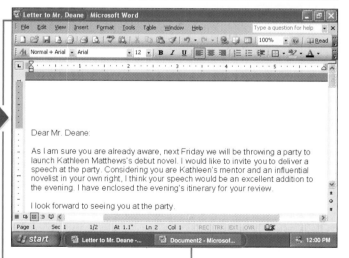

1 Click **Window** to
display a list of all the
documents you have
open.

2 Click the name of the
document you want to
switch to.

■ The document
appears.

■ This area shows the
name of the displayed
document.

■ The taskbar displays
a button for each open
document. You can also
click the buttons on the
taskbar to switch
between the open
documents.

ARRANGE OPEN DOCUMENTS

If you have several documents open, some of them may be hidden from view. You can display the contents of all your open documents at once.

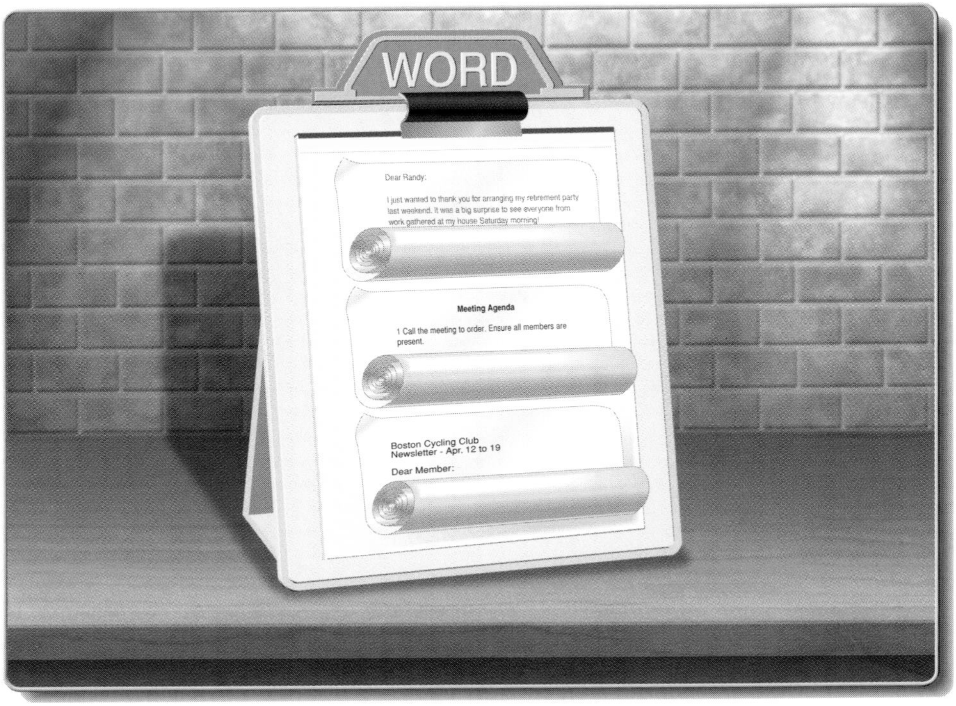

ARRANGE OPEN DOCUMENTS

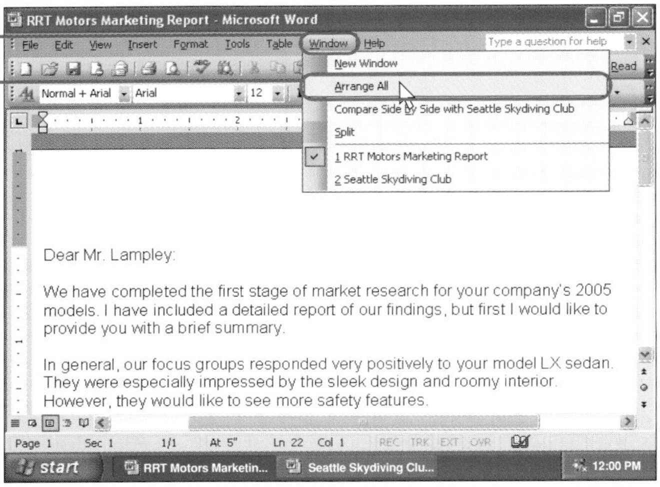

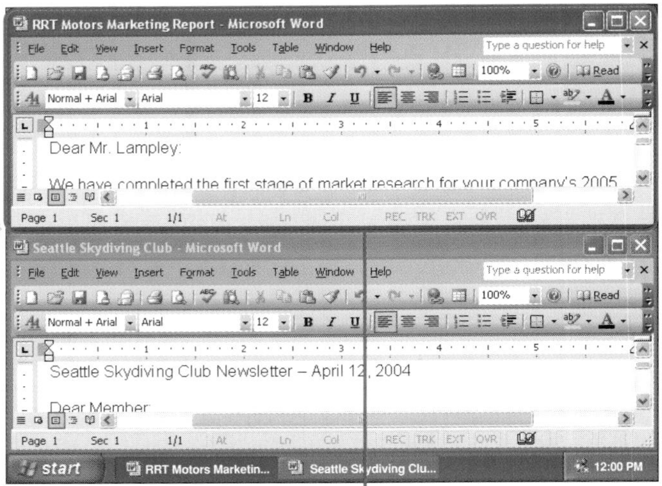

1 Click **Window**.

2 Click **Arrange All**.

Note: If Arrange All does not appear on the menu, position the mouse over the bottom of the menu to display the menu option.

■ The documents appear neatly arranged.

■ You can work with only one document at a time. The current document displays a dark title bar.

How can I display more of the arranged documents on my screen?

You can remove items, such as the ruler or a toolbar, from a document to display more of the document on your screen. To hide the ruler, see page 38. To hide a toolbar, see page 39.

Why didn't Word arrange all my open documents?

Word will not arrange an open document that is minimized to its button on the taskbar. You minimize a document when you click ▬ in the top right corner of a Microsoft Word window. To display a minimized document, click the button for the document on the taskbar. You can then repeat steps **1** and **2** below to arrange all your open documents.

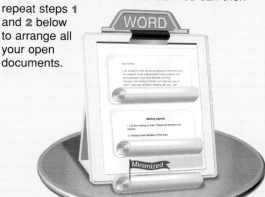

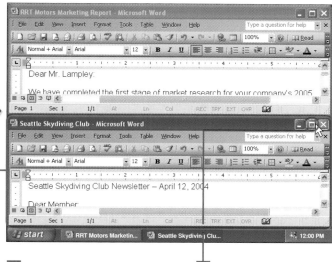

3 To make another document current, click anywhere in the document.

4 To maximize the current document to fill your screen, click ▣ .

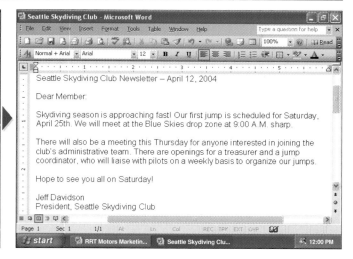

■ The document fills your screen.

■ The other document(s) are hidden behind the maximized document.

MOVE OR COPY TEXT BETWEEN DOCUMENTS

You can move
or copy text from
one document
to another. This
will save you time
when you want
to use text from
another document.

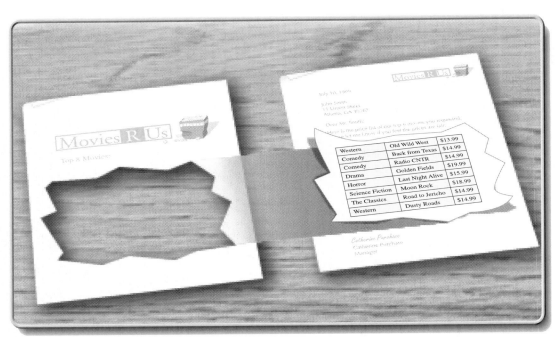

When you move text,
the text disappears
from the original
document.

When you copy text,
the text appears in
both the original and
new documents.

MOVE OR COPY TEXT BETWEEN DOCUMENTS

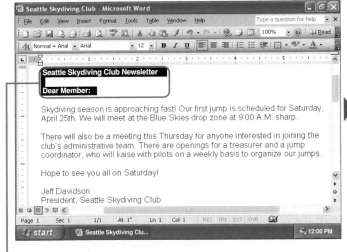

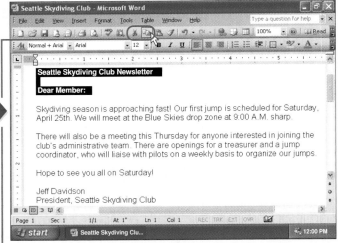

1 Select the text you
want to move or copy
to another document. To
select text, see page 8.

2 Click one of the
following buttons.

  Move text

  Copy text

■ The Clipboard task pane
may appear, displaying
items you have selected
to move or copy. To use
the Clipboard task pane,
see the top of page 185.

How can I use the Clipboard task pane to move or copy text?

The Clipboard task pane displays up to the last 24 items you have selected to move or copy. To place a clipboard item in your document, click the location where you want the item to appear and then click the item in the task pane. For more information on the task pane, see page 14.

Why does the Paste Options button (📋) appear when I move or copy text?

You can use the Paste Options button (📋) to change the format of text you have moved or copied. For example, you can choose to keep the original formatting of the text or change the formatting of the text to match the text in the new location. Click the Paste Options button to display a list of options and then select the option you want to use. The Paste Options button is available only until you perform another task.

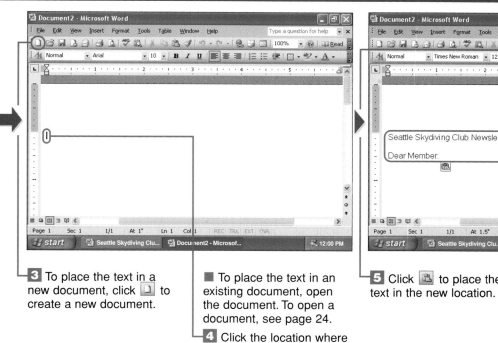

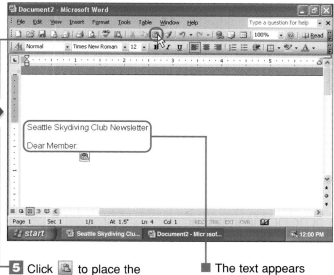

3 To place the text in a new document, click 📄 to create a new document.

■ To place the text in an existing document, open the document. To open a document, see page 24.

4 Click the location where you want to place the text.

5 Click 📋 to place the text in the new location.

■ The text appears in the new location.

COMPARE DOCUMENTS SIDE BY SIDE

You can display two documents side by side on your screen. Comparing documents side by side is useful if you want to compare an edited document to an original version of the document.

When you scroll through one document, Word automatically scrolls through the other document for you, so you can easily compare the contents of the two documents.

COMPARE DOCUMENTS SIDE BY SIDE

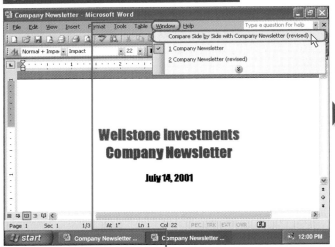

1 Open the two documents you want to compare side by side.

Note: To open a document, see page 24.

2 Click **Window** in the current document.

3 Click **Compare Side by Side with** to compare the current document with the other open document.

■ Word displays the documents side by side on your screen.

■ The Compare Side by Side toolbar also appears.

4 To scroll through the documents, drag the scroll box up or down in one document. Word automatically scrolls through the other document for you.

5 When you finish comparing the documents on your screen, click **Close Side by Side**.

CLOSE A DOCUMENT

When you finish working with a document, you can close the document to remove it from your screen.

When you close a document, you do not exit the Word program. You can continue to work with other documents.

CLOSE A DOCUMENT

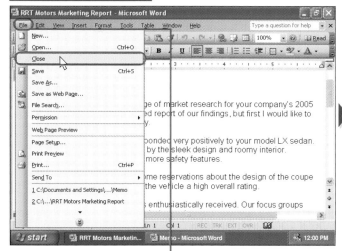

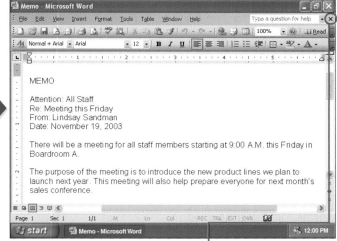

■ Before closing a document, you should save any changes you made to the document. To save a document, see page 20.

1 Click **File**.

2 Click **Close** to close the document.

■ The document disappears from your screen.

■ If you had more than one document open, the second last document you worked with appears on your screen.

QUICKLY CLOSE A DOCUMENT

■ To quickly close a document, click ⊠.

187

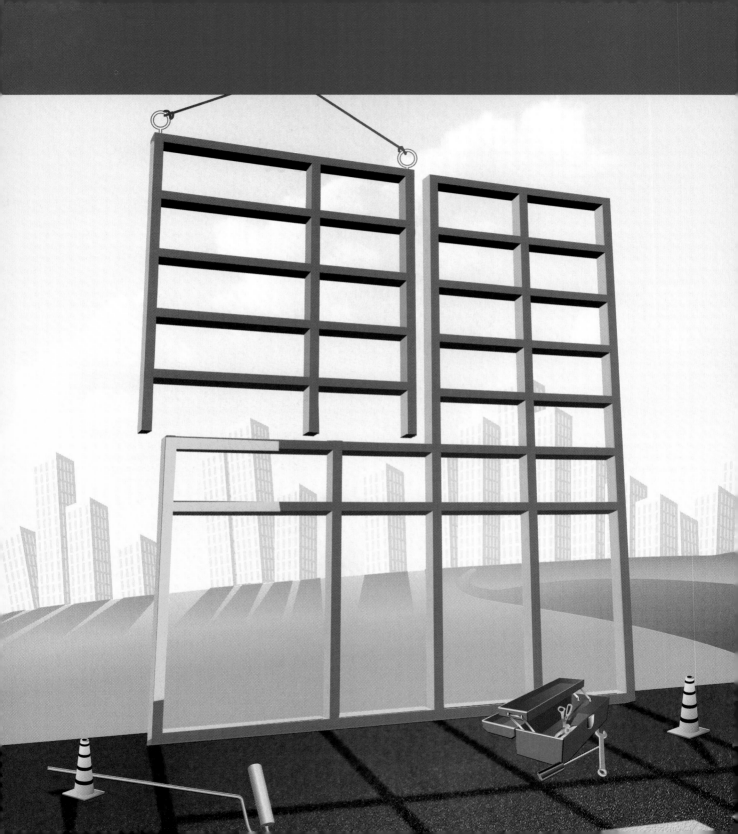

CHAPTER 11

Work With Tables

Do you want to learn how to display information in a table? This chapter teaches you how to create and work with tables.

CREATE A TABLE

You can create a table to neatly display information in your document.

CREATE A TABLE

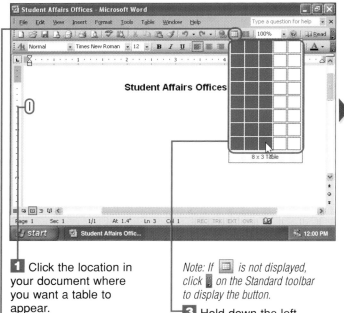

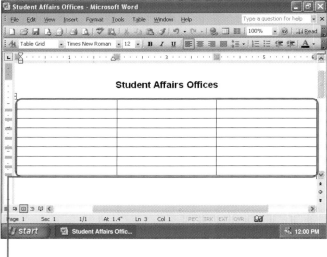

■1 Click the location in your document where you want a table to appear.

■2 Click 🔳 to create a table.

Note: If 🔳 is not displayed, click ⌄ on the Standard toolbar to display the button.

■3 Hold down the left mouse button as you move the mouse ⌖ to highlight the number of rows and columns you want the table to contain.

■ The table appears in your document.

What are the parts of a table?

A table consists of rows, columns and cells.

Row

Column

Cell

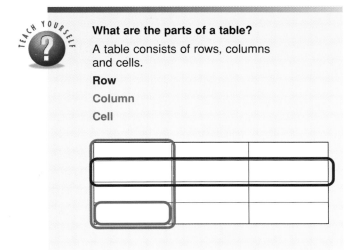

Can I change the appearance of text in a table?

Yes. You can format text in a table as you would format any text in your document. For example, you can change the font, size, color and alignment of text in a table. To format text, see pages 86 to 95.

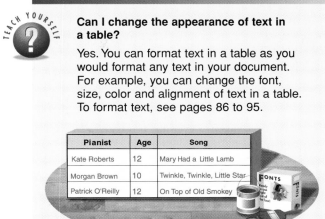

Pianist	Age	Song
Kate Roberts	12	Mary Had a Little Lamb
Morgan Brown	10	Twinkle, Twinkle, Little Star
Patrick O'Reilly	12	On Top of Old Smokey

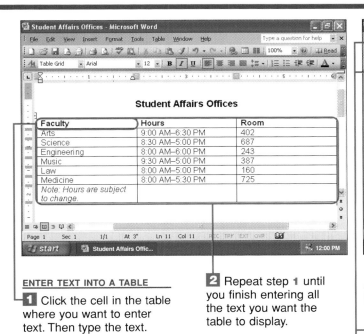

ENTER TEXT INTO A TABLE

1 Click the cell in the table where you want to enter text. Then type the text.

2 Repeat step **1** until you finish entering all the text you want the table to display.

DELETE A TABLE

1 Click anywhere in the table you want to delete.

2 Click **Table**.

3 Click **Delete**.

4 Click **Table**.

■ The table disappears from your document.

ADD A ROW OR COLUMN

You can add a row or column to your table to insert additional information.

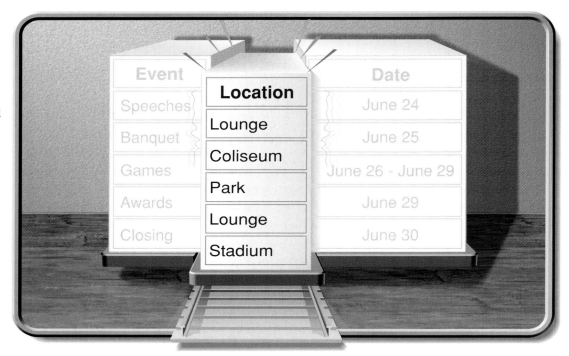

ADD A ROW

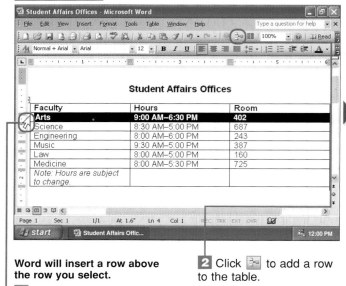

Word will insert a row above the row you select.

1 To select a row, position the mouse I to the left of the row (I changes to ⟋). Then click to select the row.

2 Click to add a row to the table.

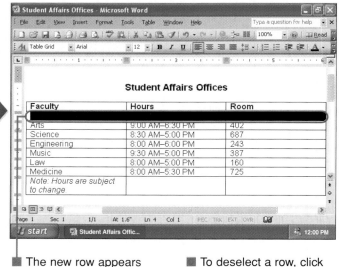

■ The new row appears in your table.

■ To deselect a row, click outside the selected area.

How do I add a row to the bottom of a table?

To add a row to the bottom of a table, click the bottom right cell in the table. Then press the `Tab` key.

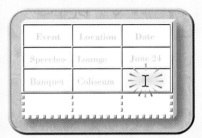

How do I add a column to the right of the last column in a table?

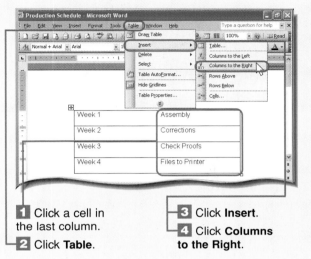

1 Click a cell in the last column.

2 Click **Table**.

3 Click **Insert**.

4 Click **Columns to the Right**.

ADD A COLUMN

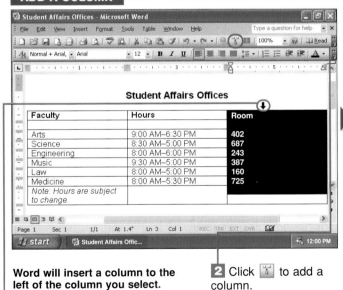

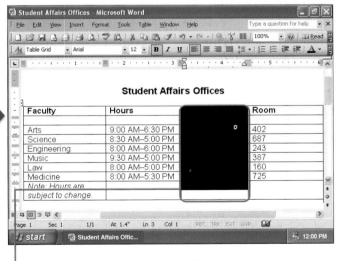

Word will insert a column to the left of the column you select.

1 To select a column, position the mouse I above the column (I changes to ↓). Then click to select the column.

2 Click to add a column.

■ The new column appears in your table.

■ To deselect a column, click outside the selected area.

DELETE A ROW OR COLUMN

You can delete a row or column you no longer need from your table.

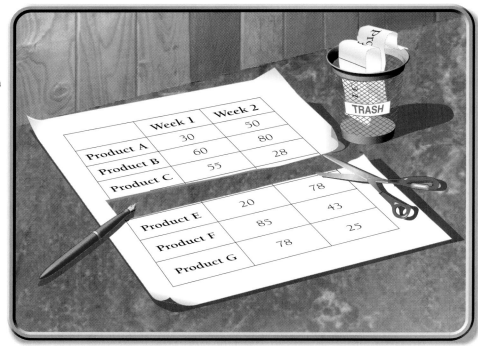

Deleting a row or column will also delete all the information in the row or column.

DELETE A ROW

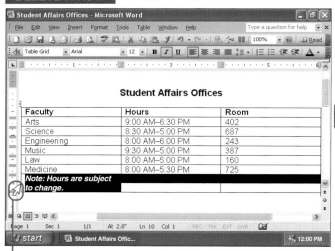

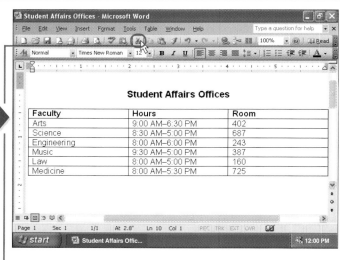

1 To select the row you want to delete, position the mouse I to the left of the row (I changes to ⏶). Then click to select the row.

2 Click ✄ to delete the row.

■ The row disappears from your table.

Can I delete the information in a row or column without removing the row or column from my table?

Yes. To select the cells in your table that contain the information you want to delete, drag the mouse I over the cells until you highlight the cells. Then press the Delete key to remove the information.

How can I restore a row or column I accidentally deleted?

If you accidentally delete a row or column, you can click the Undo button ( ) to immediately restore the row or column to your table. For more information on the Undo feature, see page 54.

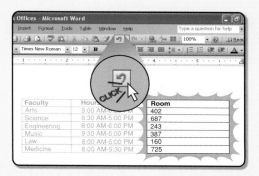

DELETE A COLUMN

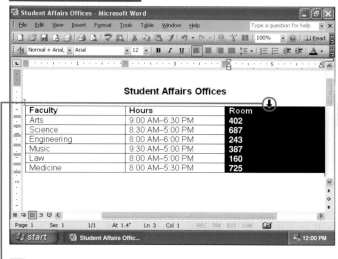

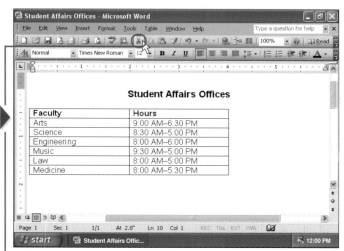

1 To select the column you want to delete, position the mouse I above the column (I changes to ↓). Then click to select the column.

2 Click to delete the column.

■ The column disappears from your table.

CHANGE ROW HEIGHT OR COLUMN WIDTH

You can change the height of rows and the width of columns to improve the layout of your table.

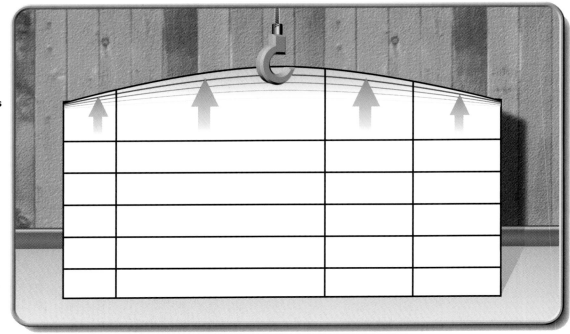

CHANGE ROW HEIGHT

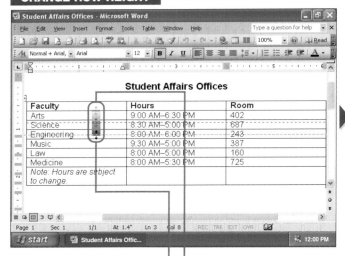

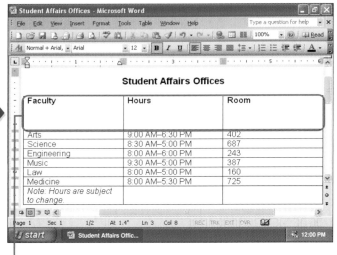

■ You can change a row height only when your document is displayed in the Print Layout or Web Layout view. To change the view of a document, see page 36.

1 Position the mouse I over the bottom edge of the row you want to change to a new height (I changes to ⬍).

2 Drag the row edge to a new position.

■ A dotted line shows the new position.

■ The row displays the new height.

Note: When you change the height of a row, the height of the entire table changes.

Can Word automatically adjust a row height or column width?

Yes. When you enter text into a table, Word automatically increases the row height or column width to accommodate the text you type.

Can I change the column width for only a few cells in a column?

Yes. To select the cells you want to change, position the mouse I over the first cell and then drag the mouse until you highlight all the cells you want to change in the column. To change the width of the selected cells, perform steps **1** and **2** on page 197.

Faculty	Hours
Arts	9:00 AM
Science	8:30 AM
Engineering	8:00 AM
Music	9:30 AM
Law	8:00 AM
Medicine	8:00 AM
Note: Hours are subject to change.	

Faculty	Hours
Arts	9:00 AM–6:30 PM
Science	8:30 AM–5:00 PM
Engineering	8:00 AM 6:00 PM
Music	9:30 AM–5:00 PM
Law	8:00 AM–5:00 PM
Medicine	8:00 AM–5:30 PM
Note: Hours are subject to change.	

CHANGE COLUMN WIDTH

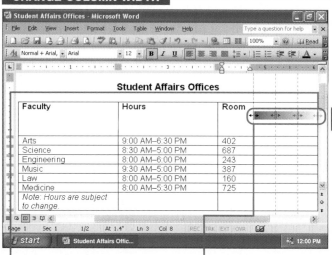 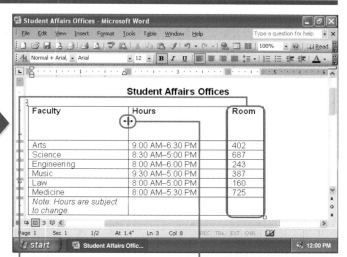

1 Position the mouse I over the right edge of the column you want to change to a new width (I changes to ◄║►).

2 Drag the column edge to a new position.

■ A dotted line shows the new position.

■ The column displays the new width.

Note: When you change the width of a column, the width of the neighboring column also changes. When you change the width of the last column, the width of the entire table changes.

FIT LONGEST ITEM

1 To quickly change a column width to fit the longest item in the column, double-click the right edge of the column.

MOVE A TABLE

You can move a table from one location in your document to another.

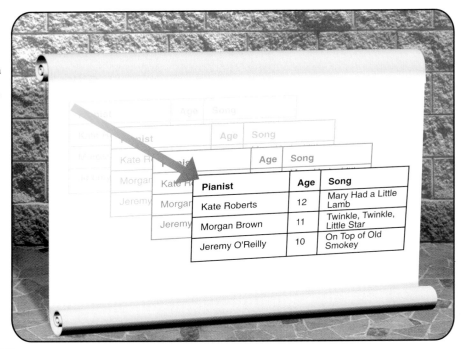

You can move a table only in the Print Layout or Web Layout view. To change the view of a document, see page 36.

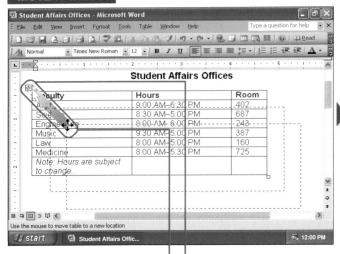

1 Position the mouse I over the table you want to move. A handle (⊞) appears.

Note: You may have to scroll to the left to view the handle.

2 Position the mouse I over the handle (I changes to ✛).

3 Drag the table to a new location.

■ A dashed outline indicates the new location.

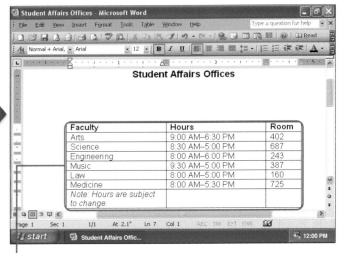

■ The table appears in the new location.

■ To copy a table, perform steps **1** to **3**, except press and hold down the **Ctrl** key as you perform step **3**.

RESIZE A TABLE

You can change the size of a table to improve the layout of the table.

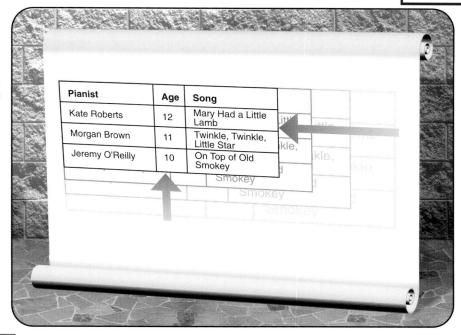

You can resize a table only in the Print Layout or Web Layout view. To change the view of a document, see page 36.

RESIZE A TABLE

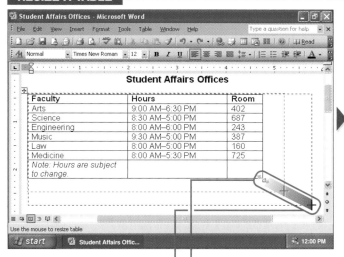

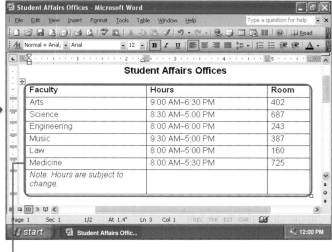

1 Position the mouse I over the table you want to resize. A handle (□) appears.

Note: You may have to scroll to the right to view the handle.

2 Position the mouse I over the handle (I changes to ↖).

3 Drag the handle until the table is the size you want.

■ A dashed outline indicates the new size.

■ The table appears in the new size.

COMBINE CELLS

You can combine two or more cells in your table to create one large cell. Combining cells is useful when you want to display a title across the top or down the side of your table.

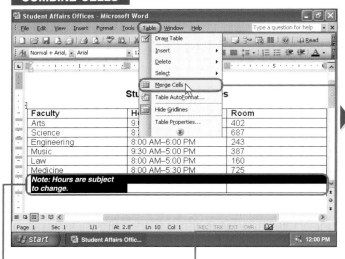

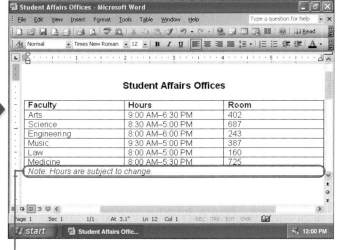

1 Position the mouse I over the first cell you want to combine with other cells.

2 Drag the mouse I until you highlight all the cells you want to combine.

3 Click **Table**.

4 Click **Merge Cells**.

Note: If Merge Cells does not appear on the menu, position the mouse ⃖ over the bottom of the menu to display the menu option.

■ The cells combine to create one large cell.

■ To deselect cells, click outside the selected area.

SPLIT CELLS

You can split one cell in your table into two or more cells.

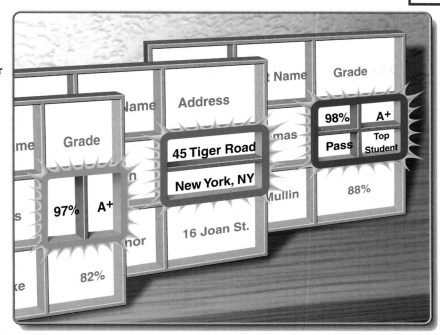

You can split a cell into columns, rows or both columns and rows.

Split cell into columns

Split cell into rows

Split cell into columns and rows

SPLIT CELLS

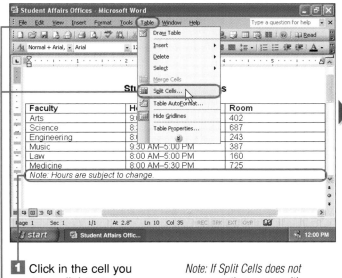

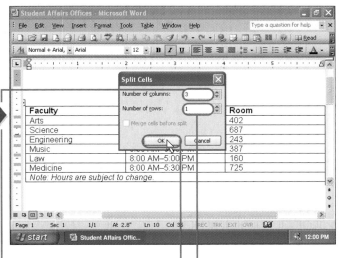

1 Click in the cell you want to split into two or more cells.

2 Click **Table**.

3 Click **Split Cells**.

Note: If Split Cells does not appear on the menu, position the mouse ⟋ over the bottom of the menu to display the menu option.

■ The Split Cells dialog box appears.

4 Double-click the number in this area and type the number of columns you want to split the cell into.

5 Double-click the number in this area and type the number of rows you want to split the cell into.

6 Click **OK** to split the cell.

ALIGN TEXT IN CELLS

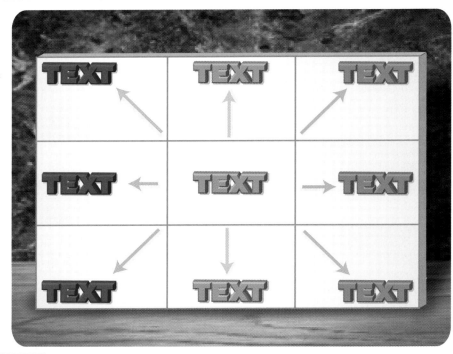

You can enhance the appearance of your table by changing the position of text in cells.

When you enter text into a cell, Word automatically aligns the text at the top left of the cell.

ALIGN TEXT IN CELLS

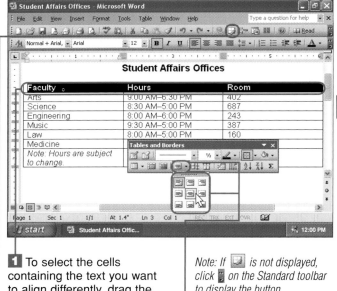

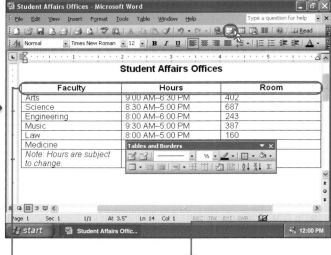

1 To select the cells containing the text you want to align differently, drag the mouse I over the cells.

2 Click 🖾 to display the Tables and Borders toolbar.

Note: If 🖾 is not displayed, click 🔧 on the Standard toolbar to display the button.

3 Click ▾ in this area.

4 Click the alignment you want to use.

■ The text displays the new alignment.

■ To deselect cells, click outside the selected area.

5 To hide the Tables and Borders toolbar, click 🖾.

You can add
shading to cells
to make the
cells stand out
in your table.

ADD SHADING TO CELLS

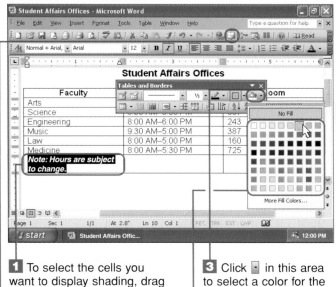

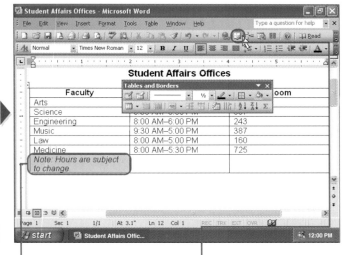

1 To select the cells you
want to display shading, drag
the mouse I over the cells.

2 Click 🖉 to display the
Tables and Borders toolbar.

*Note: If 🖉 is not displayed, click ▪
on the Standard toolbar to display the
button.*

3 Click ▪ in this area
to select a color for the
shading.

4 Click the color you
want to use.

■ The cells you selected
display the shading.

■ To deselect cells, click
outside the selected area.

5 To hide the Tables and
Borders toolbar, click 🖉.

■ To remove shading from
cells, repeat steps **1** to **5**,
selecting **No Fill** in step **4**.

CHANGE TABLE BORDERS

You can change the borders in your table to enhance the appearance of the table.

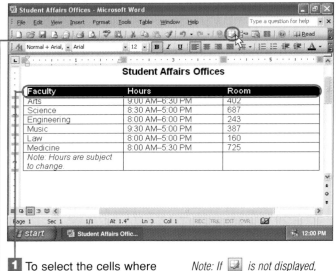

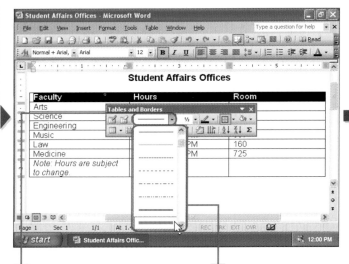

1 To select the cells where you want to change the border, drag the mouse I over the cells.

2 Click 🔲 to display the Tables and Borders toolbar.

Note: If 🔲 is not displayed, click 🔹 on the Standard toolbar to display the button.

■ The Tables and Borders toolbar appears.

3 Click this area to display a list of the available line styles for the border.

4 Click the line style you want to use.

Why would I change the border for only some of the cells in my table?

Changing the border for specific cells in your table can help you emphasize important information or divide your table into sections.

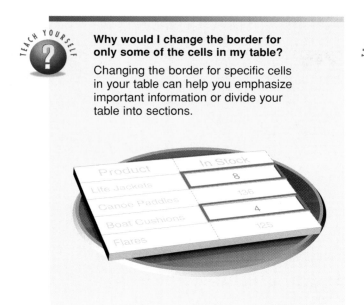

Can I remove a border from my table?

Yes. When you remove a border from your table, the border appears in gray in your document, but will not appear on a printed page. To remove a border from your table, perform steps **1** and **2** below. Then perform steps **5** to **7**, selecting ⊞ in step **6**.

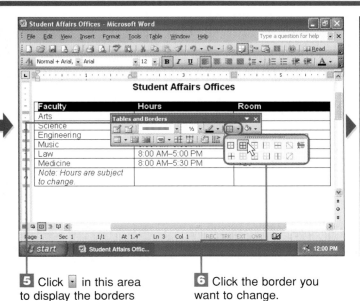

5 Click ▾ in this area to display the borders you can change.

6 Click the border you want to change.

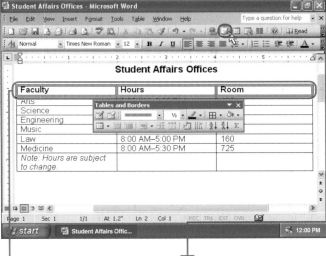

■ The cells you selected display the new border.

■ To deselect cells, click outside the selected area.

7 To hide the Tables and Borders toolbar, click 🗔.

FORMAT A TABLE

Word offers many ready-to-use designs that you can choose from to quickly give your table a professional appearance.

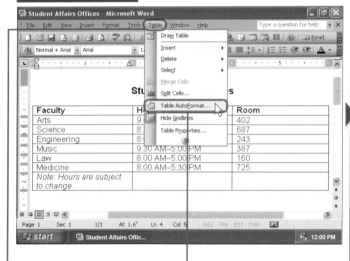

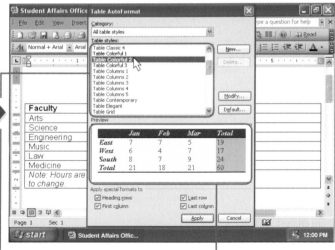

1 Click anywhere in the table you want to format.

2 Click **Table**.

3 Click **Table AutoFormat**.

■ The Table AutoFormat dialog box appears.

■ This area displays a list of the available table designs.

4 Click the table design you want to use.

■ This area displays a sample of the table design you selected.

Note: To display a sample of a different table design, repeat step 4.

What parts of a table can Word apply special formats to?

Word can apply special formats to the heading rows, the first column, the last row and the last column of a table. For example, Word can **bold text** in the heading rows of a table or apply borders to the last row of a table.

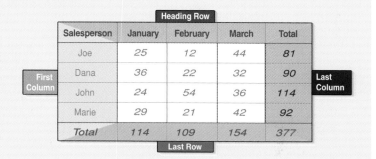

	Heading Row			
Salesperson	January	February	March	Total
Joe	25	12	44	81
Dana	36	22	32	90
John	24	54	36	114
Marie	29	21	42	92
Total	114	109	154	377

First Column

Last Column

Last Row

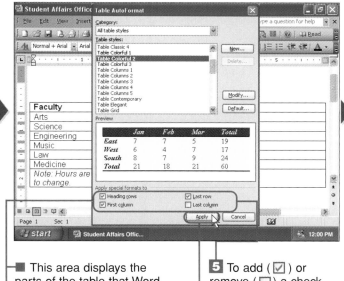

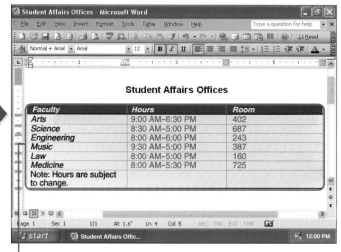

■ This area displays the parts of the table that Word can apply special formats to.

■ A check mark (✓) beside an option indicates that Word will apply special formats to that part of the table.

5 To add (☑) or remove (☐) a check mark beside an option, click the option.

6 Click **Apply** or press the Enter key to apply the design to your table.

■ The table displays the design you selected.

■ To remove a table design from a table, repeat steps **1** to **4**, selecting **Table Grid** in step **4**. Then press the Enter key.

CHAPTER 12

Work With Graphics

Are you interested in using graphics to enhance the appearance of your document? This chapter shows you how.

Drawing Canvas

ADD AN AUTOSHAPE

Word provides ready-made shapes, called AutoShapes, that you can add to your document.

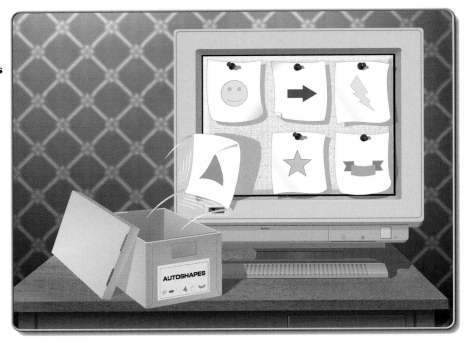

Word offers several types of AutoShapes such as lines, arrows, stars and banners.

Word can display AutoShapes only in the Print Layout, Web Layout and Reading Layout views. To change the view of a document, see page 36.

ADD AN AUTOSHAPE

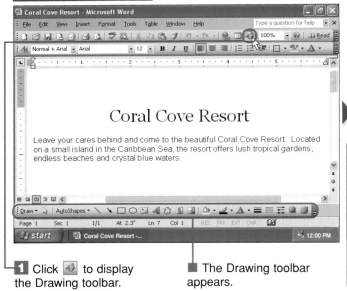

1 Click  to display the Drawing toolbar.

Note: If [icon] is not displayed, click [icon] on the Standard toolbar to display the button.

■ The Drawing toolbar appears.

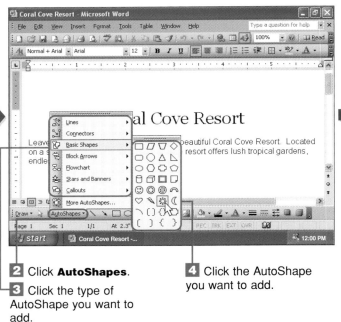

2 Click **AutoShapes**.

3 Click the type of AutoShape you want to add.

4 Click the AutoShape you want to add.

How can I add text to an AutoShape?

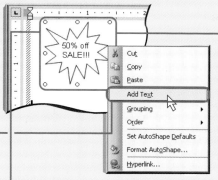

3 Type the text you want the AutoShape to display.

4 When you finish typing the text, click outside the AutoShape.

1 Right-click an edge of the AutoShape you want to display text. A menu appears.

2 Click **Add Text**.

Note: If Add Text does not appear on the menu, you cannot add text to the AutoShape you selected.

How do I delete an AutoShape?

To delete an AutoShape, click an edge of the AutoShape and then press the `Delete` key.

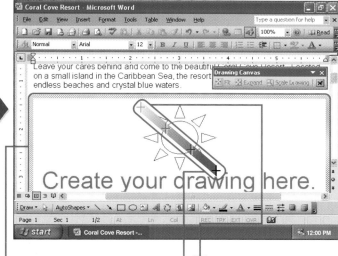

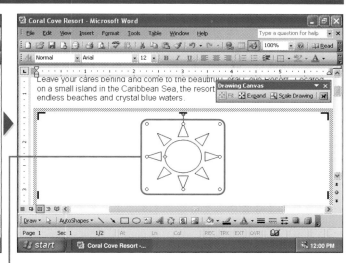

■ Word adds a drawing canvas to your document. A drawing canvas provides an area that allows you to arrange graphics and move several graphics at once.

Note: For more information on using a drawing canvas, see page 228.

5 Position the mouse + where you want to begin drawing the AutoShape.

6 Drag the mouse + until the AutoShape is the size you want.

■ The AutoShape appears. The handles (○) around the AutoShape allow you to change the size of the AutoShape. To move or resize an AutoShape, see page 222.

■ To deselect an AutoShape, click outside the AutoShape.

■ To hide the drawing canvas, click outside the drawing canvas or press the `Esc` key.

Note: To hide the Drawing toolbar, repeat step 1.

ADD WORDART

You can add WordArt to your document to create an eye-catching title or draw attention to important information.

WordArt allows you to create decorative text that is skewed, curved, rotated, stretched, three-dimensional or even vertical.

ADD WORDART

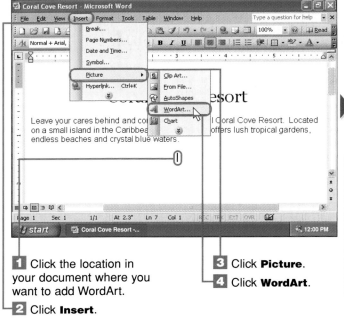

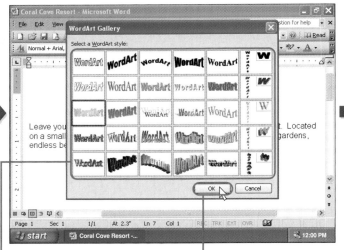

1 Click the location in your document where you want to add WordArt.

2 Click **Insert**.

3 Click **Picture**.

4 Click **WordArt**.

■ The WordArt Gallery dialog box appears.

5 Click the WordArt style you want to use.

6 Click **OK** to confirm your selection.

How do I edit WordArt text?

To edit WordArt text, double-click the WordArt to display the Edit WordArt Text dialog box. Then perform steps **7** and **8** below to specify the new text you want the WordArt to display.

Why does the WordArt toolbar appear when I select WordArt in a document?

The WordArt toolbar contains buttons that allow you to change the appearance of WordArt. For example, you can click one of the following buttons to alter the appearance of WordArt.

Aa Display all the letters in the WordArt at the same height.

Ab Display the WordArt text vertically rather than horizontally.

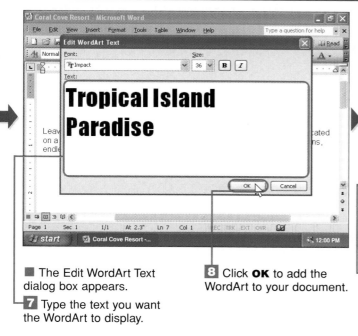

■ The Edit WordArt Text dialog box appears.

7 Type the text you want the WordArt to display.

8 Click **OK** to add the WordArt to your document.

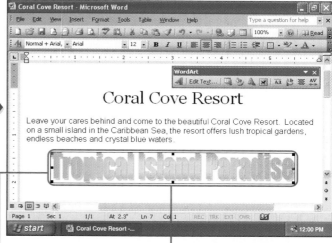

■ The WordArt appears in your document.

Note: To move or resize WordArt, see page 222.

DELETE WORDART

1 Click the WordArt you want to delete. Handles (■) appear around the WordArt.

2 Press the Delete key to delete the WordArt.

ADD A TEXT BOX

You can add a text box to your document. Text boxes are useful for controlling the placement of text in a document.

Word can display text boxes only in the Print Layout, Web Layout and Reading Layout views. To change the view of a document, see page 36.

To change the view of a document, see page 36.

ADD A TEXT BOX

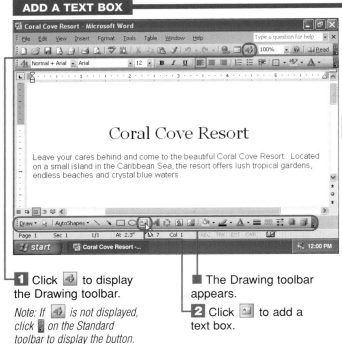

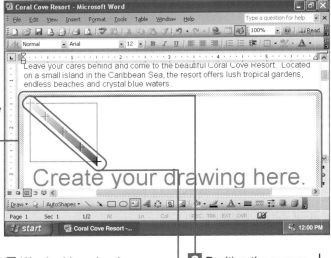

1 Click [icon] to display the Drawing toolbar.

Note: If [icon] is not displayed, click [icon] on the Standard toolbar to display the button.

■ The Drawing toolbar appears.

2 Click [icon] to add a text box.

■ Word adds a drawing canvas to your document. A drawing canvas provides an area that allows you to arrange graphics and move several graphics at once.

Note: For more information on using a drawing canvas, see page 228.

Note: For more information on using a drawing canvas, see page 228.

3 Position the mouse + where you want to begin drawing the text box.

4 Drag the mouse + until the text box is the size you want.

How do I edit the text in a text box?

To edit the text in a text box, click the text box and then edit the text as you would edit any text in a document. To edit text, see page 50. When you finish editing the text, click outside the text box.

Can I format the text in a text box?

Yes. You can format the text in a text box as you would format any text in a document. For example, you can bold, italicize and change the font of text in a text box. To format text, see pages 86 to 99.

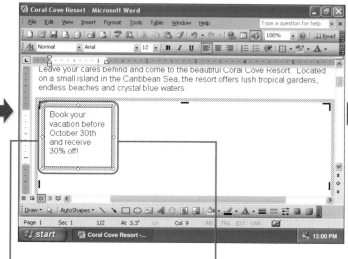

■ The text box appears. The handles (○) around the text box allow you to change the size of the text box. To move or resize a text box, see page 222.

5 Type the text you want the text box to display.

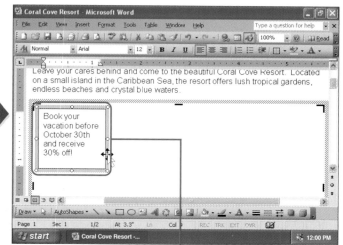

■ To deselect a text box, click outside the text box.

■ To hide the drawing canvas, click outside the drawing canvas or press the **Esc** key.

Note: To hide the Drawing toolbar, repeat step 1.

DELETE A TEXT BOX

1 Click an edge of the text box you want to delete. Handles (○) appear around the text box.

2 Press the **Delete** key to delete the text box.

ADD A PICTURE

You can add a picture stored on your computer to your document.

Adding a picture is useful when you want to display your company logo or illustrate a concept.

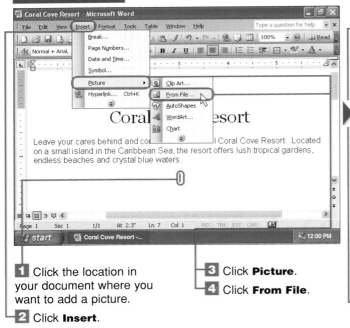

1 Click the location in your document where you want to add a picture.

2 Click **Insert**.

3 Click **Picture**.

4 Click **From File**.

■ The Insert Picture dialog box appears.

■ This area shows the location of the displayed pictures. You can click this area to change the location.

■ This area allows you to access pictures stored in commonly used locations. You can click a location to display the pictures stored in the location.

Note: For information on the commonly used locations, see the top of page 21.

Where can I get pictures that I can add to my documents?

You can purchase collections of pictures at stores that sell computer software or obtain pictures on the Internet. You can also use a scanner to scan pictures into your computer or create your own pictures using an image editing program, such as Adobe Photoshop.

How can I change the appearance of a picture?

When you click a picture, the Picture toolbar appears, displaying buttons that allow you to change the appearance of the picture. For example, you can click ⬛ or ⬛ to increase or decrease the brightness of the picture.

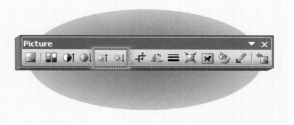

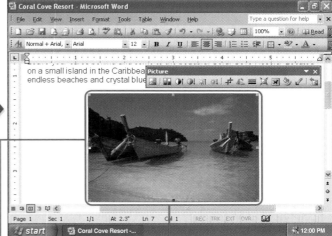

5 Click the picture you want to add to your document.

6 Click **Insert** to add the picture to your document.

■ The picture appears in your document.

Note: To move or resize a picture, see page 222.

DELETE A PICTURE

1 Click the picture you want to delete. Handles (■) appear around the picture.

2 Press the Delete key to delete the picture.

ADD A CLIP ART IMAGE

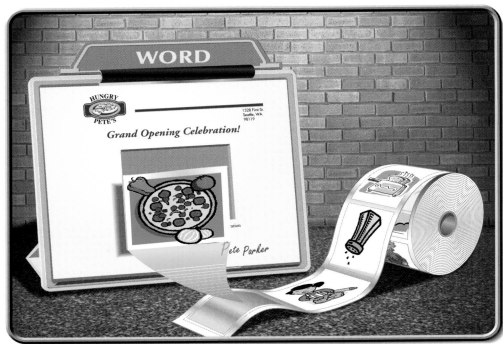

You can add professionally designed clip art images to your document. Clip art images can help illustrate concepts and make your document more interesting.

ADD A CLIP ART IMAGE

1 Click **Insert**.

2 Click **Picture**.

3 Click **Clip Art**.

■ The Clip Art task pane appears.

4 Click **Organize clips** to view all the available clip art images in the Microsoft Clip Organizer.

*Note: The first time you add a clip art image to a document, the Add Clips to Organizer dialog box appears. To catalog the clip art images and other media files on your computer, click **Now** in the dialog box.*

In the Microsoft Clip Organizer, what type of clip art images will I find in each collection?

My Collections

Displays images that came with Microsoft Windows and images you created or obtained on your own.

Office Collections

Displays the images that came with Microsoft Office.

Web Collections

Displays the images that are available at Microsoft's Web site and at Web sites in partnership with Microsoft.

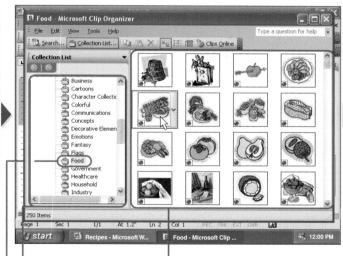

■ The Microsoft Clip Organizer window appears.

■ This area displays the folders that contain the clip art images you can add to your document. A folder displaying a plus sign (⊞) contains hidden folders.

5 To display the hidden folders within a folder, click the plus sign (⊞) beside the folder (⊞ changes to ⊟).

Note: You must be connected to the Internet to view the contents of the Web Collections folder.

■ The hidden folders appear.

6 Click a folder of interest.

■ This area displays the clip art images in the folder you selected.

7 Click the clip art image you want to add to your document.

CONTINUED ▶

ADD A CLIP ART IMAGE

After you locate an image you want to add to your document, you can copy the image to the clipboard and then place the image in your document.

The clipboard temporarily stores information you have selected to move or copy.

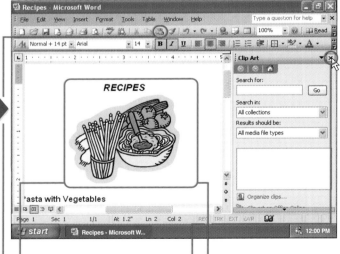

8 Click 🔳 to copy the image you selected to the clipboard.

9 Click ⊠ to close the Microsoft Clip Organizer.

■ A dialog box appears, stating that you have one or more clip art images on the clipboard.

10 Click **Yes** to continue.

11 Click the location in your document where you want to add the image.

12 Click 🔳 to place the image in your document.

■ The image appears in your document.

13 To close the Clip Art task pane, click ⊠.

How do I resize a clip art image?

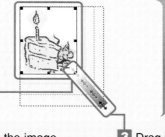

1 Click the image you want to resize. Handles (■) appear around the image.

2 Position the mouse over one of the handles (changes to ↖, ↗, ↕ or ↔).

3 Drag the handle until the image is the size you want.

■ A dashed line shows the new size.

How do I delete a clip art image?

Click the clip art image you want to delete. Handles (■) appear around the image. Press the Delete key to delete the image.

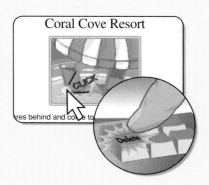

Coral Cove Resort

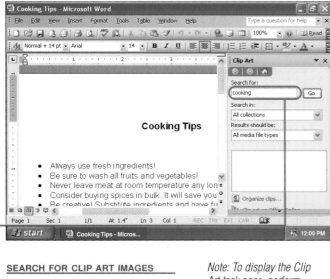

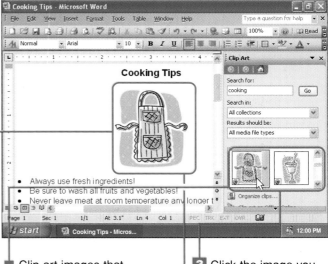

SEARCH FOR CLIP ART IMAGES

You can search for clip art images by specifying one or more words of interest in the Clip Art task pane.

1 Double-click this area and type one or more words that describe the image you want to find. Then press the Enter key.

Note: To display the Clip Art task pane, perform steps 1 to 3 on page 218.

■ Clip art images that match the words you specified appear in this area.

2 Click the location in your document where you want to add an image.

3 Click the image you want to add to your document.

■ The image appears in your document.

MOVE OR RESIZE A GRAPHIC

You can change the location and size of a graphic in your document.

Word can display all types of graphics in the Print Layout and Web Layout views. To change the view of a document, see page 36.

MOVE A GRAPHIC

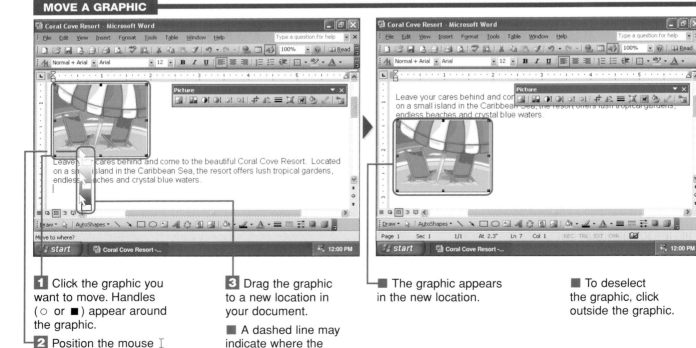

1 Click the graphic you want to move. Handles (○ or ■) appear around the graphic.

2 Position the mouse I over an edge of the graphic (I changes to ↕ or ⊹).

3 Drag the graphic to a new location in your document.

■ A dashed line may indicate where the graphic will appear.

■ The graphic appears in the new location.

■ To deselect the graphic, click outside the graphic.

222

Which handle should I use to resize a graphic?

The handles that appear at the top and bottom of a graphic (■ or ●) allow you to change the height of the graphic. The handles at the sides of a graphic (■ or ●) allow you to change the width of the graphic. The handles at the corners of a graphic (■ or ●) allow you to change the height and width of the graphic at the same time.

How can I change the way a graphic is moved or resized?

To move a graphic only horizontally or vertically, press and hold down the Shift key as you move the graphic.

To keep the center of a graphic in the same location while resizing the graphic, press and hold down the Ctrl key as you resize the graphic.

RESIZE A GRAPHIC

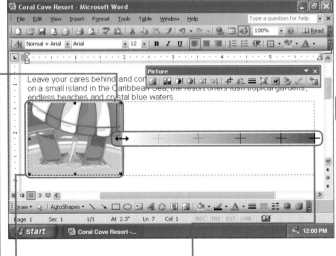

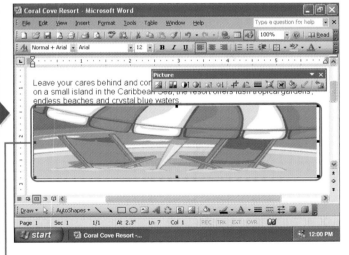

1 Click the graphic you want to resize. Handles (○ or ■) appear around the graphic.

2 Position the mouse I over one of the handles (I changes to ↔, ↕, ↖ or ↗).

3 Drag the handle until the graphic is the size you want.

■ A dashed line indicates the new size.

■ The graphic appears in the new size.

■ To deselect the graphic, click outside the graphic.

CHANGE THE COLOR OF A GRAPHIC

You can change the color of a graphic in your document.

You cannot change the color of some clip art images and pictures.

CHANGE THE COLOR OF A GRAPHIC

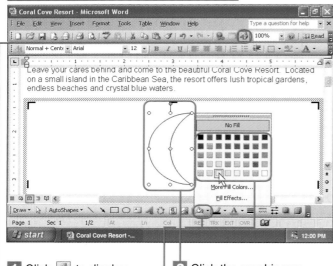

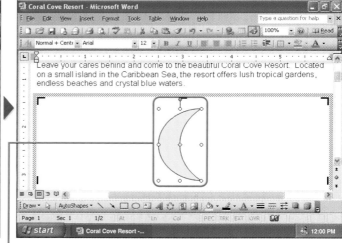

1 Click ⬛ to display the Drawing toolbar.

Note: If ⬛ is not displayed, click ⬛ on the Standard toolbar to display the button.

2 Click the graphic you want to change to a different color. Handles (○ or ■) appear around the graphic.

3 Click ⬛ in this area to display the available colors.

4 Click the color you want to use.

■ The graphic appears in the color you selected.

■ To deselect a graphic, click outside the graphic.

Note: To hide the Drawing toolbar, repeat step 1.

ROTATE A GRAPHIC

You can rotate a graphic in your document.

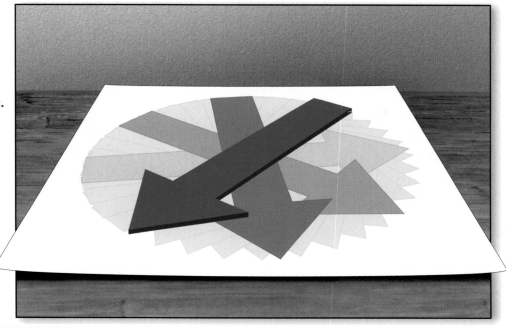

You cannot rotate text boxes and some AutoShapes.

ROTATE A GRAPHIC

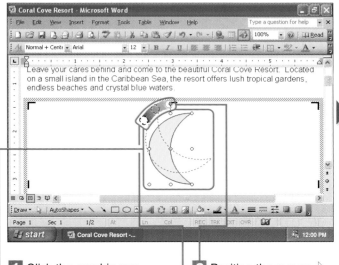

1 Click the graphic you want to rotate. Handles (○) appear around the graphic.

Note: If ■ handles appear around the graphic, you cannot rotate the graphic.

2 Position the mouse ⌖ over the green dot (⌖ changes to ↻).

3 Drag the mouse ⟡ in the direction you want to rotate the graphic.

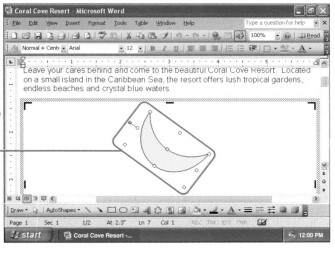

■ The graphic appears in the new position.

■ To deselect a graphic, click outside the graphic.

225

ADD A SHADOW TO A GRAPHIC

You can add a shadow to add depth to a graphic in your document.

ADD A SHADOW TO A GRAPHIC

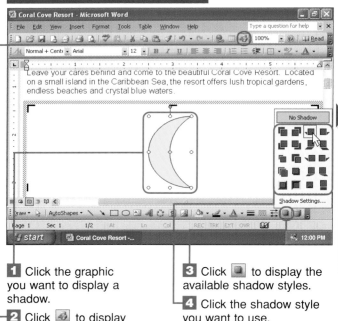

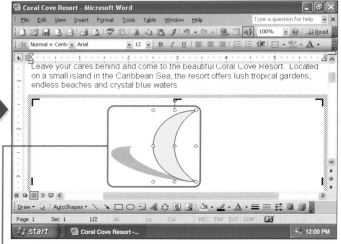

1 Click the graphic you want to display a shadow.

2 Click 🔲 to display the Drawing toolbar.

Note: If 🔲 is not displayed, click ⁝ on the Standard toolbar to display the button.

3 Click 🔲 to display the available shadow styles.

4 Click the shadow style you want to use.

Note: If a shadow style is dimmed, the style is not available for the graphic you selected.

■ The graphic displays the shadow.

Note: To hide the Drawing toolbar, repeat step 2.

■ To remove a shadow from a graphic, repeat steps **1** to **4**, selecting **No Shadow** in step **4**.

MAKE A GRAPHIC 3-D

You can make a
graphic in your
document appear
three-dimensional.

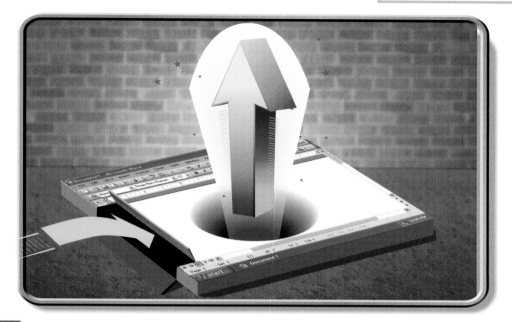

MAKE A GRAPHIC 3-D

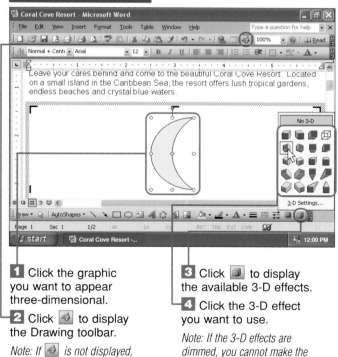

1 Click the graphic
you want to appear
three-dimensional.

2 Click 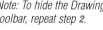 to display
the Drawing toolbar.

*Note: If ⬚ is not displayed,
click ⬚ on the Standard
toolbar to display the button.*

3 Click ⬚ to display
the available 3-D effects.

4 Click the 3-D effect
you want to use.

*Note: If the 3-D effects are
dimmed, you cannot make the
graphic you selected three-
dimensional.*

■ The graphic
displays the 3-D effect.

*Note: To hide the Drawing
toolbar, repeat step 2.*

■ To remove a 3-D
effect from a graphic,
repeat steps **1** to **4**,
selecting **No 3-D** in
step **4**.

CREATE A DRAWING CANVAS

You can add a drawing canvas to your document. A drawing canvas provides an area that allows you to arrange graphics and move several graphics at once.

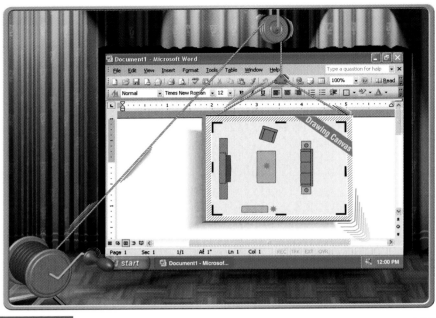

Word can display a drawing canvas only in the Print Layout, Web Layout and Reading Layout views. To change the view of a document, see page 36.

Word automatically creates a drawing canvas when you add some types of graphics to your document, such as AutoShapes and text boxes.

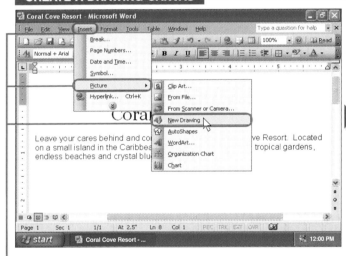

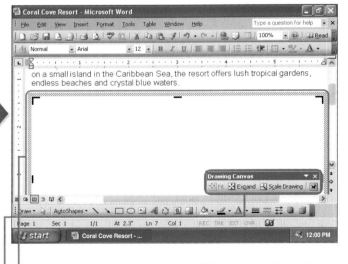

1 Click **Insert**.

2 Click **Picture**.

3 Click **New Drawing**.

Note: If New Drawing does not appear on the menu, position the mouse ⌖ over the bottom of the menu to display the menu option.

■ A drawing canvas appears in your document.

■ The Drawing Canvas toolbar also appears, displaying buttons you can use to work with the drawing canvas.

Note: If the Drawing Canvas toolbar does not appear, right-click the drawing canvas and then select **Show Drawing Canvas Toolbar***.*

■ You can add graphics, such as an AutoShape, text box or picture, to the drawing canvas.

■ To deselect the drawing canvas, click outside the drawing canvas or press the **Esc** key.

How do I delete a drawing canvas?

To delete a drawing canvas, click a blank area inside the canvas and then press the Delete key. Deleting a drawing canvas will delete all the graphics on the canvas. If you want to keep the graphics, you must move the graphics off the drawing canvas before deleting the canvas. To move a graphic, see page 222.

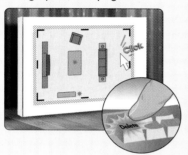

How can I change the size of a drawing canvas and the graphics on the canvas at the same time?

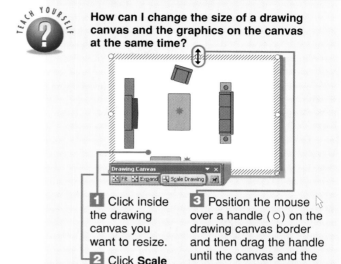

1 Click inside the drawing canvas you want to resize.

2 Click **Scale Drawing**.

3 Position the mouse over a handle (○) on the drawing canvas border and then drag the handle until the canvas and the graphics are the size you want.

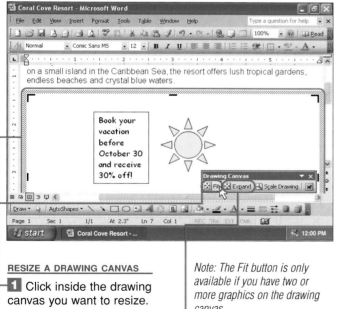

RESIZE A DRAWING CANVAS

1 Click inside the drawing canvas you want to resize.

2 Click **Fit** to make the drawing canvas border fit tightly around the graphics.

Note: The Fit button is only available if you have two or more graphics on the drawing canvas.

■ To enlarge the drawing canvas, click **Expand** until the drawing canvas is the size you want.

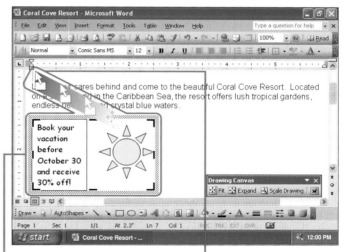

MOVE A DRAWING CANVAS

1 Click inside the drawing canvas you want to move.

2 Position the mouse over the border of the drawing canvas (changes to).

3 Drag the drawing canvas to a new location.

Note: The drawing canvas will appear where you position the dotted insertion point on your screen.

WRAP TEXT AROUND A GRAPHIC

After you add a graphic to your document, you can choose how you want to wrap text around the graphic.

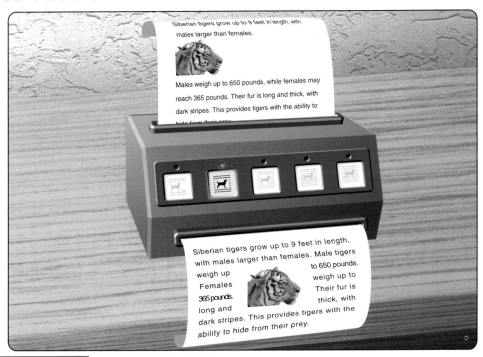

WRAP TEXT AROUND A GRAPHIC

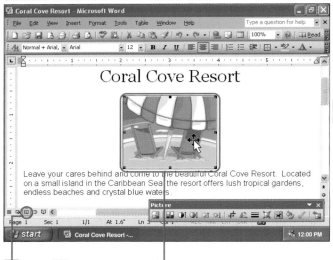

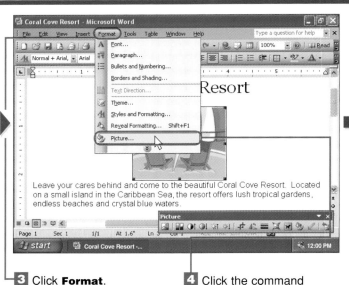

1 Click ▣ to display your document in the Print Layout view.

2 Click the graphic in your document you want to wrap text around. Handles (○ or ■) appear around the graphic.

Note: For information on wrapping text around a graphic on a drawing canvas, see the top of page 231.

3 Click **Format**.

4 Click the command for the type of graphic you selected, such as **AutoShape**, **Picture** or **WordArt**.

■ The Format dialog box appears.

How can Word align a graphic with text?

Word can align a graphic to the left, center or right of text.

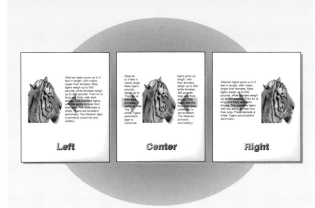

Left Center Right

Can I wrap text around a graphic on a drawing canvas?

Yes. To wrap text around a graphic on a drawing canvas, perform steps **1** to **8** below, except click a blank area on the drawing canvas in step **2** and select **Drawing Canvas** in step **4**. For information on using a drawing canvas, see page 228.

Here is the new layout of the family room. By adding a large area rug, scented candles, and some green plants. I think you can really add a lot of warmth to this large room. You can also try adding a few throw pillows to the couches.

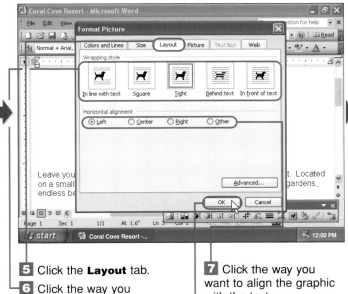

5 Click the **Layout** tab.

6 Click the way you want to wrap text around the graphic.

7 Click the way you want to align the graphic with the text.

8 Click **OK** to confirm your changes.

■ The text wraps around the graphic.

■ To deselect a graphic, click outside the graphic.

ADD A DIAGRAM

You can add a diagram to a document to illustrate a concept or idea. Word provides several types of diagrams for you to choose from.

Word can display diagrams only in the Print Layout, Web Layout and Reading Layout views. To change the view of a document, see page 36.

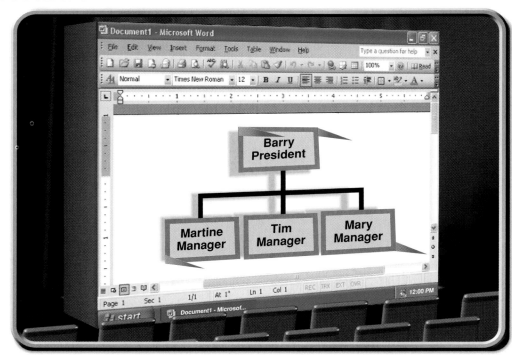

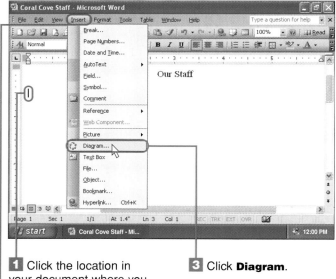

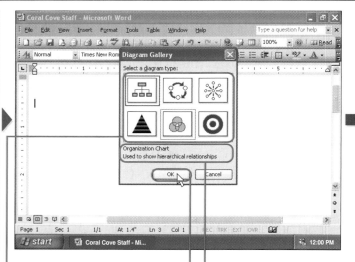

1 Click the location in your document where you want to add a diagram.

2 Click **Insert**.

3 Click **Diagram**.

Note: If Diagram does not appear on the menu, position the mouse ⌖ over the bottom of the menu to display the menu option.

■ The Diagram Gallery dialog box appears.

4 Click the type of diagram you want to add to your document.

Note: For information on the types of diagrams, see the top of page 233.

■ This area displays a description of the diagram you selected.

5 Click **OK** to add the diagram to your document.

232

What types of diagrams can I add to my document?

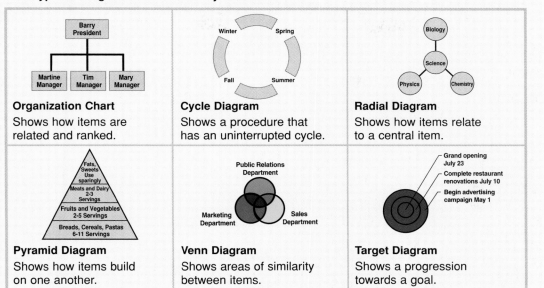

Organization Chart
Shows how items are related and ranked.

Cycle Diagram
Shows a procedure that has an uninterrupted cycle.

Radial Diagram
Shows how items relate to a central item.

Pyramid Diagram
Shows how items build on one another.

Venn Diagram
Shows areas of similarity between items.

Target Diagram
Shows a progression towards a goal.

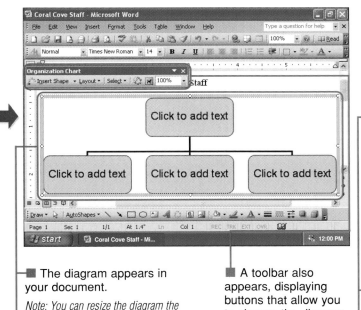

■ The diagram appears in your document.

Note: You can resize the diagram the same way you would resize any graphic.

■ A border appears around the diagram. The border will not appear when you print your document.

■ A toolbar also appears, displaying buttons that allow you to change the diagram.

■ To deselect a diagram, click outside the diagram or press the **Esc** key.

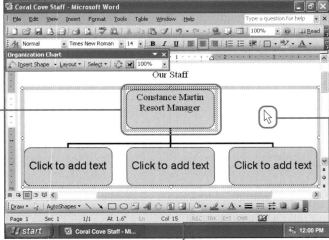

ADD TEXT

1 Click an area where you want to add text.

■ A border appears around the area if you can add text to the area.

2 Type the text you want to add.

3 When you finish typing the text, click outside the text area.

■ Repeat steps **1** to **3** for each area of text you want to add.

CONTINUED

ADD A DIAGRAM

You can add
a new shape
to a diagram
to include
additional
information
in the diagram.

ADD A DIAGRAM (CONTINUED)

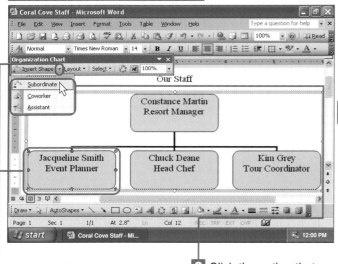

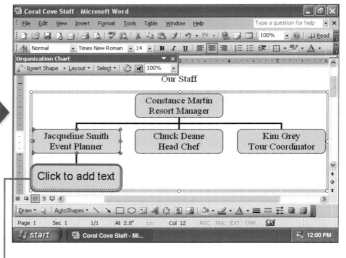

ADD A SHAPE

1 Click the shape above
or beside where you want
the new shape to appear.

2 To add a shape to an
organization chart, click ⬝
beside **Insert Shape**.

3 Click the option that
describes where you want
to position the shape.

■ To add a shape to all
other types of diagrams,
click **Insert Shape**.

■ The new shape appears
in the diagram.

■ You can add text to the
new shape.

■ To delete a shape, click
an edge of the shape you
want to delete and then
press the Delete key.

Where can I position a shape I add to an organization chart?

Subordinate
Adds a shape below the shape you selected.

Subordinate

Coworker
Adds a shape beside the shape you selected.

Coworker

Assistant
Uses an elbow connector to add a shape below the shape you selected.

Assistant

How do I delete a diagram?

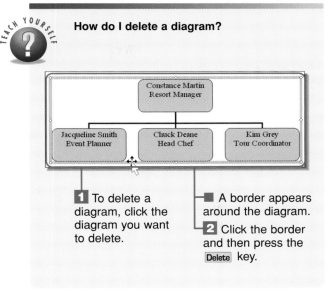

1 To delete a diagram, click the diagram you want to delete.

■ A border appears around the diagram.

2 Click the border and then press the Delete key.

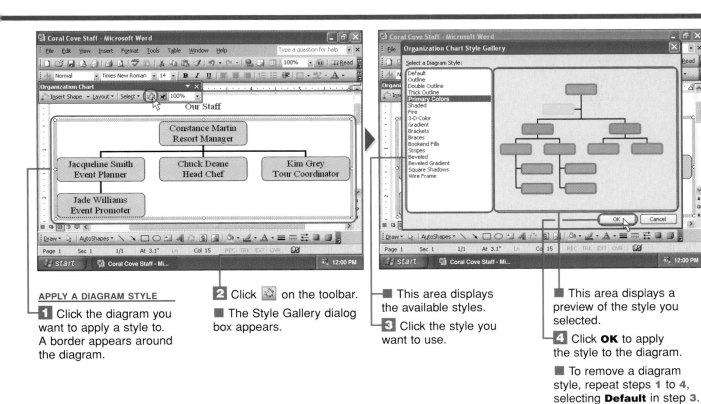

APPLY A DIAGRAM STYLE

1 Click the diagram you want to apply a style to. A border appears around the diagram.

2 Click ⬚ on the toolbar.

■ The Style Gallery dialog box appears.

■ This area displays the available styles.

3 Click the style you want to use.

■ This area displays a preview of the style you selected.

4 Click **OK** to apply the style to the diagram.

■ To remove a diagram style, repeat steps 1 to 4, selecting **Default** in step 3.

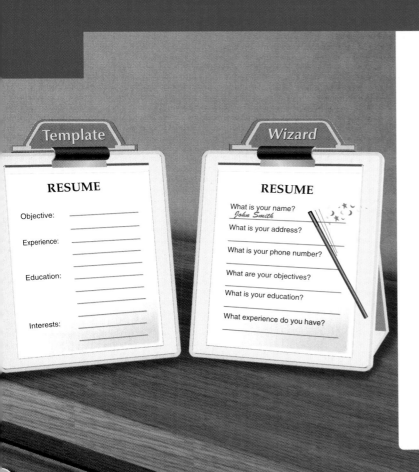

CHAPTER 13

Time-Saving Features

Do you want to learn how to save time when creating documents? In this chapter, you will learn how to perform tasks using smart tags, create a document using a template and more.

USING SMART TAGS

Word labels certain types of information, such as dates and addresses, with smart tags. You can use a smart tag to perform an action, such as scheduling a meeting on a specific date or displaying a map for an address.

You can change the options for smart tags to specify the types of information you want Word to recognize and label with a smart tag.

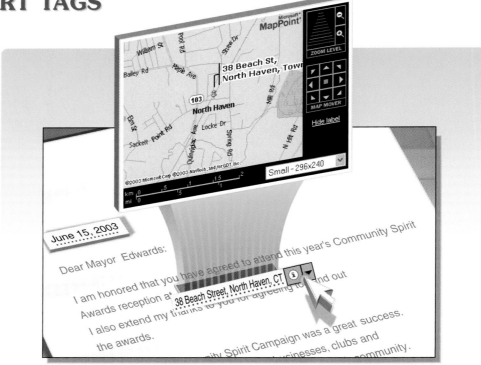

USING SMART TAGS

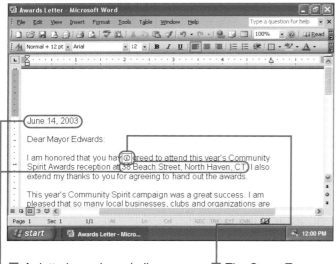

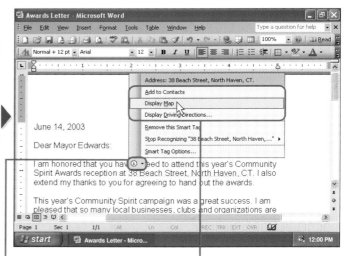

■ A dotted, purple underline appears below text Word has labeled as a smart tag.

1 To perform an action using a smart tag, position the mouse I over the text labeled as a smart tag.

■ The Smart Tag Actions button (⊡) appears.

2 Click the Smart Tag Actions button (⊡) to display a list of actions you can perform using the smart tag.

3 Click the action you want to perform.

■ The program that allows you to perform the action will appear on your screen.

How can I remove a smart tag from text in my document?

To remove a smart tag from text in your document, perform steps **1** to **3** on page 238, selecting **Remove this Smart Tag** in step **3**.

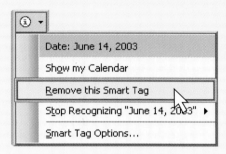

What types of information can Word label with smart tags?

Word can label people's names, dates, times, addresses, places and telephone numbers with smart tags. Word can also label e-mail addresses of people to whom you sent messages using Microsoft Office Outlook and financial symbols you type in capital letters, such as MSFT.

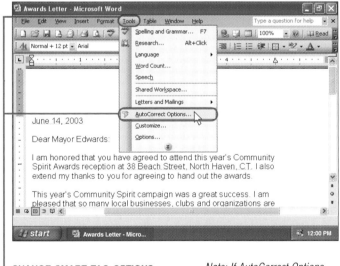

CHANGE SMART TAG OPTIONS

1 Click **Tools**.

2 Click **AutoCorrect Options**.

Note: If AutoCorrect Options does not appear on the menu, position the mouse ▷ over the bottom of the menu to display the menu option.

■ The AutoCorrect dialog box appears.

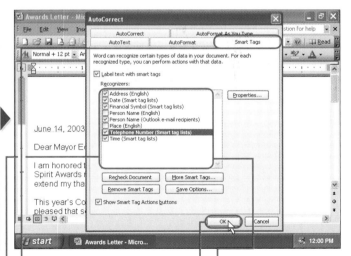

3 Click the **Smart Tags** tab to display the smart tag options.

■ This area displays the types of information Word can label as smart tags. Smart tags are currently turned on for each type of information that displays a check mark (✔).

4 You can click the check box beside a type of information to turn smart tags on (☑) or off (☐) for the information.

5 Click **OK** to confirm your changes.

USING TEMPLATES AND WIZARDS

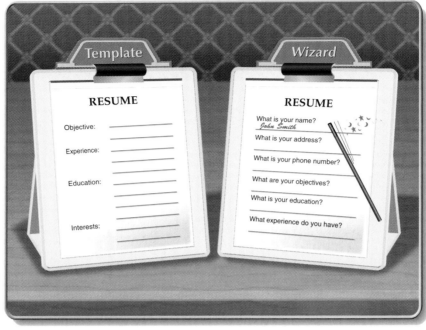

You can use templates and wizards to save time when creating common types of documents, such as letters, memos and reports.

Template

A template is a document that provides areas for you to fill in your personalized information.

Wizard

A wizard asks you a series of questions and then uses your answers to create a document.

USING TEMPLATES AND WIZARDS

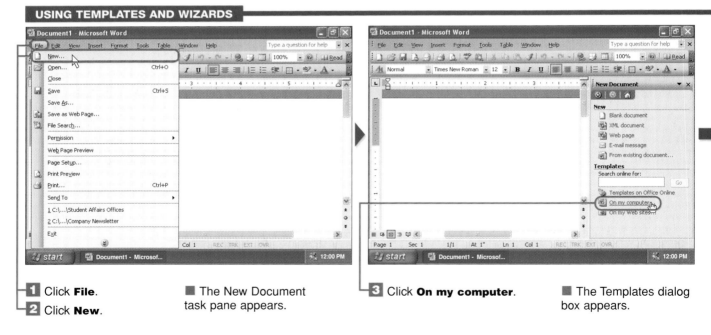

1 Click **File**.

2 Click **New**.

■ The New Document task pane appears.

3 Click **On my computer**.

■ The Templates dialog box appears.

Are there other templates available that I can use to create documents?

Yes. The Microsoft Office Online Web site offers many templates that you can download to use on your computer. For example, you can find templates to help you create resumes, newsletters and more.

Perform steps **1** and **2** below to display the New Document task pane. Then click **Templates on Office Online**. Your Web browser will open, displaying a Web site where you can browse through many different templates.

How can I quickly begin using a template or wizard I recently worked with?

The New Document task pane displays the names of the last four templates or wizards you worked with. To display the New Document task pane, perform steps **1** and **2** on page 240.

1 To quickly begin using a template or wizard, click the name of the template or wizard you want to use.

Note: You may need to click ▼ at the bottom of the task pane to view the templates and wizards.

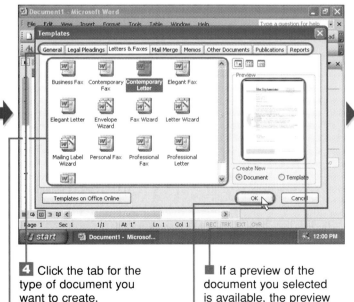

4 Click the tab for the type of document you want to create.

5 Click the template or wizard for the document you want to create.

Note: The icon for a wizard displays a magic wand (✨).

■ If a preview of the document you selected is available, the preview appears in this area.

6 Click **OK** to create the document.

■ The document appears on your screen.

Note: If you selected a wizard in step 5, Word will ask you a series of questions before creating the document.

7 Type your personalized information in the appropriate areas to complete the document.

CREATE A TEMPLATE

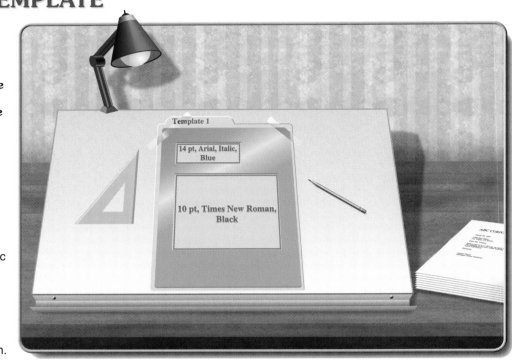

You can create a template from any document. You can then use the template to quickly create other documents that use the same graphics, text, formatting and page settings.

A template provides the basic structure of a document and can contain formatting, such as fonts, text alignment, line spacing and borders. A template can also contain page settings, such as margins and page orientation.

CREATE A TEMPLATE

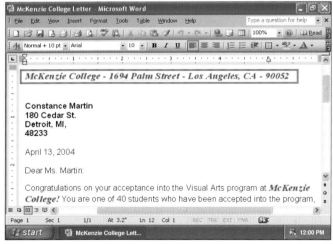

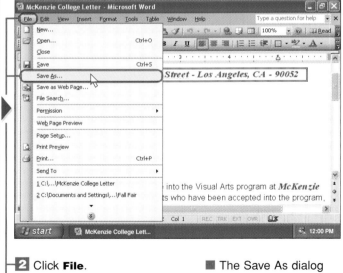

1 Open the document you want to use as the basis for the template. To open a document, see page 24.

2 Click **File**.

3 Click **Save As**.

■ The Save As dialog box appears.

How do I use a template I created?

Word stores templates you create in the Templates folder. To use a template stored in the Templates folder, perform steps **1** to **7** starting on page 240, selecting the **General** tab in step **4**.

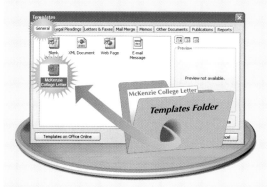

Can I create a template that displays my company logo?

Yes. Adding your company logo to the document you use as the basis of your template allows you to display the logo in each document you create using the template.

You add a company logo to a document the same way you add any picture to a document. For information on adding a picture, see page 216.

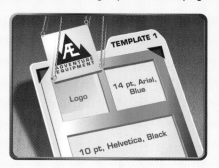

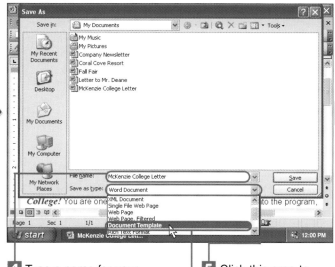

4 Type a name for your template.

Note: A template name cannot contain the * : ? > < | or " characters.

5 Click this area to specify you want to save your document as a template.

6 Click **Document Template**.

■ This area indicates Word will store your template in the Templates folder.

7 Click **Save** to save your document as a template.

CUSTOMIZE A TOOLBAR

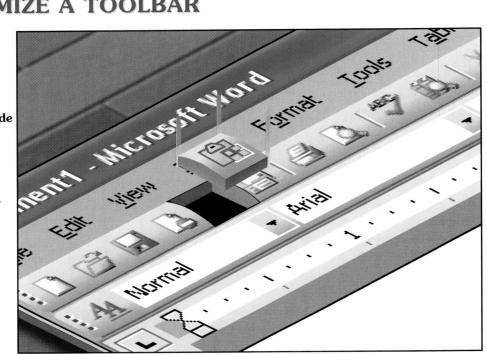

You can add buttons to a toolbar to provide quick access to the commands you use most often. This can help you work more efficiently.

Word offers hundreds of buttons for you to choose from.

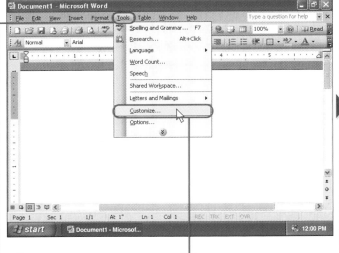

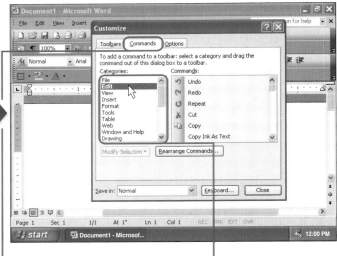

1 Display the toolbar you want to customize. To display a toolbar, see page 39.

2 Click **Tools**.

3 Click **Customize**.

■ The Customize dialog box appears.

4 Click the **Commands** tab.

5 Click the category that contains the button you want to add to the toolbar.

**I don't like my customized toolbar. How can I
return the toolbar to its original appearance?**

1 Perform steps **2** and **3** below to display the Customize dialog box.

2 Click the **Toolbars** tab.

3 Click the name of the toolbar you want to return to its original appearance.

4 Click **Reset**.

5 In the confirmation dialog box that appears, click **OK** to undo all the changes you have made to the toolbar.

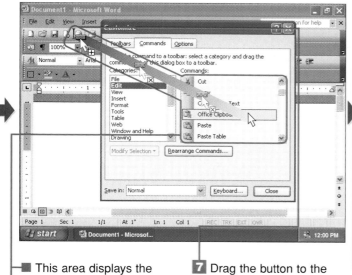

■ This area displays the buttons in the category you selected.

6 Position the mouse over the button you want to add to the toolbar.

7 Drag the button to the toolbar. A line (I) indicates where the button will appear.

■ The button appears on the toolbar.

■ You can repeat steps **5** to **7** for each button you want to add to the toolbar.

8 When you finish adding buttons to the toolbar, click **Close** to close the Customize dialog box.

CONTINUED

CUSTOMIZE A TOOLBAR

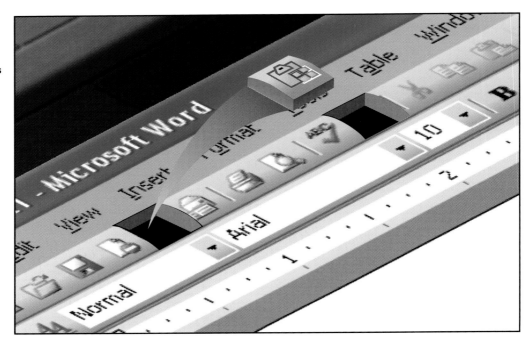

You can move buttons on a toolbar to place buttons for related tasks together. This can make it easier to find the buttons you need.

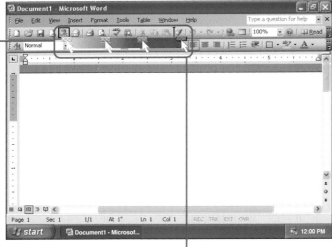

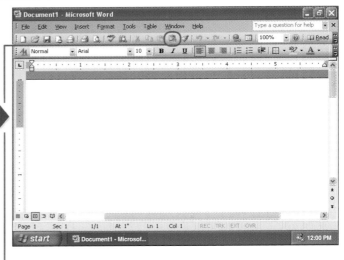

1 Display the toolbar you want to customize. To display a toolbar, see page 39.

2 Position the mouse over the button you want to move to a new location.

3 Press and hold down the **Alt** key as you drag the button to a new location. A line (I) indicates where the button will appear.

■ The button appears in the new location on the toolbar.

You can remove
buttons you do
not use from a
toolbar.

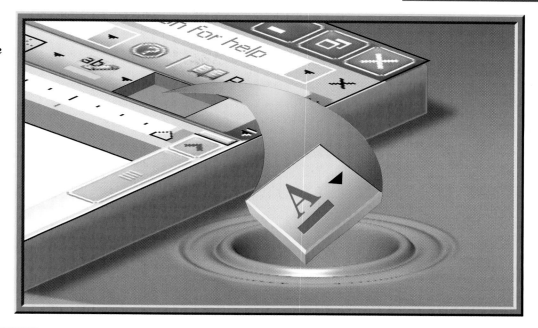

REMOVE A BUTTON

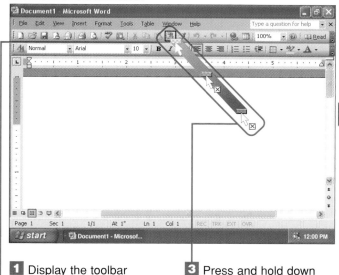

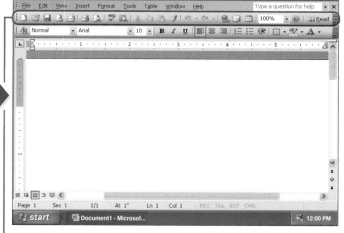

1 Display the toolbar
you want to customize.
To display a toolbar, see
page 39.

2 Position the mouse
over the button you want
to remove from the toolbar.

3 Press and hold down
the **Alt** key as you drag
the button downward off
the toolbar.

■ The button disappears
from the toolbar.

CREATE A NEW TOOLBAR

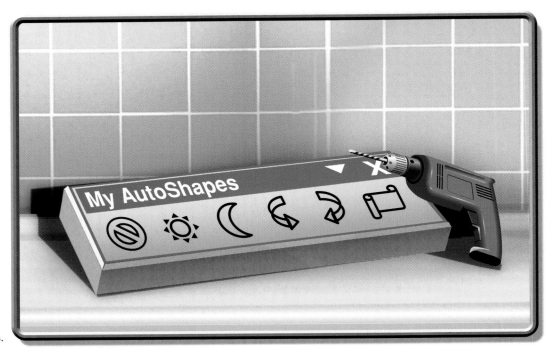

You can create a new toolbar containing buttons you frequently use.

Creating a toolbar allows you to have a specific toolbar for a task you regularly perform, such as printing documents or adding AutoShapes.

CREATE A NEW TOOLBAR

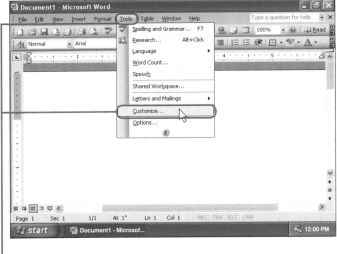

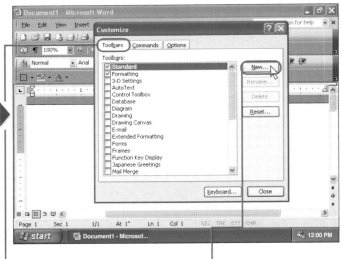

█1 Click **Tools**.

█2 Click **Customize**.

■ The Customize dialog box appears.

█3 Click the **Toolbars** tab.

█4 Click **New** to create a new toolbar.

■ The New Toolbar dialog box appears.

How can I move a toolbar I created?

After you create a new toolbar, you can move the toolbar to a new location on your screen. To move a toolbar, position the mouse ⊳ over the title bar and then drag the toolbar to a new location (⊳ changes to ✛).

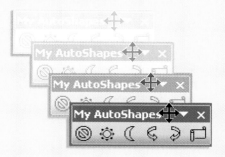

How can I hide a toolbar I created?

You can hide or display a toolbar you created as you would any toolbar. To hide or display a toolbar, see page 39.

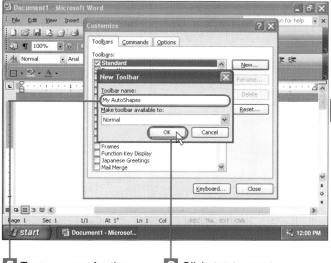

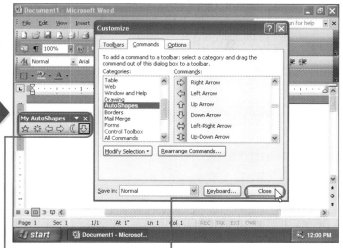

5 Type a name for the toolbar.

6 Click **OK** to create the toolbar.

■ The new toolbar appears on your screen.

7 You can now add the buttons you want the toolbar to display. To add buttons to a toolbar, see page 244.

Note: You can move or remove buttons you add to the toolbar. To move or remove buttons on a toolbar, see page 246 or 247.

8 When you finish adding buttons to the toolbar, click **Close** to close the Customize dialog box.

CREATE A MACRO

A macro saves you time by combining a series of actions into a single command. Macros are ideal for tasks you frequently perform.

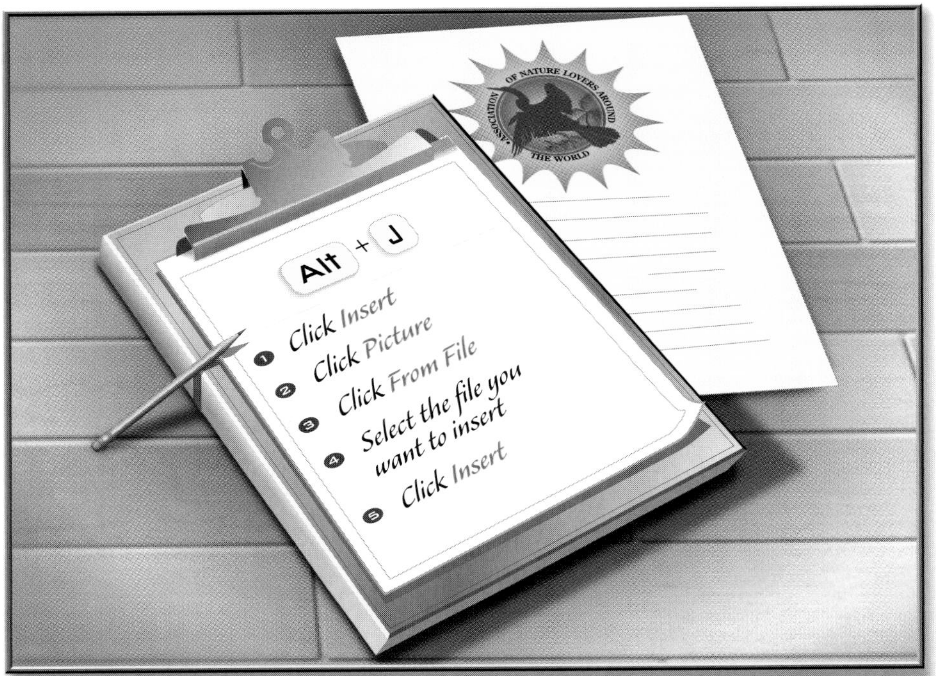

CREATE A MACRO

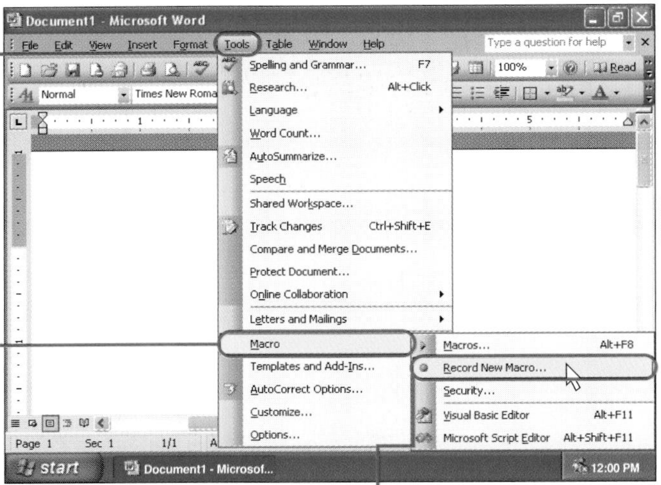

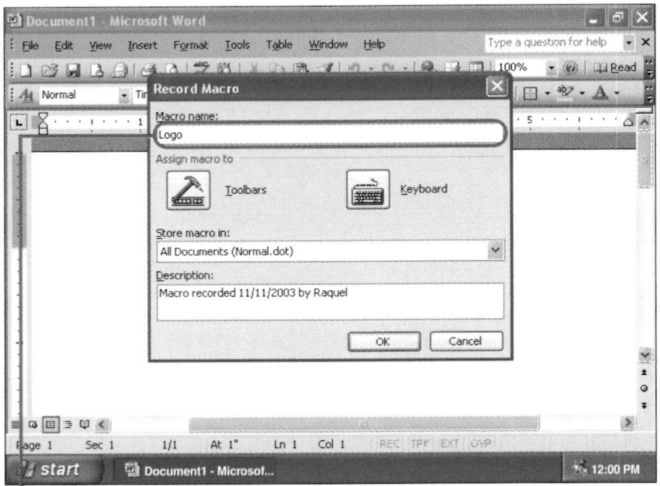

1 Click **Tools**.

2 Click **Macro**.

Note: If Macro does not appear on the menu, position the mouse over the bottom of the menu to display the menu option.

3 Click **Record New Macro**.

■ The Record Macro dialog box appears.

4 Type a name for the macro.

Note: A macro name must begin with a letter and cannot contain spaces.

Why would I create a macro?

Macros can help speed up many repetitive formatting and editing tasks, such as removing extra spaces from text. Macros are also useful for inserting items, such as pictures or symbols, into your documents.

Should I practice before I record a macro?

Yes. Before recording a macro, you should plan and practice all the actions you want the macro to include. Word will record any mistakes and corrections you make while recording the macro.

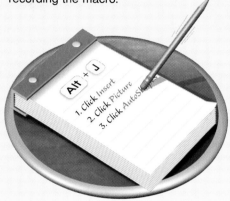

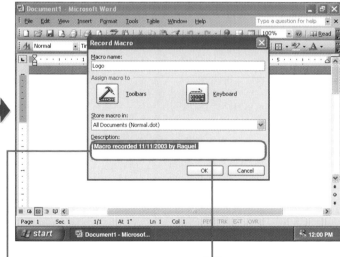

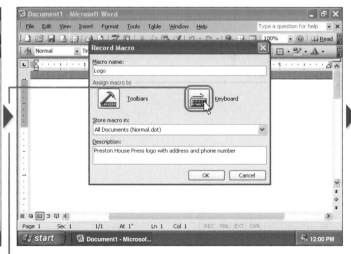

■ Word displays the date and your name as a description for the macro.

5 To enter a different description, drag the mouse I over the text in this area until you highlight the text. Then type a new description.

6 Click **Keyboard** to assign a keyboard shortcut to the macro.

■ The Customize Keyboard dialog box appears.

CONTINUED ▶

CREATE A MACRO

You can assign a keyboard shortcut, such as `Alt` + `J`, to a macro you create. A keyboard shortcut allows you to quickly run the macro.

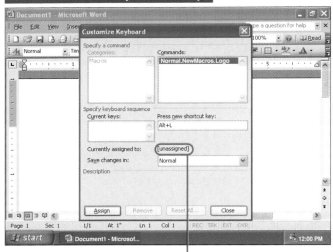

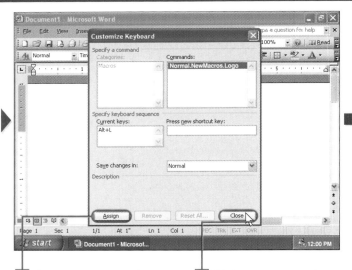

7 To specify a keyboard shortcut for the macro, press and hold down the `Alt` key as you press a letter or number key.

■ This area displays the word **[unassigned]**.

*Note: If the word **[unassigned]** is not displayed, the keyboard shortcut you specified is already assigned to another command. Press the `◆Backspace` key to delete the shortcut and then repeat step 7, using a different letter or number.*

8 Click **Assign** to assign the keyboard shortcut to your macro.

9 Click **Close** to continue.

Can I use the mouse while recording a macro?

While recording a macro, you can only use the mouse to select toolbar buttons or menu commands. You must use the keyboard to move the insertion point on your screen and to select text. To move the insertion point on your screen using the keyboard, press the ↑, ↓, ← or → key. To select text using the keyboard, position the insertion point at the beginning of the text you want to select. Then press and hold down the **Shift** key as you press the → key.

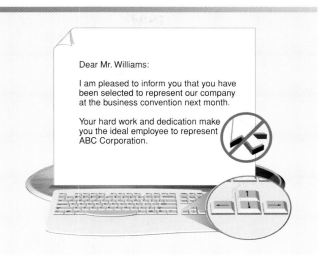

Dear Mr. Williams:

I am pleased to inform you that you have been selected to represent our company at the business convention next month.

Your hard work and dedication make you the ideal employee to represent ABC Corporation.

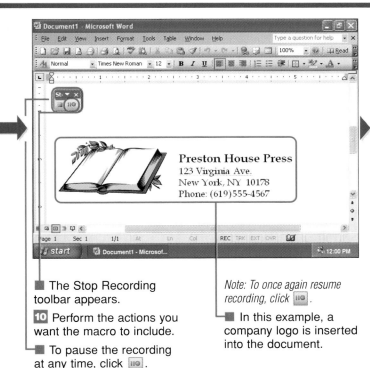

■ The Stop Recording toolbar appears.

10 Perform the actions you want the macro to include.

■ To pause the recording at any time, click ▐▐●.

Note: To once again resume recording, click ▐▐●.

■ In this example, a company logo is inserted into the document.

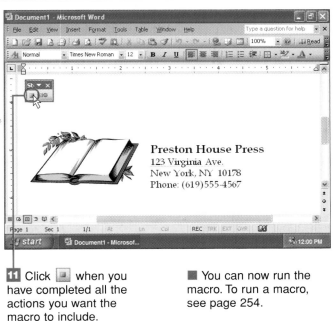

11 Click ■ when you have completed all the actions you want the macro to include.

■ You can now run the macro. To run a macro, see page 254.

RUN A MACRO

When you run a macro, Word automatically performs the actions you recorded.

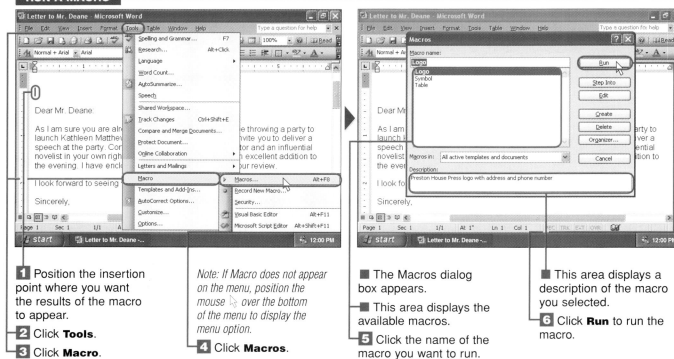

1 Position the insertion point where you want the results of the macro to appear.

2 Click **Tools**.

3 Click **Macro**.

Note: If Macro does not appear on the menu, position the mouse ⬡ over the bottom of the menu to display the menu option.

4 Click **Macros**.

■ The Macros dialog box appears.

■ This area displays the available macros.

5 Click the name of the macro you want to run.

■ This area displays a description of the macro you selected.

6 Click **Run** to run the macro.

Can I run the macro in all my documents?

After you have recorded a macro, you can run the macro in any Word document.

Press Release

Marketing Meeting

Proposal

How do I delete a macro I no longer need?

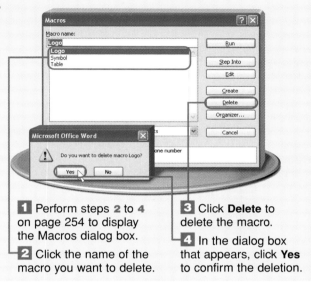

1 Perform steps **2** to **4** on page 254 to display the Macros dialog box.

2 Click the name of the macro you want to delete.

3 Click **Delete** to delete the macro.

4 In the dialog box that appears, click **Yes** to confirm the deletion.

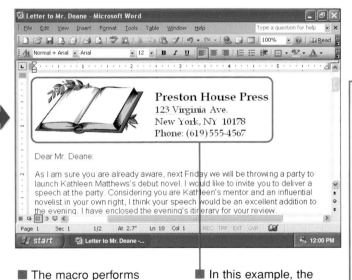

■ The macro performs the actions you recorded.

■ In this example, the macro inserted a company logo into the document.

RUN A MACRO USING THE KEYBOARD SHORTCUT

1 Position the insertion point where you want the results of the macro to appear.

2 Press the keyboard shortcut you assigned to the macro.

■ The macro performs the actions you recorded.

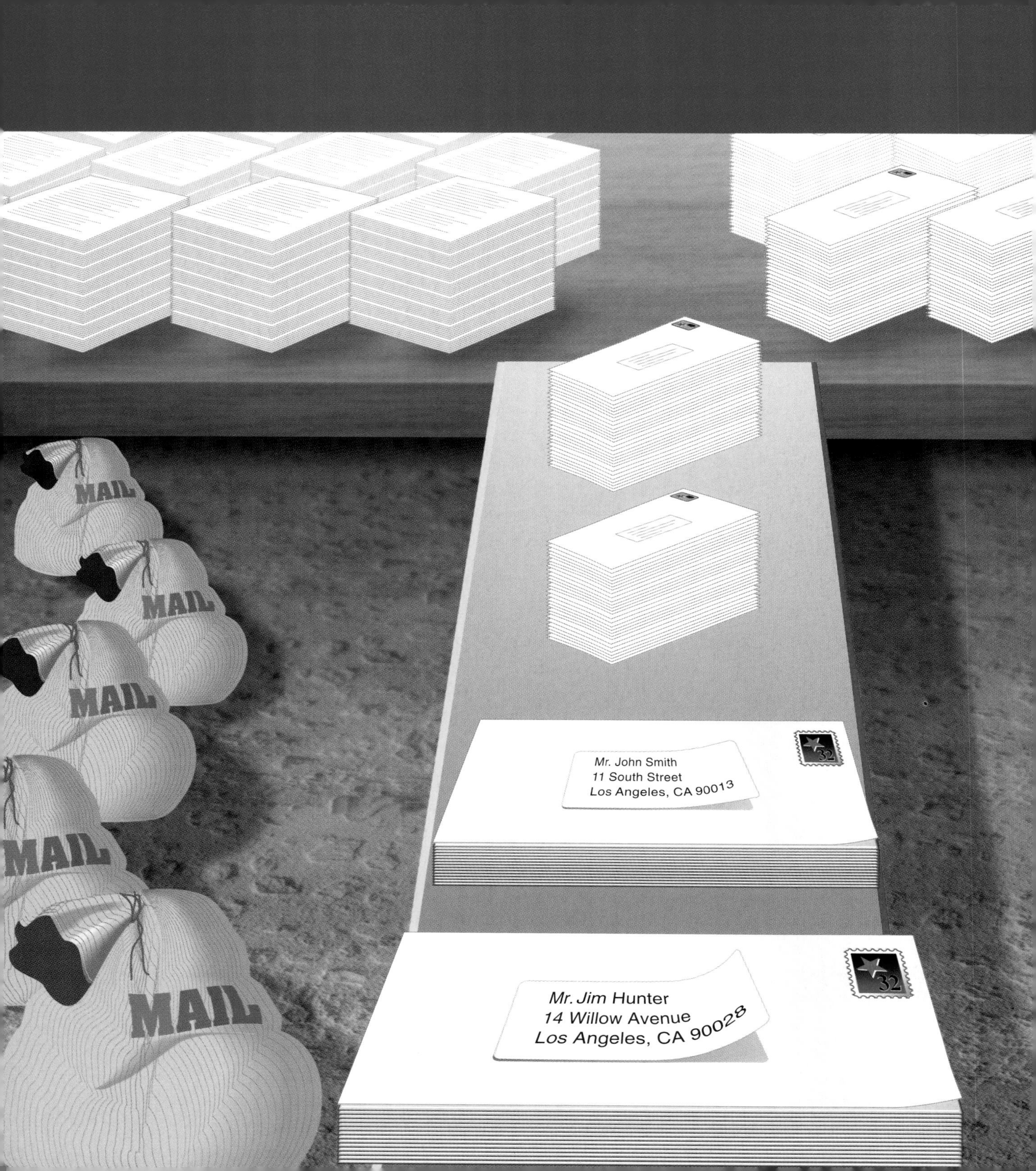

Mr. John Smith
11 South Street
Los Angeles, CA 90013

32

Mr. Jim Hunter
14 Willow Avenue
Los Angeles, CA 90028

32

MAIL
MAIL
MAIL
MAIL
MAIL
MAIL

CHAPTER 14

Using Mail Merge

Would you like to quickly produce a personalized letter for each person on a mailing list? This chapter teaches you how.

CREATE LETTERS USING MAIL MERGE

You can use the Mail Merge feature to produce a personalized letter for each person on your mailing list.

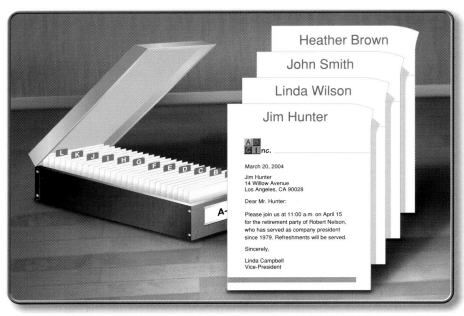

Performing a mail merge is useful if you want to send the same document, such as an announcement or advertisement, to many people.

Word guides you step by step through the mail merge process.

CREATE LETTERS USING MAIL MERGE

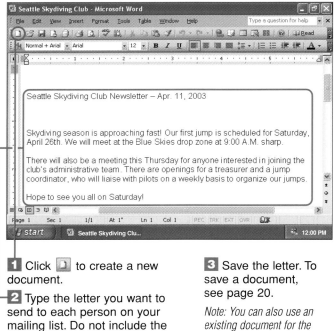

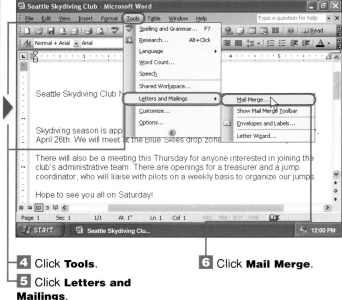

1 Click 🗋 to create a new document.

2 Type the letter you want to send to each person on your mailing list. Do not include the information that will change in each letter, such as a person's name or address.

3 Save the letter. To save a document, see page 20.

Note: You can also use an existing document for the letter. To open an existing document, see page 24.

4 Click **Tools**.

5 Click **Letters and Mailings**.

6 Click **Mail Merge**.

What other types of documents can I create using the Mail Merge feature?

E-mail messages

Creates an e-mail message for each person on your mailing list.

Envelopes

Creates an envelope for each person on your mailing list.

Labels

Creates a label for each person on your mailing list. For information on creating labels using the Mail Merge feature, see page 268.

Directory

Creates a document that contains information about each person on your mailing list.

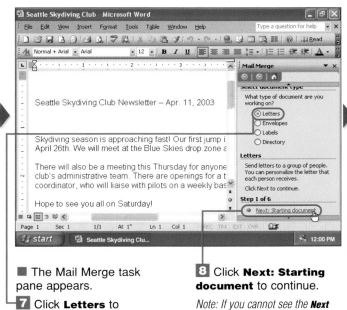

■ The Mail Merge task pane appears.

7 Click **Letters** to create a letter for each person on your mailing list (○ changes to ⊙).

8 Click **Next: Starting document** to continue.

*Note: If you cannot see the **Next** option, click ▼ to scroll down through the Mail Merge task pane.*

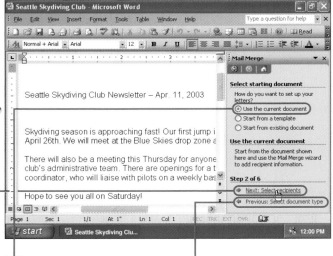

9 Click **Use the current document** to use the displayed document as the letter you will send to each person on your mailing list (○ changes to ⊙).

10 Click **Next: Select recipients** to continue.

■ You can click **Previous** at any time to return to a previous step and change your selections.

CONTINUED

CREATE LETTERS USING MAIL MERGE

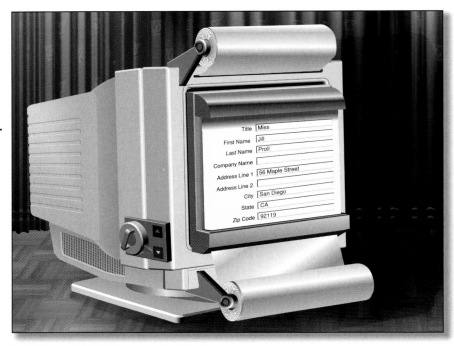

You can specify the address information for each person on your mailing list.

Once you create a mailing list, you can use the mailing list for all your mailings. For example, you can use a Customer mailing list for each newsletter and sales brochure you send to your customers.

CREATE LETTERS USING MAIL MERGE (CONTINUED)

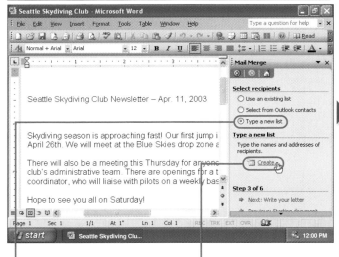

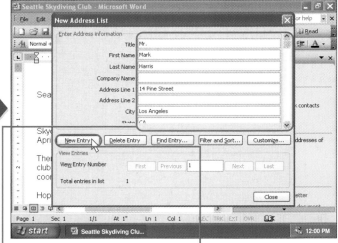

11 Click **Type a new list** to create your mailing list (○ changes to ⊙).

12 Click **Create** to enter the names and addresses of the people on your mailing list.

■ The New Address List dialog box appears, displaying areas where you can enter the information for each person on your mailing list.

13 Click each area and type the appropriate information for a person. You do not have to fill in every area.

14 To enter the information for another person, click **New Entry**.

How can I remove a person I accidentally added to my mailing list?

While creating your mailing list, you can display the information for the person you want to remove and then click the **Delete Entry** button. To confirm the deletion, click **Yes** in the dialog box that appears.

How do I use an existing mailing list to perform a mail merge?

Perform steps **1** to **10** starting on page 258 to begin the mail merge. To select the mailing list you want to use, perform steps **15** to **18** on page 271. Then skip to step **19** on page 262 to continue with the mail merge.

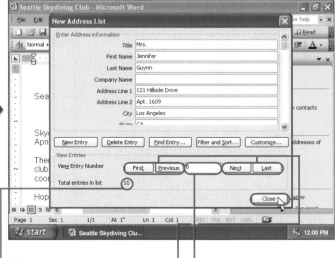

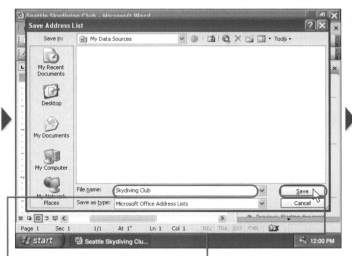

15 Repeat steps **13** and **14** for each person on your mailing list.

■ This area displays the number of people you have added.

■ This area displays the number of the entry that is currently displayed.

■ To browse through the entries, click a button to display the first, previous, next or last entry.

16 When you finish creating your mailing list, click **Close**.

■ The Save Address List dialog box appears.

17 Type a name for the file that will store your mailing list.

18 Click **Save** to save the file.

■ The Mail Merge Recipients dialog box appears.

CONTINUED

261

CREATE LETTERS USING MAIL MERGE

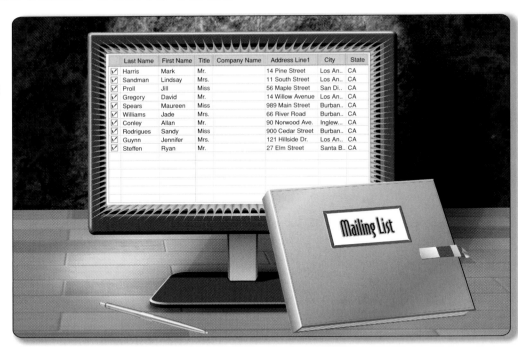

When you finish creating your mailing list, Word displays the information for each person on the list. You can select the people you want to receive a personalized letter.

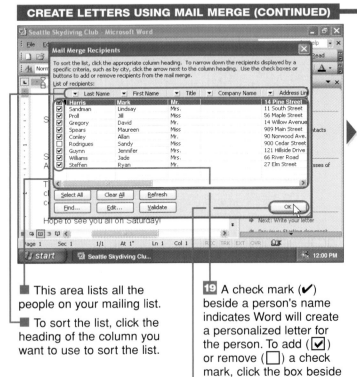

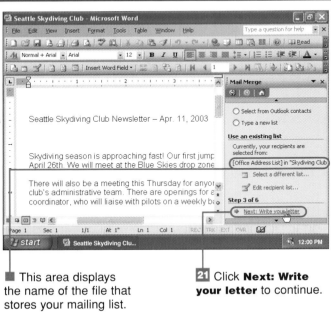

■ This area lists all the people on your mailing list.

■ To sort the list, click the heading of the column you want to use to sort the list.

19 A check mark (✔) beside a person's name indicates Word will create a personalized letter for the person. To add (☑) or remove (☐) a check mark, click the box beside a person's name.

20 Click **OK**.

■ This area displays the name of the file that stores your mailing list.

21 Click **Next: Write your letter** to continue.

What type of information can I add to my letters?

Mr. Mark Harris
14 Pine Street
Los Angeles, CA 90023

Address block

Displays the address of a person on your mailing list.

Dear Mr. Harris,

Greeting line

Displays a greeting for a person on your mailing list.

mharris@abccorp.com

More items

Displays a piece of information for a person on your mailing list, such as the person's home phone number or e-mail address.

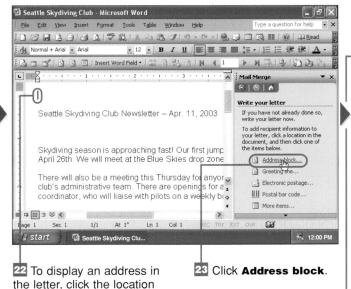

22 To display an address in the letter, click the location in the letter where you want to display the address.

23 Click **Address block**.

■ The Insert Address Block dialog box appears.

24 Click the way you want each person's name to appear in the letter.

■ This area displays a preview of how the address will appear in the letter.

25 Click **OK** to confirm your selection.

CONTINUED

CREATE LETTERS USING MAIL MERGE

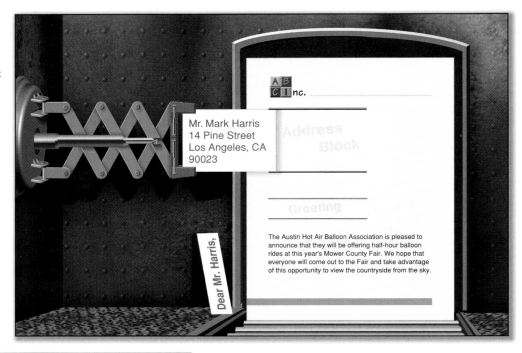

Word helps you insert special instructions, called merge fields, into your letter. A merge field acts as a placeholder for information from your mailing list.

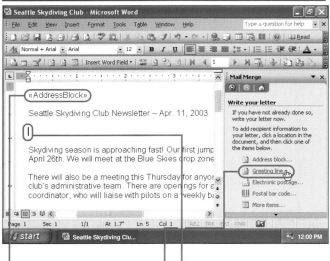

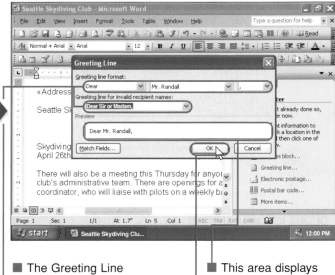

■ A merge field for the address appears in the letter. Word will replace the merge field with an address from your mailing list.

26 To add a greeting to the letter, click the location in the letter where you want to display the greeting.

Note: If you do not want to add a greeting to the letter, skip to step 29.

27 Click **Greeting line**.

■ The Greeting Line dialog box appears.

■ These areas display the available formats for the greeting. You can click ▼ in an area to select a different format.

■ This area displays a preview of how the greeting will appear in the letter.

28 Click **OK** to add the greeting to the letter.

264

How do I delete a merge field I accidentally inserted?

To delete a merge field you accidentally inserted, drag the mouse I over the merge field until you highlight the field. Then press the Delete key.

When previewing the letters, can I exclude a person from the mail merge?

Yes. When the letter you do not want to send is displayed on your screen, click the **Exclude this recipient** button on the Mail Merge task pane. Word will not create a letter for the person when you complete the mail merge.

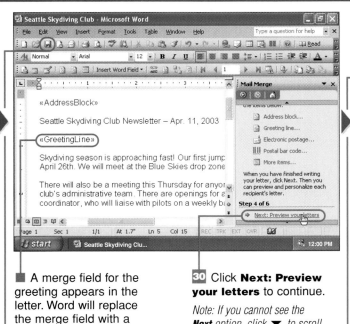

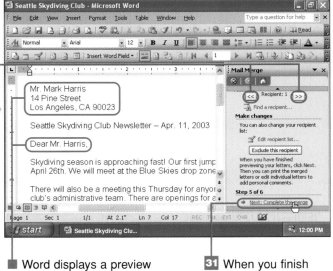

■ A merge field for the greeting appears in the letter. Word will replace the merge field with a greeting for each letter.

29 Click 🖫 to save the changes you made to the letter.

30 Click **Next: Preview your letters** to continue.

*Note: If you cannot see the **Next** option, click ▼ to scroll down through the Mail Merge task pane.*

■ Word displays a preview of one of the merged letters. Word replaces the merge fields with the corresponding information for one person on your mailing list.

■ To preview another letter, click ⟨⟨ or ⟩⟩ to display the previous or next letter.

31 When you finish previewing your letters, click **Next: Complete the merge** to continue.

CONTINUED ▶

CREATE LETTERS USING MAIL MERGE

Once you complete your letter, Word can combine the letter with the information from your mailing list to create a personalized letter for each person.

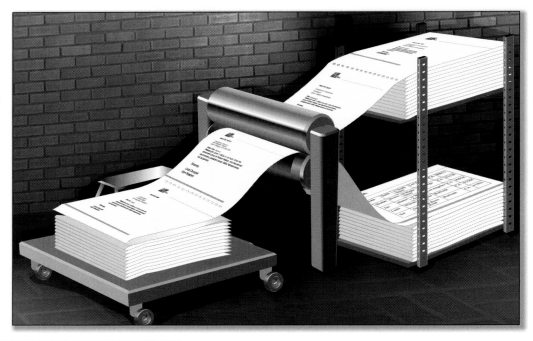

CREATE LETTERS USING MAIL MERGE (CONTINUED)

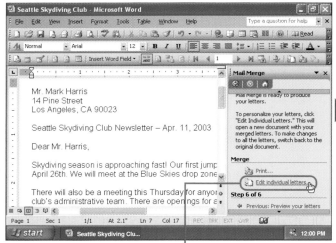

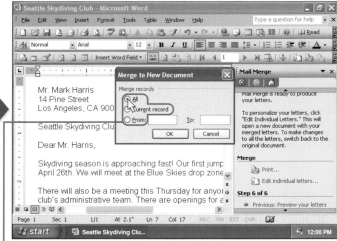

■ Word is ready to produce the letters.

32 Click **Edit individual letters** to combine the letter with the information from your mailing list.

■ The Merge to New Document dialog box appears.

33 Click an option to specify which people from your mailing list you want to create letters for (◯ changes to ◉).

All
All the people on your mailing list.

Current record
Only the displayed person.

From
People on your mailing list that you specify.

Can I print the letters from the Mail Merge task pane?

Yes. Printing letters from the Mail Merge task pane is useful when you know the letters are ready to print and do not require further editing. To print your letters from the Mail Merge task pane, select the **Print** option in step **32** below.

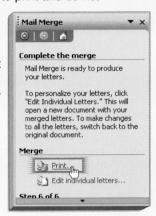

 Should I save the document containing the personalized letters?

There is no need to save the document. You can easily perform another mail merge at any time to recreate the personalized letters.

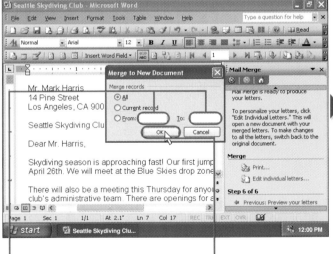

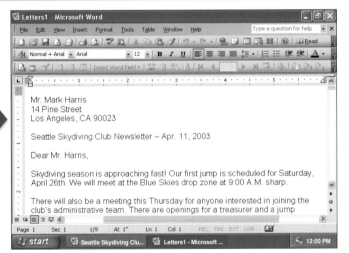

■ If you selected From in step **33**, click this area and type the number of the first person you want to create a letter for. Then press the Tab key and type the number of the last person you want to create a letter for.

34 Click **OK** to create the letters.

■ Word opens a new document and creates the personalized letters in the document.

■ You can edit and print the letters as you would edit and print any document. Editing a letter allows you to include additional information in the letter. To edit a document, see page 50. To print a document, see page 168.

CREATE LABELS USING MAIL MERGE

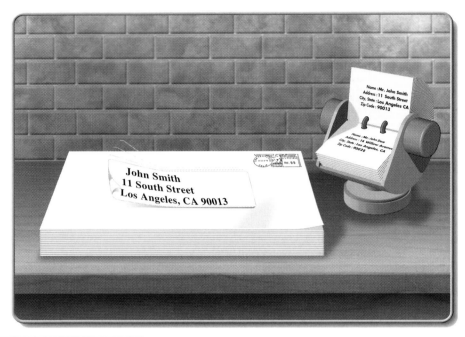

You can use the Mail Merge feature to print a personalized label for each person on your mailing list. This saves you from having to type each label individually.

You can use labels for addressing envelopes and packages.

Word takes you step by step through the mail merge process.

CREATE LABELS USING MAIL MERGE

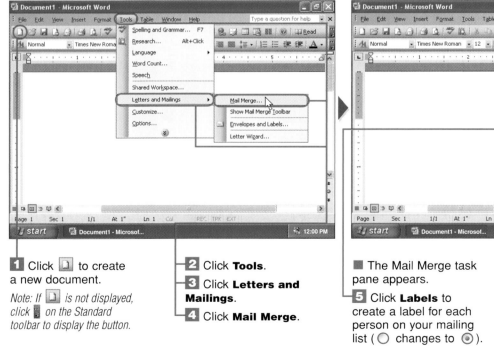

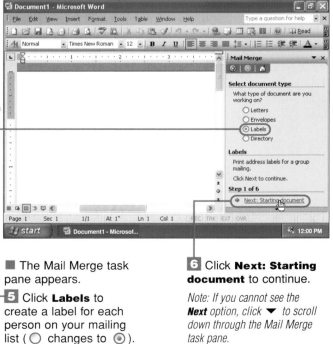

1 Click 🗋 to create a new document.

Note: If 🗋 is not displayed, click 📋 on the Standard toolbar to display the button.

2 Click **Tools**.

3 Click **Letters and Mailings**.

4 Click **Mail Merge**.

■ The Mail Merge task pane appears.

5 Click **Labels** to create a label for each person on your mailing list (○ changes to ◉).

6 Click **Next: Starting document** to continue.

*Note: If you cannot see the **Next** option, click ▼ to scroll down through the Mail Merge task pane.*

Can I use the Mail Merge feature to print envelopes?

Yes. You can use the Mail Merge feature to print a personalized envelope for each person on your mailing list. Perform steps **1** to **5** below, selecting **Envelopes** in step **5**. Then follow the instructions on your screen to set up the envelopes.

Can I create labels without using the Mail Merge feature?

Yes. If you want to create only a few labels, you can type the text you want to appear on each label yourself. For information on printing labels without using the Mail Merge feature, see page 172.

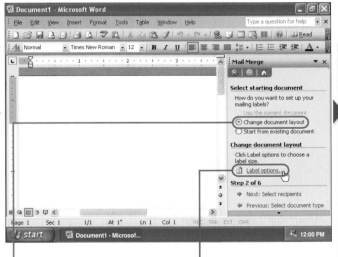

7 Click **Change document layout** to set up the current document for labels (○ changes to ◉).

8 Click **Label options** to specify options for the labels.

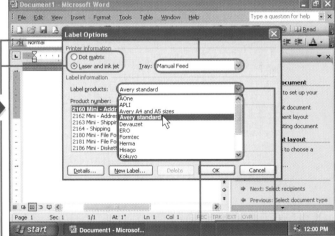

■ The Label Options dialog box appears.

9 Click an option to specify the type of printer you will use to print the labels (○ changes to ◉).

■ This area displays the printer tray that will contain the labels. You can click this area to specify a different tray.

10 Click this area to display a list of the available label products.

11 Click the label product you will use.

CONTINUED

CREATE LABELS USING MAIL MERGE

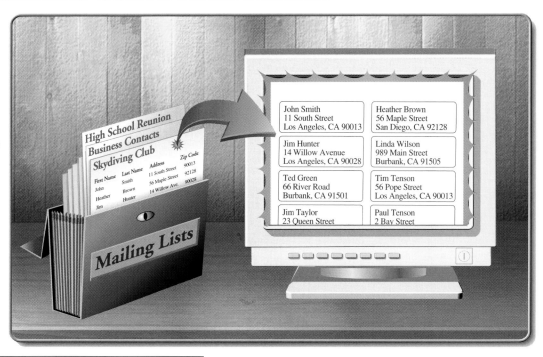

After Word sets up a document for the labels, you must specify which mailing list stores the address information you want to appear on the labels.

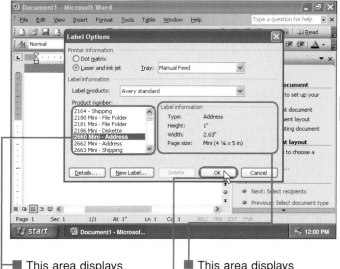

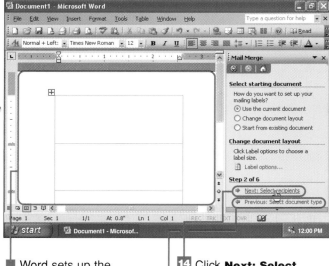

■ This area displays the types of labels available for the label product you selected.

12 Click the type of label you will use.

■ This area displays information about the type of label you selected.

13 Click **OK** to confirm your selections.

■ Word sets up the document for labels.

14 Click **Next: Select recipients** to continue.

■ You can click **Previous** at any time to return to a previous step and change your selections.

270

Which label product and type should I choose?

You can check your label packaging to determine which label product and type you should choose when printing labels.

Can I create a mailing list when I create labels?

If you have not created a mailing list that stores the address information you want to use, you can create a mailing list during the process of creating labels. After performing step **14** below, perform steps **11** to **18** starting on page 260 to create a mailing list for the labels. Then skip to step **19** on page 272 to continue with the mail merge.

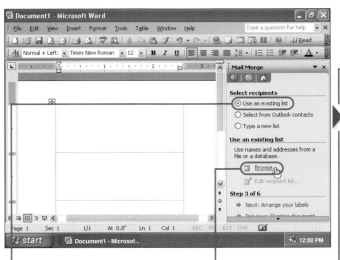

15 Click **Use an existing list** to use a mailing list you created in a previous mail merge (○ changes to ●).

Note: If you have not previously created a mailing list, see the top of this page.

16 Click **Browse** to select the mailing list you want to use.

■ The Select Data Source dialog box appears.

17 Click the file that stores the mailing list you want to use.

18 Click **Open** to open the file.

■ The Mail Merge Recipients dialog box appears.

CONTINUED

CREATE LABELS USING MAIL MERGE

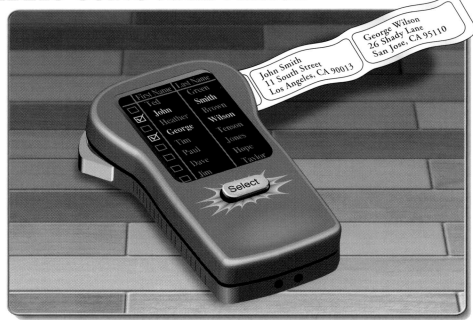

Word displays the information for each person on your mailing list. You can select each person you want to create a label for.

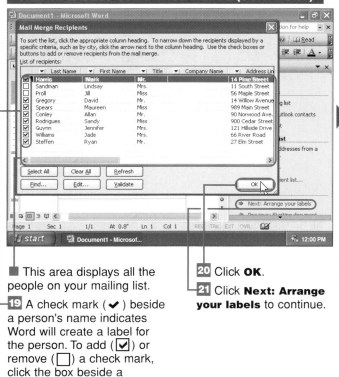

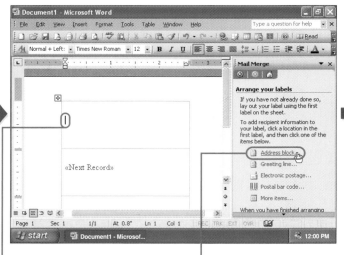

■ This area displays all the people on your mailing list.

19 A check mark (✔) beside a person's name indicates Word will create a label for the person. To add (☑) or remove (☐) a check mark, click the box beside a person's name.

20 Click **OK**.

21 Click **Next: Arrange your labels** to continue.

■ You use the first label to set up all of the labels.

22 To display an address on the first label, click the location on the label where you want to display the address.

23 Click **Address block**.

Can I sort my mailing list?

You can sort your mailing list when the Mail Merge Recipients dialog box is displayed. To sort your mailing list, click the heading of the column you want to use to sort the list. For example, if you want to sort the list alphabetically by last name, click the **Last Name** column heading.

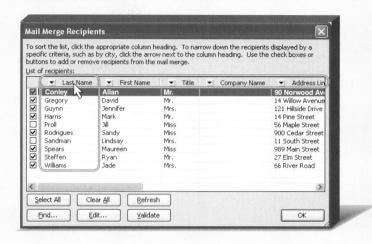

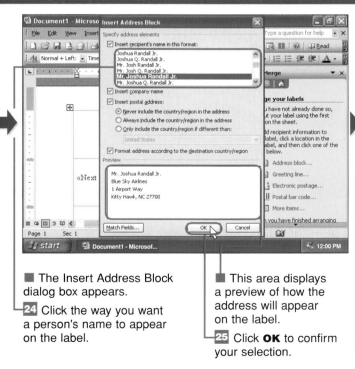

■ The Insert Address Block dialog box appears.

24 Click the way you want a person's name to appear on the label.

■ This area displays a preview of how the address will appear on the label.

25 Click **OK** to confirm your selection.

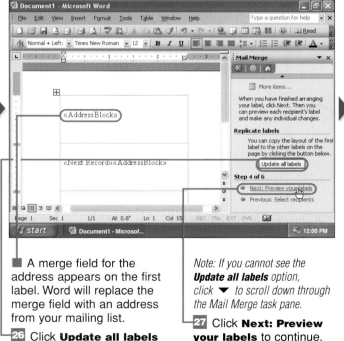

■ A merge field for the address appears on the first label. Word will replace the merge field with an address from your mailing list.

26 Click **Update all labels** to copy the layout of the first label to all the other labels.

*Note: If you cannot see the **Update all labels** option, click ▼ to scroll down through the Mail Merge task pane.*

27 Click **Next: Preview your labels** to continue.

CONTINUED

CREATE LABELS USING MAIL MERGE

After you finish setting up your labels, Word can combine the labels with the information from your mailing list to create a personalized label for each person.

You do not need to save the labels you create. You can easily perform another mail merge at any time to recreate the labels.

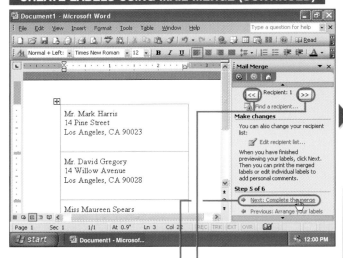

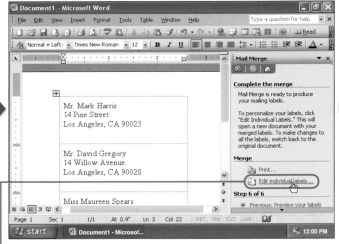

■ Word displays a preview of one page of the labels. Word replaces the merge fields with the corresponding information from your mailing list.

■ To preview other labels, click ‹‹ or ›› to display the previous or next label at the top of the page.

28 When you finish previewing your labels, click **Next: Complete the merge** to continue.

■ Word is ready to produce the labels.

29 Click **Edit individual labels** to combine the labels with the information from your mailing list.

■ The Merge to New Document dialog box appears.

Which people on my mailing list can I create labels for?

All

Creates labels for all the people on your mailing list.

Current record

Creates labels for only the people shown on the current page.

From

Creates labels for people on your mailing list that you specify.

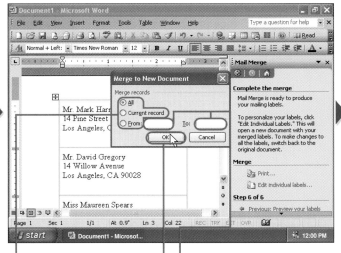

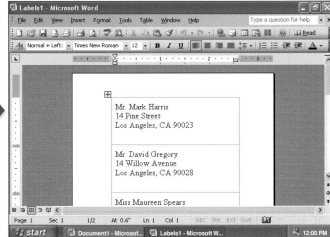

30 Click an option to specify which people on your mailing list you want to create labels for (○ changes to ◉).

■ If you selected **From** in step **30**, click this area and type the number of the first person you want to create a label for. Then press the **Tab** key and type the number of the last person you want to create a label for.

31 Click **OK** to create the labels.

■ Word opens a new document and creates the personalized labels in the document.

■ You can edit and print the labels as you would edit and print any document. Editing a label allows you to include additional information on the label. To edit a document, see page 50. To print a document, see page 168.

CHAPTER 15

Using Speech Recognition

Would you like to use your voice to enter text into a document? Read this chapter to learn how to enter text and select commands using your voice.

SET UP SPEECH RECOGNITION

Speech recognition allows you to use your voice to enter data into a document and select commands from menus and toolbars. Before you can use speech recognition, you must set up the feature on your computer.

Before setting up speech recognition, make sure your microphone and speakers are connected to your computer.

SET UP SPEECH RECOGNITION

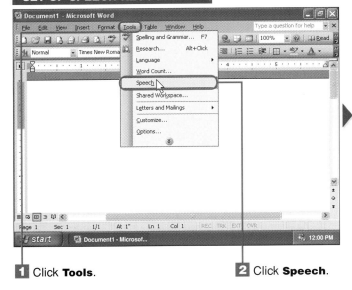

1 Click **Tools**.

2 Click **Speech**.

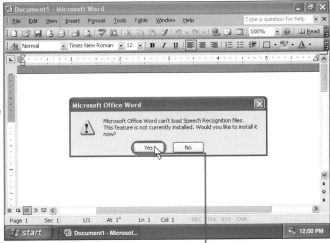

■ A message appears, stating that speech recognition is not currently installed.

3 Click **Yes** to install speech recognition on your computer.

What are the minimum hardware requirements for using speech recognition?

Speech recognition requires a 400 MHz computer with at least 128 MB of memory to run. You cannot set up speech recognition if your computer does not meet the minimum hardware requirements.

 What type of microphone should I use with speech recognition?

You should use a high quality headset microphone that supports gain adjustment. Gain adjustment allows your computer to automatically make your speech louder. For best results, you should position the microphone approximately one inch from the side of your mouth so that you are not breathing directly into the microphone.

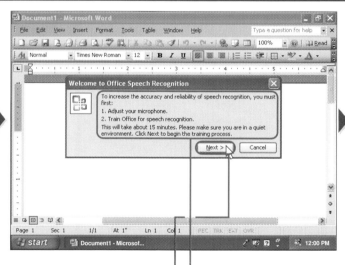

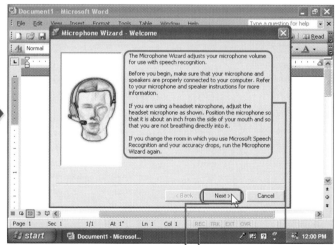

■ When the installation is complete, the Welcome to Office Speech Recognition dialog box appears.

■ This area describes the process of setting up speech recognition on your computer.

4 To begin setting up speech recognition, click **Next**.

■ The Microphone Wizard appears. The wizard will help you adjust your microphone for use with speech recognition.

■ This area describes the wizard and provides instructions for positioning your microphone.

5 To begin adjusting your microphone, click **Next**.

CONTINUED ▶

SET UP SPEECH RECOGNITION

The Microphone Wizard helps you adjust the volume and position of your microphone for best results with speech recognition.

Once your microphone is properly set up, you can follow the step-by-step instructions in the Microsoft Speech Recognition Training Wizard to train speech recognition to recognize how you speak.

SET UP SPEECH RECOGNITION (CONTINUED)

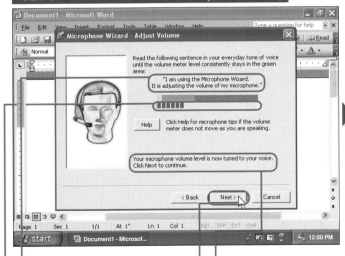

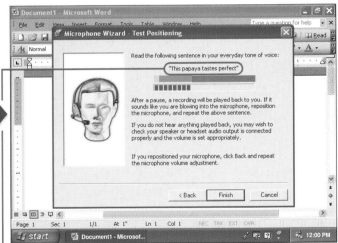

6 Read this text aloud to adjust the volume of your microphone.

■ As you read the text aloud, the volume meter in this area indicates the volume of your microphone.

7 Repeat step **6** until a message appears in this area, indicating that the volume level is tuned to your voice.

8 Click **Next** to continue.

9 Read this text aloud to test the position of your microphone.

■ After a few moments, your voice will be played back to you. If it sounds like you are blowing into the microphone, adjust your microphone's position and then repeat step **9**.

Do I have to train speech recognition?

If you do not train speech recognition, the feature may not work properly. During the training, the Microsoft Speech Recognition Training Wizard gathers information about your voice. The speech recognition feature uses this information to recognize the words you say when entering data or selecting commands.

How should I speak during the training process?

You should speak in your everyday tone of voice, pronouncing words clearly and not pausing between words. You should also speak at a consistent speed.

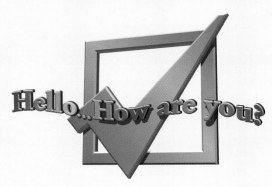

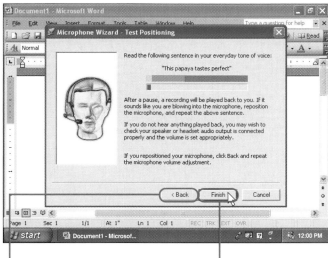

■ If you change the position of your microphone, click **Back** and then repeat steps **6** to **9** to adjust the volume of the microphone in the new position.

10 When you finish positioning your microphone, click **Finish**.

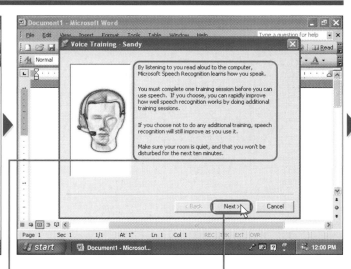

■ The Voice Training dialog box appears.

■ This area describes the Microsoft Speech Recognition Training Wizard.

11 To begin training speech recognition to recognize how you speak, click **Next**.

CONTINUED

SET UP SPEECH RECOGNITION

The Microsoft Speech Recognition Training Wizard provides text you can read aloud to train speech recognition.

You should train speech recognition in a quiet area so that background noise does not interfere with the sound of your voice.

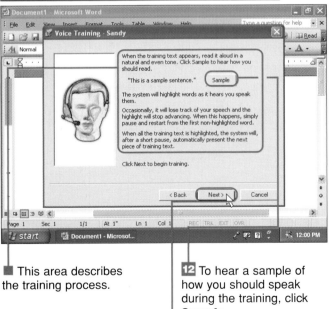

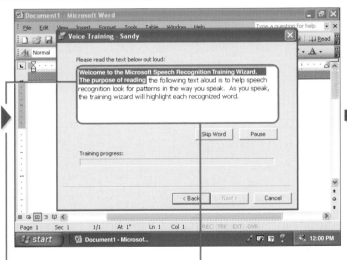

■ This area describes the training process.

12 To hear a sample of how you should speak during the training, click **Sample**.

13 Click **Next** to continue.

■ The training wizard will display a series of screens containing text for you to read aloud.

14 Read the text displayed in this area of each screen.

■ As you read aloud, the training wizard highlights the words it recognizes.

■ If the training wizard does not recognize a word, it stops highlighting the text. If this happens, begin reading again, starting with the first word that is not highlighted.

I have repeated a word several times, but the wizard still does not recognize the word. What should I do?

If the wizard cannot recognize a word you say, you can click the **Skip Word** button to move on to the next word.

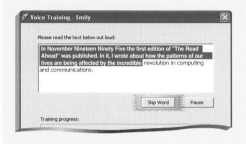

Can I perform more training?

Yes. Microsoft Speech Recognition provides additional training sessions you can perform to improve the accuracy of speech recognition.

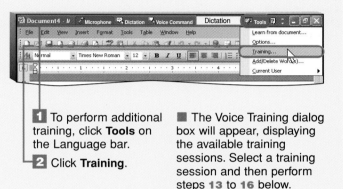

1 To perform additional training, click **Tools** on the Language bar.

2 Click **Training**.

■ The Voice Training dialog box will appear, displaying the available training sessions. Select a training session and then perform steps **13** to **16** below.

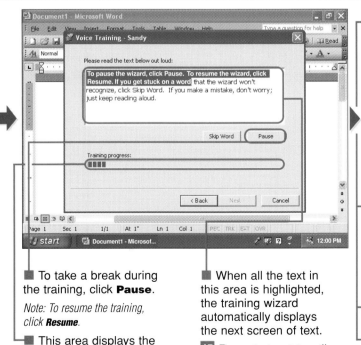

■ To take a break during the training, click **Pause**.

Note: To resume the training, click Resume.

■ This area displays the progress of the training.

■ When all the text in this area is highlighted, the training wizard automatically displays the next screen of text.

15 Repeat step **14** until you have read all the training text.

■ This message appears when the training is complete.

16 Click **Finish** to close the Voice Training dialog box.

■ This area displays the Language bar, which contains buttons you can use to perform tasks using speech recognition.

■ You can now use speech recognition in Word.

Note: A window will appear, displaying a video that introduces you to speech recognition. When the video is finished, click ✕ to close the window.

USING DICTATION MODE

Once you have set up speech recognition on your computer, you can use Dictation mode to enter text into a document using your voice.

Speech recognition is designed to be used along with your mouse and keyboard. You can use your voice to enter text into a document and then use your mouse and keyboard to edit the text you entered.

USING DICTATION MODE

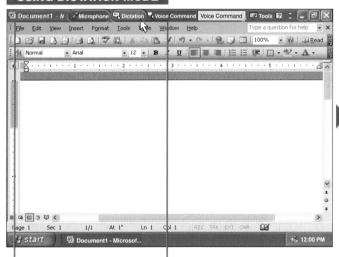

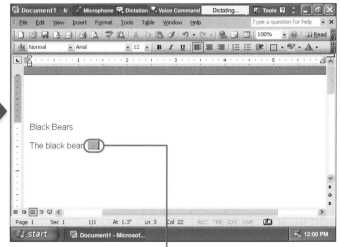

1 If your microphone is turned off, click **Microphone** on the Language bar to turn on the microphone.

Note: When your microphone is turned on, the Dictation and Voice Command buttons appear on the Language bar.

2 Click **Dictation** to turn on Dictation mode.

3 Speak into your microphone to enter text into the document.

Note: The text will appear where the insertion point flashes on your screen.

■ As you speak, a gray bar appears on the screen to indicate that the computer is processing your voice. You can continue to speak while the gray bar is displayed on the screen.

■ You should not use your mouse or keyboard while the gray bar is displayed on the screen.

What are some of the punctuation marks I can enter using my voice?

To enter:	Say:
.	"Period"
,	"Comma"
:	"Colon"
;	"Semicolon"
?	"Question mark"
!	"Exclamation point"
(	"Open parenthesis"
)	"Close parenthesis"
"	"Open quote"
"	"Close quote"

Note: To begin a new line, say "new line." To begin a new paragraph, say "new paragraph."

How should I speak when using speech recognition?

You should speak to your computer in your everyday tone of voice, pronouncing words clearly and not pausing between words. You should also speak at a consistent speed. If you speak too quickly or too slowly, the computer may not be able to recognize what you say.

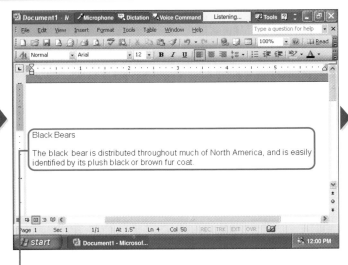

■ As the computer processes your voice, words appear on the screen.

4 To enter punctuation, say the name of the punctuation mark you want to enter.

Note: For a list of punctuation marks you can enter using your voice, see the top of this page.

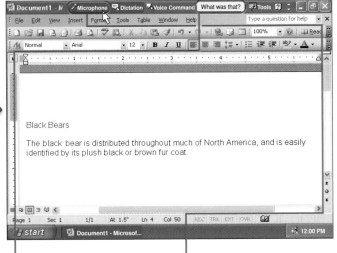

■ As you enter text using your voice, this area may display a message to help you use Dictation mode. For example, the message "What was that?" indicates you should repeat your last words.

5 When you finish entering text using your voice, click **Microphone** to turn off your microphone.

■ You can now edit the text you entered using your voice as you would edit any text. To edit text, see page 50.

USING VOICE COMMAND MODE

You can use Voice Command mode to select commands from menus and toolbars using your voice.

You can also use Voice Command mode to select options in dialog boxes.

USING VOICE COMMAND MODE

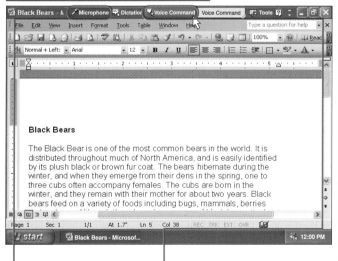

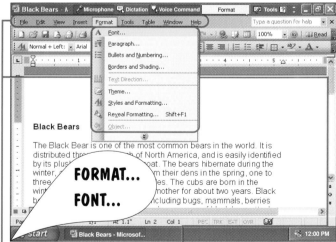

1 If your microphone is turned off, click **Microphone** on the Language bar to turn on the microphone.

Note: When your microphone is turned on, the Dictation and Voice Command buttons appear on the Language bar.

2 Click **Voice Command** to turn on Voice Command mode.

SELECT MENU COMMANDS

1 To select a command from a menu, say the name of the menu.

■ A short version of the menu appears, displaying the most commonly used commands.

Note: To expand the menu and display all the commands, say "expand."

2 To select a command from the menu, say the name of the command.

■ To close a menu without selecting a command, say "escape."

Can I use Voice Command mode to select an option in the task pane?

Yes. Task panes display links that allow you to perform common tasks. To select a link in a task pane using your voice, say the full name of the link. For more information on task panes, see page 14.

Can I use Voice Command mode to perform other tasks?

Yes. In addition to selecting commands, you can use Voice Command mode to perform the following tasks.

To:	Say:
Move up one line	"Up"
Move down one line	"Down"
Move left one character	"Left"
Move right one character	"Right"
Enter a tab	"Tab"
Enter a blank space	"Space"
Delete a character	"Backspace"

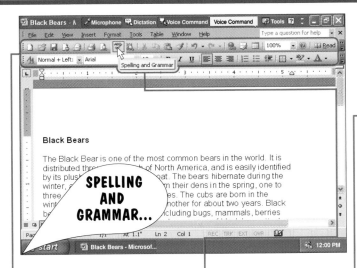

SELECT TOOLBAR COMMANDS

1 To select a command from a toolbar, say the name of the toolbar button.

■ To determine the name of a toolbar button, position the mouse over the button. After a few seconds, the name of the button appears in a yellow box.

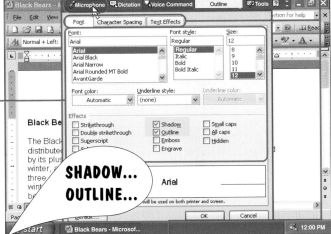

SELECT DIALOG BOX OPTIONS

■ A dialog box may appear when you select a menu or toolbar command.

1 To select an option in a dialog box, say the name of the option.

■ If the dialog box contains tabs, you can say the name of a tab to display the tab.

2 When you finish selecting commands using your voice, click **Microphone** to turn off your microphone.

Boston Cycling Club

Welcome to the Boston Cycling Club Network. We have been riding in Boston for 15 years and we are still going strong. To learn about the club, click one of the following links.

Boston Cycling Club Newsletter

List of Upcoming Events Organized by the Club

History of the Boston Cycling Club

How to Become a Member

Contact Information

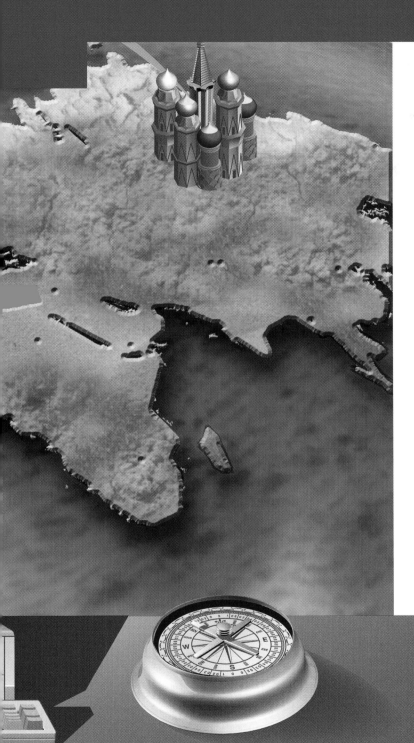

CHAPTER 16

Word and the Internet

Are you wondering how you can use Word to share information with other people on the Internet? In this chapter, you will learn how to e-mail a document, save a document as a Web page and more.

E-MAIL A DOCUMENT

You can e-mail the document displayed on your screen to a friend, family member or colleague.

Before you can e-mail a document, an e-mail program, such as Microsoft Office Outlook 2003, must be set up on your computer.

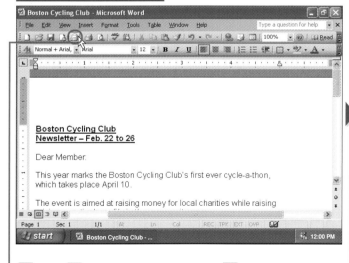

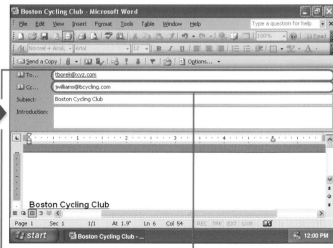

1 Click 📧 to e-mail the displayed document.

Note: If 📧 is not displayed, click ⏷ on the Standard toolbar to display the button.

■ An area appears for you to address the message.

2 Click this area and type the e-mail address of the person you want to receive the message.

3 To send a copy of the message to another person, click this area and type the person's e-mail address.

Note: To enter more than one e-mail address in step 2 or 3, separate each e-mail address with a semicolon (;).

How can I address an e-mail message?

To

Sends the message to the person you specify.

Carbon Copy (Cc)

Sends an exact copy of the message to a person who is not directly involved, but would be interested in the message.

Why would I include an introduction for the document I am e-mailing?

Including an introduction allows you to provide the recipient of the message with additional information about the document. For example, the recipient may require instructions or an explanation of the content of the document.

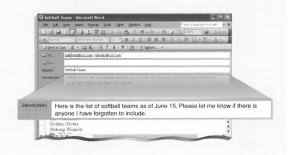

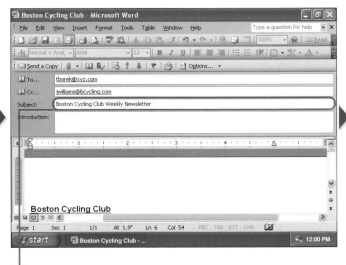

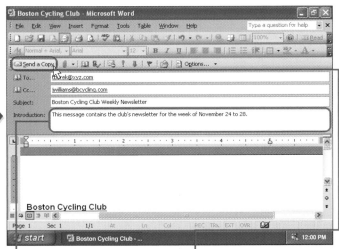

4 Click this area and type a subject for the message.

Note: If a subject already exists, you can drag the mouse I over the existing subject and then type a new subject.

5 To include an introduction for the document you are e-mailing, click this area and type the introduction.

Note: You can include an introduction only if you are using the Microsoft Outlook e-mail program.

6 Click **Send a Copy** to send the message.

Note: If you are not currently connected to the Internet, a dialog box may appear, allowing you to connect.

CREATE A HYPERLINK

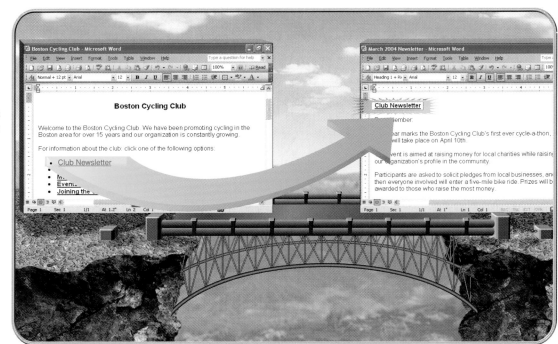

You can create a hyperlink to connect a word, phrase or graphic in your document to another document or Web page on your computer, network or the Internet.

Hyperlinks are also known as links. You can easily identify hyperlinks in your document. Hyperlinks appear underlined and in color.

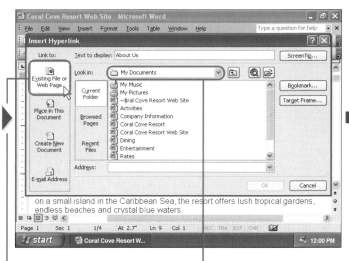

■1 Select the text or click the graphic you want to link to another document or Web page. To select text, see page 8.

■2 Click 🔗 to create a hyperlink.

Note: If 🔗 is not displayed, click ┇ on the Standard toolbar to display the button.

■ The Insert Hyperlink dialog box appears.

■3 Click **Existing File or Web Page**.

■ This area shows the location of the displayed documents. You can click this area to change the location.

Can Word automatically create a hyperlink for me?

When you type the address of a Web page and then press the **Spacebar** or the [Enter] key, Word will automatically change the address to a hyperlink.

How can I remove a hyperlink?

To remove a hyperlink completely, select the text or click the graphic and then press the [Delete] key. To select text, see page 8.

To remove a hyperlink but keep the text or graphic, right-click the hyperlink and then select **Remove Hyperlink** from the menu that appears.

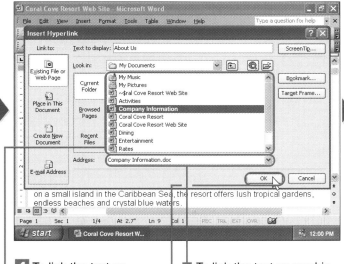

4 To link the text or graphic to a document on your computer or network, click the name of the document in this area.

■ To link the text or graphic to a page on the Web, click this area and then type the address of the Web page.

5 Click **OK** to create the hyperlink.

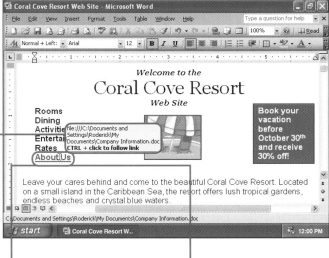

■ Word creates the hyperlink. Text hyperlinks appear underlined and in color.

■ When you position the mouse I over a hyperlink, a yellow box appears, indicating where the hyperlink will take you.

■ To display the document or Web page connected to the hyperlink, press and hold down the [Ctrl] key as you click the hyperlink.

Note: If the hyperlink connects to a Web page, your Web browser will open and display the page.

SAVE A DOCUMENT AS A WEB PAGE

You can save a document as a Web page. This allows you to place the document on the Internet or your company's intranet.

An intranet is a small version of the Internet within a company or organization.

SAVE A DOCUMENT AS A WEB PAGE

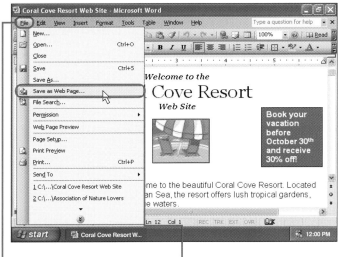

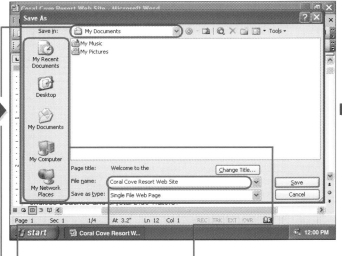

1 Open the document you want to save as a Web page. To open a document, see page 24.

2 Click **File**.

3 Click **Save as Web Page**.

■ The Save As dialog box appears.

4 Type a file name for the Web page.

■ This area shows the location where Word will store the Web page. You can click this area to change the location.

■ This area allows you to access commonly used locations. You can click a location to save the Web page in the location.

Note: For information on the commonly used locations, see the top of page 21.

What is the difference between the file name and the title of a Web page?

The file name is the name you use to store the Web page on your computer. The title is the text that will appear at the top of the Web browser window when a person views your Web page.

How do I make my Web page available for other people to view?

After you save a document as a Web page, you can transfer the page to a computer that stores Web pages, called a Web server. Once the Web page is stored on a Web server, the page will be available for other people to view. For information on transferring a Web page to a Web server, contact your network administrator or Internet service provider.

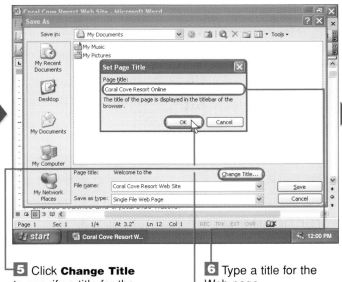

■5 Click **Change Title** to specify a title for the Web page.

■ The Set Page Title dialog box appears.

Note: A default title may appear in the dialog box.

■6 Type a title for the Web page.

■7 Click **OK** to confirm the title.

■ This area displays the title you specified for the Web page.

■8 Click **Save** to save the document as a Web page.

■ Word saves the document as a Web page and displays the document in the Web Layout view. This view displays the document as it will appear on the Web. For more information on the Web Layout view, see page 37.

INDEX

INDEX

Introducing Our New Consumer Books...

Our new Teach Yourself VISUALLY Consumer books are an excellent resource for people who want to learn more about general interest topics. We have launched this new groundbreaking series with three exciting titles: *Teach Yourself VISUALLY Weight Training*, *Teach Yourself VISUALLY Yoga* and *Teach Yourself VISUALLY Guitar*. These books maintain the same design and structure of our computer books—graphical, two-page lessons that are jam-packed with useful, easy-to-understand information.

Each full-color book includes over **500** photographs, accompanied by step-by-step instructions to guide you through the fundamentals of each topic. "Teach Yourself" sidebars also provide practical tips and tricks to further fine tune your skills and introduce more advanced techniques.

By using top experts in their respective fields to consult on our books, we offer our readers an extraordinary opportunity to access first-class, superior knowledge in conjunction with our award winning communication process. Teach Yourself VISUALLY Consumer is simply the best way to learn!

Teach Yourself VISUALLY **WEIGHT TRAINING**

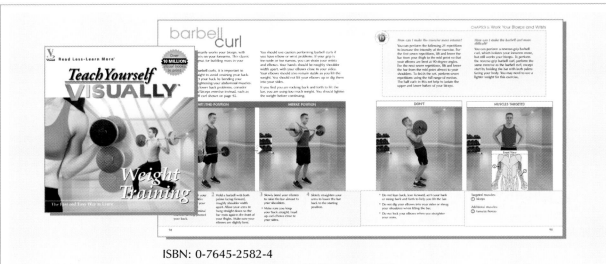

ISBN: 0-7645-2582-4
Price: $24.99 US; $36.99 CDN; £14.99 UK
Page count: 320

Teach Yourself VISUALLY **YOGA**

ISBN: 0-7645-2580-8

Price: $24.99 US; $36.99 CDN; £14.99 UK

Page count: 320

Teach Yourself VISUALLY **GUITAR**

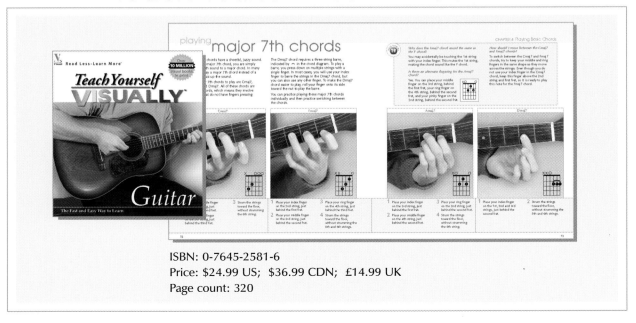

ISBN: 0-7645-2581-6

Price: $24.99 US; $36.99 CDN; £14.99 UK

Page count: 320

Read Less – Learn More™

Visual

Simplified®

Simply the Easiest Way to Learn

For visual learners who are brand-new to a topic and want to be shown, not told, how to solve a problem in a friendly, approachable way.

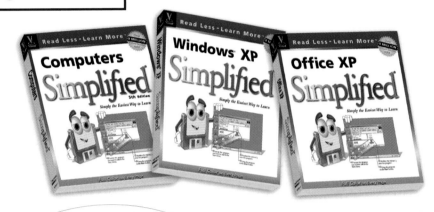

All *Simplified*® books feature friendly Disk characters who demonstrate and explain the purpose of each task.

Title	ISBN	U.S. Price
America Online Simplified, 3rd Ed. (Version 7.0)	0-7645-3673-7	$24.99
Computers Simplified, 5th Ed.	0-7645-3524-2	$27.99
Creating Web Pages with HTML Simplified, 2nd Ed.	0-7645-6067-0	$27.99
Excel 97 Simplified	0-7645-6022-0	$27.99
Excel 2002 Simplified	0-7645-3589-7	$27.99
FrontPage 2000 Simplified	0-7645-3450-5	$27.99
FrontPage 2002 Simplified	0-7645-3612-5	$27.99
Internet and World Wide Web Simplified, 3rd Ed.	0-7645-3409-2	$27.99
Microsoft Excel 2000 Simplified	0-7645-6053-0	$27.99
Microsoft Office 2000 Simplified	0-7645-6052-2	$29.99
Microsoft Word 2000 Simplified	0-7645-6054-9	$27.99
More Windows 98 Simplified	0-7645-6037-9	$27.99
Office XP Simplified	0-7645-0850-4	$29.99
Office 97 Simplified	0-7645-6009-3	$29.99
PC Upgrade and Repair Simplified, 2nd Ed.	0-7645-3560-9	$27.99
Windows 98 Simplified	0-7645-6030-1	$27.99
Windows Me Millennium Edition Simplified	0-7645-3494-7	$27.99
Windows XP Simplified	0-7645-3618-4	$27.99
Word 2002 Simplified	0-7645-3588-9	$27.99

Over 10 million *Visual* books in print!

with these full-color Visual™ guides

The Fast and Easy Way to Learn

Title	ISBN	U.S. Price
Teach Yourself FrontPage 2000 VISUALLY	0-7645-3451-3	$29.99
Teach Yourself HTML VISUALLY	0-7645-3423-8	$29.99
Teach Yourself the Internet and World Wide Web VISUALLY, 2nd Ed.	0-7645-3410-6	$29.99
Teach Yourself Microsoft Access 2000 VISUALLY	0-7645-6059-X	$29.99
Teach Yourself Microsoft Excel 2000 VISUALLY	0-7645-6056-5	$29.99
Teach Yourself Microsoft Office 2000 VISUALLY	0-7645-6051-4	$29.99
Teach Yourself Microsoft Word 2000 VISUALLY	0-7645-6055-7	$29.99
Teach Yourself VISUALLY Access 2003	0-7645-3995-7	$29.99
Teach Yourself VISUALLY Access 2002	0-7645-3591-9	$29.99
Teach Yourself VISUALLY Adobe Acrobat 5 PDF	0-7645-3667-2	$29.99
Teach Yourself VISUALLY Adobe Premiere 6	0-7645-3664-8	$29.99
Teach Yourself VISUALLY Computers, 3rd Ed.	0-7645-3525-0	$29.99
Teach Yourself VISUALLY Digital Photography	0-7645-3565-X	$29.99
Teach Yourself VISUALLY Digital Video	0-7645-3688-5	$29.99
Teach Yourself VISUALLY Dreamweaver 3	0-7645-3470-X	$29.99
Teach Yourself VISUALLY Dreamweaver MX	0-7645-3697-4	$29.99
Teach Yourself VISUALLY E-commerce with FrontPage	0-7645-3579-X	$29.99
Teach Yourself VISUALLY Excel 2003	0-7645-3945-0	$29.99
Teach Yourself VISUALLY Excel 2002	0-7645-3594-3	$29.99
Teach Yourself VISUALLY Fireworks 4	0-7645-3566-8	$29.99
Teach Yourself VISUALLY Flash 5	0-7645-3540-4	$29.99
Teach Yourself VISUALLY Flash MX	0-7645-3661-3	$29.99
Teach Yourself VISUALLY FrontPage 2002	0-7645-3590-0	$29.99
Teach Yourself VISUALLY Illustrator 10	0-7645-3654-0	$29.99
Teach Yourself VISUALLY iMac	0-7645-3453-X	$29.99
Teach Yourself VISUALLY Investing Online	0-7645-3459-9	$29.99
Teach Yourself VISUALLY Mac OS X Panther	0-7645-4393-8	$29.99
Teach Yourself VISUALLY Mac OS X Jaguar	0-7645-1802-X	$29.99
Teach Yourself VISUALLY Macromedia Web Collection	0-7645-3648-6	$29.99
Teach Yourself VISUALLY Networking, 2nd Ed.	0-7645-3534-X	$29.99
Teach Yourself VISUALLY Office 2003	0-7645-3980-9	$29.99
Teach Yourself VISUALLY Office XP	0-7645-0854-7	$29.99
Teach Yourself VISUALLY Photoshop 6	0-7645-3513-7	$29.99
Teach Yourself VISUALLY Photoshop 7	0-7645-3682-6	$29.99
Teach Yourself VISUALLY Photoshop Elements 2.0	0-7645-2515-8	$29.99
Teach Yourself VISUALLY PowerPoint 2002	0-7645-3660-5	$29.99
Teach Yourself VISUALLY Quicken 2001	0-7645-3526-9	$29.99
Teach Yourself VISUALLY Restoration & Retouching with Photoshop Elements 2.0	0-7645-2601-4	$29.99
Teach Yourself VISUALLY Windows 2000 Server	0-7645-3428-9	$29.99
Teach Yourself VISUALLY Windows Me Millennium Edition	0-7645-3495-5	$29.99
Teach Yourself VISUALLY Windows XP	0-7645-3619-2	$29.99
Teach Yourself VISUALLY MORE Windows XP	0-7645-3698-2	$29.99
Teach Yourself VISUALLY Word 2003	0-7645-3997-3	$29.99
Teach Yourself VISUALLY Word 2002	0-7645-3587-0	$29.99
Teach Yourself Windows 95 VISUALLY	0-7645-6001-8	$29.99
Teach Yourself Windows 98 VISUALLY	0-7645-6025-5	$29.99
Teach Yourself Windows 2000 Professional VISUALLY	0-7645-6040-9	$29.99

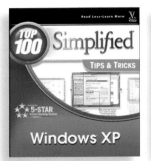
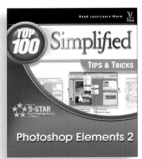
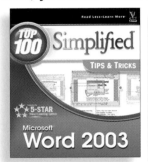

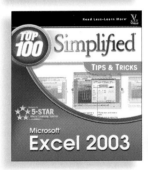

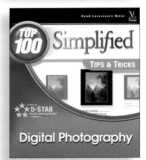
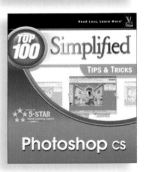